PRAISE FOR THE

Best Food Writing

SERIES

"What is so great about this annual series is that editor Holly Hughes curates articles that likely never crossed your desk, even if you're an avid reader of food content. Nearly every piece selected is worth your time."
—The Huffington Post

"There's a mess of vital, provocative, funny and tender stuff . . . in these pages." —*USA Today*

"Some of these stories can make you burn with a need to taste what they're writing about." —*Los Angeles Times*

"The essays are thought-provoking and moving . . . This is an absolutely terrific and engaging book . . . There is enough variety, like a box of chocolates, that one can poke around the book looking for the one with caramel and find it." —*New York Journal of Books*

"Stories for connoisseurs, celebrations of the specialized, the odd, or simply the excellent." —*Entertainment Weekly*

"This book is a menu of delicious food, colorful characters, and tales of strange and wonderful food adventures that make for memorable meals and stories."—*Booklist*

"This collection has something for connoisseurs, short story fans, and anyone hungry for a good read." —*Library Journal*

WRITING

2016

best Food
WRITING
2016

edited by

Holly
Hughes

Da Capo
∞
LIFE
LONG

Design by Jeff Williams
Set in 11 point Arno Pro by the Perseus Books Group

Cataloging-in-Publication data for this book is available from the Library of Congress.

First Da Capo Press edition 2016
ISBN: 978-0-7382-1944-8 (paperback)
ISBN: 978-0-7382-1945-5 (e-book)

Published by Da Capo Press, an imprint of Perseus Books, LLC, a subsidiary of Hachette Book Group, Inc.
www.dacapopress.com

Da Capo Press books are available at special discounts for bulk purchases in the U.S. by corporations, institutions, and other organizations. For more information, please contact the Special Markets Department at the Perseus Books Group, 2300 Chestnut Street, Suite 200, Philadelphia, PA, 19103, or call (800) 810-4145, ext. 5000, or e-mail special.markets@perseusbooks.com.

10 9 8 7 6 5 4 3 2 1

Contents

COOKING THE BOOKS

THE FAMILY TABLE

Introduction

I t was all the talk of the Upper Upper West Side. Despite everything else there was to lament in these sad and strange modern times—*What's up with D'Agostino's?*

Shopping at that neighborhood grocery store had become like visiting Iron Curtain Bulgaria. One day, there was no canned dog food; the next day, the dog food had arrived, but there was no toilet paper. Apple juice disappeared in June (except for that lone bottle of Mott's Natural that hung on for weeks). Stock clerks kept pulling items to the front of the shelves, one deep, hoping that ten boxes of elbow macaroni could make the pasta section seem full. (It didn't.)

Sadly, there's a pattern here. In the past three years, three other supermarkets in our neighborhood have closed, and none of them have been replaced. If (when) D'Agostino's goes, there won't be a single mainstream food market in a forty-block swath of Manhattan.

Well, it's not as if I live in a food desert (as, sadly, far too many Americans do). Our neighborhood is blessed with a lovely family-run greengrocer/deli on the corner and a natural foods store a block up. There's a Whole Foods seven blocks north, and real estate blogs claim a Trader Joe's is coming this fall. Still, I've tried to do The Big Weekly Shopping at each of them—but honestly, none of these stock everything I need. And in New York City, where you do your food shopping on foot, lugging packages home from multiple stores is quite frankly a pain in the ass.

You see, for nearly three decades, D'Agostino's was where I did The Big Weekly Shopping. This is where I stood in line to buy bottled water after 9/11, and candles in the blackout of 2003. Where I bought milk, bread, and eggs before blizzards (1996, 2006, 2010, 2016—thanks, climate change!). It was the store that didn't lose power after Hurricane Sandy.

And even more important, it was where I bought baby food (aisle 2) for my kids, until they graduated to blue box macaroni (aisle 3) and chicken nuggets (the end of aisle 7). Where I bought last-minute soccer snacks, the cake mix for birthday cupcakes, frozen pigs-in-a-blanket for my son's annual Super Bowl party. The summer my daughter went vegan, I found almond milk, tofu, and hummus there. After my son's nut allergy was diagnosed, I vetted all their baked goods to find the ones that were safe for him to eat.

D'Agostino's had a decent produce section, where automatic misters kept the lettuce fresh (and cooled off my kids on a hot summer day). It had a sushi bar, fresh baked goods, and a very obliging butcher. But it was also the store where I could buy cat litter, a case of Diet Coke, Tide detergent, and Bounty paper towels—all the name-brand products we secretly need. Everything in one place—*and then they'd deliver it.*

And then it struck me—that's what I've tried to provide in each edition of *Best Food Writing.*

Every year, I delve into piles of magazines and newspapers, scan endless websites, and forage through bookstores (a shout-out here to Matt and Nach at the indispensable Manhattan culinary bookstore Kitchen Arts and Letters). After seventeen years of doing this—the first edition of BFW came out in 2000—my end goal remains the same: to provide a robust mix of what's up in the world of food writing. To assemble in one place a wide-ranging sample of all the intriguing food writing that's been published this year.

On one hand, there's the topical—reflections on the trends that made this year different, from meal kits (Corby Kummer, page 26) to extreme dining experiences (Jennifer Cockrall-King, page 21) to the failures of farm-to-table pieties (Debbie Weingarten, page 31). We've got John Birdsall turning the proper noun "Brooklyn" into an adjective for an entire artisanal mind-set (page 12), and Matt Buchanan archly describing high-end coffee orthodoxy (page 40).

But on the other hand, we've also got a reaction against trends and PC food snobbery, from Helen Rosner's chicken tenders (page 8) to Kat Kinsman's gumbos and goulashes (page 13) to Keith Pandolfi's drip coffee (page 55) and Max Ufberg's classic diner food (page 166). Kathleen Purvis (page 90) cries wolf on one chic "lifestyle" cookbook writer, while Rachel Levin (page 286) hands us a poignant shortcut around an uber-trendy San Francisco breakfast spot.

Within the covers of this book, I've also tried to strike a balance between cooking and dining, between everyday meals and special meals. There are pieces that focus on home cooking, with or without kids, from Phyllis Grant (page 82) trying out cookbook recipes with her children, to Andrew Sean Greer (page 276) remembering his mother's dinner parties, and Pete Wells (page 271) embracing his role as home chef on vacation. Flip a few pages, however, and you can shift gears to contemplate the culinary wizards who create meals we could never reproduce at home—such as Jason Tesauro's piece on Danish chef Bo Bech (page 210), Brett Martin's homage to Jacques Pepin (page 249), or Daniel Duane's frantic afternoon with Dominque Crenn (page 86).

I keep coming back to the fact that as humans, we're somehow hardwired for breaking bread together. During a four-months-long kitchen renovation (see *Best Food Writing 2011* for that tale), I could always pick up a tasty rotisserie chicken and bagged salad at my grocery store to create the semblance of a family meal, even if it was eaten on the living room sofa off the four plastic plates we hadn't packed up. There's a powerful lure to the foods we eat together as families—as we learn from Laura Donohue, cleaning out her mother's kitchen (page 96), Besha Rodell revisiting the beach shacks of her peripatetic childhood (page 107), and Victoria Pesce-Elliott hungering for her ailing mother's meatball recipe (page 114). It doesn't even have to be a happy memory to be powerful, as Betsy Andrews (page 103) brings home.

Even when we don't cook at home, we long for that human connection. I turn to Tove Danovich's profile of a commuter bar (page 170), James Nolan's essay on the right way to dine alone (page 175), or Michael Procopio's valedictory blog post after his mother's funeral (page 119). Of course, that connection can be just as strong when the subjects are drinking in company—as Rowan Jacobsen (page 44) and Wells Tower (page 48) so skillfully evoke.

The beauty of a full-service grocery store is also that it can offer a wider and more diverse range of products than you can find at the simple corner store or at the specialty shop. So do food writers, in our increasingly globalized food culture, help us expand our horizons. In these pages, you'll find guides to exotic fare such as puffin (Brian Kevin, page 132), Swiss fondue (Tim Neville, page 240), Soba noodles (Francis

Lam, page 264), or the legendary Cockentrice (Chris Newens, page 126). Howie Kahn takes us on a dizzying culinary tour of Singapore (page 187), topped only by Todd Kliman's phantasmagoric journey to Mexico City (page 193). And it's not just about taste-testing these foods; their cultural connections matter just as much. Which brings us to L. Kasimu Harris, jonesing for the New Orleans cure-all Yakamein (page 141); or Mikki Kendall (page 146), explaining why Beyonce carries hot sauce in her bag. Pableaux Johnson (page 158) writes his life in gumbo while Oliver Sacks (page 290) wrote his in gefilte fish.

Superstitiously, I still carry a crumpled "$5 Off" D'Agostino coupon in my wallet. It's true, I could do all of my shopping online or at a cavernous, anonymous big box store. But it won't be the same.

I ache for the check-out clerks and delivery guys I've dealt with for twenty-plus years. And I'll admit, I'm also grieving the fact that I no longer am feeding small children—the realization that my kids have grown and will soon be moving out of our family home.

But I also mourn something bigger—the passing of a culture wherein we shop in person, in real time, fondling the produce and eyeing the meat. I mourn the loss, in our increasingly gentrified neighborhood, of this community nexus, where old and young, black and white, rich and poor met face-to-face. In an America that's increasingly factionalized and incensed over the differences among us, here was a place where folks of all stripes came to buy the simplest of all things: food.

Where we smiled at each other and took our turns at the deli counter.

Where we let shoppers with only three items go ahead of us in the checkout line.

Where we practiced being human.

I refuse to lose that. I've just got to go out and find me a new store.

The Way We Eat Now

Brooklyn Is Everywhere

By John Birdsall

From *Bon Appétit*

Though he lives in Oakland, California, John Birdsall's wide-
ranging food writing—*Saveur, Lucky Peach, Eater, Chow, Serious
Eats*—covers trends across the country. So he knows you'll
know what he means when he calls something "Brooklyn,"
even when it's nowhere near New York.

T he local beer is "craft."
It costs $8 for a small plastic cup of stout that tastes like choco-
late porridge. I set it on the bar and watch the liquid heave and crater
from waves of feral folk-rock thrashing the packed room, coming from a
bandanna'd blond kid onstage with a guitar, hair pasted to his pink face
by righteous sweat.

Band stickers cover random surfaces of this old building like scales
on a half-scraped salmon. Upstairs it's open studio night, and women in
wool beanies and art bros in Woolrich snowflake pullovers hustle past
the galleries, cocking their heads to ponder installations referencing
Star Wars circa '77.

It's my first time in this place. Maybe like you, though, I've been
here before—anyone who's walked through Williamsburg or seen an
episode of *Girls* has. It's a landscape of under-35s, bristling with locally
brewed IPAs, restaurant pop-ups, and new kinds of mustard. And everybody—literally everybody—is flaunting freestyle forearm ink.

But tonight I'm not in Williamsburg. I'm in Indianapolis. And what's
playing in Indy, on this raw December night in Fountain Square, is a

specific language of food, style, and cultural appreciation now spoken all over America and, damn, all over the world.

Go to Roma Norte in Mexico City, where you'll stroll past guys with waxed mustaches and women in '80s jumpsuits, nibbling expensive *paletas* from a mod turquoise cart. In Old Town Bangkok, around the corner from an illicit cockfight on the street, there's a young Thai dude who set up a tiny Third Wave coffee bar. If you ask, he'll tell you it's modeled after San Francisco's Blue Bottle. North, in Chiang Mai, a couple of Thai hipsters preside over the kind of barbershop that's the anchor tenant of any Brooklyn block—in the chair, you can throw back a shot of whiskey.

It was less than a decade ago that urban America first got into this revived notion of homesteading, raising Ameraucana chickens and wearing overalls to take all-day butchering classes or make things in their tiny home kitchens (so many mason jars full of so many pickles). The Brooklyn Flea launched in 2008 with its mix of food and vintage, and by the next year an editor of *Edible Brooklyn* described a new demographic to the *New York Times*: "It's that guy in the band with the big plastic glasses who's already asking for grass-fed steak and knows about nibs."

In Oakland, California, where I live, neighborhoods like Temescal are mourning braiding salons and African-American fried-fish shacks. You can buy vegan Earl Grey ice cream, or a terrarium of succulents, then head to the boutique for $129 hand-dyed shirts that aren't so different from those at Le Bon Marché, the Paris department store, during last year's "Brooklyn Rive Gauche" pop-up.

None of these objects is definitively Brooklyn, but the sum total nudges certain enclaves—Chicago's Wicker Park, Los Angeles's Silver Lake, and Stockholm's SoFo—or cities like Austin and Portland (Oregon and Maine) into places where a near-spiritual reverence for anything "local" and a resolutely dialed-in personal style can tip into caricature. One that, astonishingly, looks and feels the same no matter where you are.

You see it even in smaller cities like Tulsa and Indianapolis, where I'm pushing through the crowd at The HI-FI before I head out to taste Indiana-distilled Backbone Bourbon at another bar. It's late when I start to think about whether this city can hit all those Brooklyn notes and still feel distinctively like Indianapolis. In other words, once you look beyond the throwback cocktails and cheesemongers, can our seemingly universal food codes act as a shortcut for cities to hit on their real potential? That's what I came to Indianapolis to find out.

Just up Virginia Avenue is a car-strafed condo strip called Fletcher Place. That's where Milktooth is.

It's best to sit at the counter at Milktooth, kitty-corner from chef and owner Jonathan Brooks as he works the sauté pans. The restaurant does brunch daily—opens at seven for coffee, passes out menus at nine, and closes at three—inside a rehabbed garage. It's bright and open; looks like it was decorated by a thrifter with a good eye.

Brooks is 31, though he could pass for younger, wearing an apron with strings that pinch his back. He has a rooster tattooed on his hand, a pig's skull on his neck, and something on his upper arm that resembles a fat ear of shucked corn.

For the next 40 minutes, he hands me plates from the line: a warm, delicately crumbly biscuit made with wild-rice flour, topped with a thick, cool disk of persimmon butter that tastes like raw Christmas-cookie dough; a Dutch baby pancake with craggy bits of oatmeal-dukka streusel, dabbed with spheres of puréed parsnip so smooth it's like the whipped butter at IHOP; a grilled cheese sandwich of Indiana raclette. The bread is black—Brooks took it astonishingly far in the pan—and it's perfect that way.

A cocktail arrives: Del Maguey mezcal and poppy-seed liqueur, shaken along with some egg white. It has tannins that filter up through the mousse-y cloud—like smoke through a bong's diffuser, it's been de-harshed. It's the best egg-white drink I've ever had.

Everything I taste that day at Milktooth shows off tight technical skills and an easy, loping confidence. The food is brilliant.

Then I begin to ask him how a kid in Indianapolis has the life experience to produce food at this level, then wonder to myself whether I'd be asking the same of a 31-year-old chef in L.A. or Chicago. I must look like a total snob, because as I hustle into my coat, making plans to meet up with Brooks later that night, I stop to tell the cook who made the cocktail how perfect it was.

He says thanks and asks where I'm from. "New York?"

"California," I say.

"Here's what I always wanted to know," he asks: "When a maga-zine tells you they're sending you to Indianapolis, are you like, 'Damn, really? Indy?'"

Later that evening, Jonathan Brooks interrupts himself and points behind me. "I think that's Sleater-Kinney!"

I turn to see the backs of two women leaving the restaurant, Blue-beard. It's attached to Amelia's bakery, which produces very good fen-nel seed–sprinkled semolina bread.

A smiling man is looming above our table. If any one person bears re-sponsibility for the Brooklynization of Indy, it's probably this guy, Tom Battista.

Battista, who looks like he's settled softly into his 60s, used to man-age tours for big acts. He got his start on the road with David Bowie's Diamond Dogs tour in 1974, and now he's into seeing that other kinds of young artists—Brooks and Bluebeard chef Abbi Merriss, to name two—are giving his city an identity beyond pork tenderloin sand-wiches and the Indy 500.

He acquires evocative old buildings, then rehabs and leases them to young restaurateurs who promise to do something interesting. That's one huge difference with Brooklyn: There, restaurant owners struggle to make rent. In Indy, Tom Battista plays benevolent papa.

That's what happened with Amelia's too, and with Black Market, where I ate delicious hunks of roasted beef heart, and with Calvin Fletcher's Coffee Company, a chilled-out café nearby. Battista bought the old garage where Milktooth sits, then got in touch with Brooks to tell him he had a place he should check out.

Over drinks and a plate of Parmesan-loaded spaghetti, Brooks tells me he used to hate Indianapolis. He followed his older brother, a col-lege professor, to Missoula, Montana, a place he liked for its hunting, fishing, and lack of bullshit. He'd sometimes drive the eight hours to Portland or Seattle just to eat in solid restaurants. Cooking's call was too loud to keep Brooks in Missoula, so he moved to Chicago, staged around for a while till he was broke, then did the thing he swore he wouldn't: He came back to Indianapolis.

That sort of migration helps explain why things that once defined Brooklyn—pottery studios, mead distilleries, or millennials selling their crafts—have turned up all over. Folks like Brooks read about them online, or got into them while traveling or while living in Brooklyn proper, then decided there was no reason their hometowns shouldn't have them too. It helps that a greater percentage of young people are moving to cities than ever before. And why would they choose Brooklyn itself, where the average one-bedroom apartment rents for more than $2,500 monthly? That doesn't even include a garden for growing stuff.

Brooks and I move on to Pioneer, where we swab toast through a smooth pink puck of chicken liver mousse. The bartender is saying something quietly to Brooks, who nods. "What did he say?" I ask. Brooks explains they're talking about Sleater-Kinney being in Fountain Square, but only two of them, without Carrie Brownstein, the one from *Portlandia*. It's never the famous ones who show up, he jokes.

Our last stop is Marrow, where John Adams, who used to be at Bluebeard, is the executive chef. It's after ten on a weeknight, and we down old-fashioneds made with bone marrow–infused rye whiskey as Adams delivers chitlins fried crisp, delicate as curls of sloughed-off snakeskin, in a shallow bowl with red chile mash. It's fantastic, if a bit overwrought.

At some point, I tell Brooks how I'm in Indianapolis to find Brooklyn, and to see how America's dominant food trends play out in a place with an emerging restaurant scene. I see his face drop, like I've delivered the ultimate insult, regarding these young chefs as cartoon characters.

I worry he's going to get up and bail. Instead he tells me, basically, that I haven't looked hard enough.

"We have people who come into Milktooth and say, 'This feels like New York,'" Brooks says. "I'm like, it's not f*#%ing Brooklyn. It's Indianapolis."

As I try to smooth things over, telling him I think what he and chefs like Adams are doing is amazing, I feel like the lamest guy in the room. These young people distilling gin and smoking elk—for a lot of them, Brooklyn is the Disney version of their lives. It's a gesture, but not substantial. Few of them have their sights on moving to the coasts, because the real achievement isn't getting out of the place where you were born to build a new identity for yourself. It's better to stay put and change the culture—genuinely transform—where you are. And while it's easy for visitors like me to grouse that all these restaurants in all these cities feel similar, the fact that you can eat this well in Indianapolis is alone worth celebrating.

"The moment I knew something was going on," Brooks says, "was when I looked and saw there were more people ordering chicken livers than waffles."

From the backseat, my Uber driver is just this wall of long auburn hair. "I haven't been in this part of Indy in a long time," she says. "It's changed."

Chris and Ally Benedyk opened their sandwich spot, Love Handle, less than six months ago. It's inside a former Subway franchise, complete with fake wood-grain tiles and bolted-down benches. The Benedyks grew up in Indy, left for Milwaukee for a while, and now they're back with their own place, pioneering on the Near Eastside, which looks like it has a way to go despite the food co-op.

I order the Darger, a roast pork belly sandwich: pale, tender slices of meat, with chips of rose-colored turnip that have been pickled in pink lemonade. It comes with popcorn dusty with nutritional yeast mixed with pork fat and fennel butter. "Darger," Chris tells me, is a reference to Henry Darger, an outsider artist whose work was discovered after he died. Chris likes to name his sandwiches for misunderstood geniuses, he says.

As I finish the sandwich, I'm curious if the rawness of a place like Love Handle—the energy of young chefs, the grand narrative built from little pieces of this and that—is how actual Brooklyn used to feel before Paris pop-ups and million-dollar condos. What if it isn't so much Indianapolis trying to be Brooklyn, as Brooklyn wanting to capture something of Indianapolis? I think of the kid I saw onstage at The HI-FI, who told me that it was his first paid gig. Maybe someday, if everything falls right, he'll be playing Brooklyn.

Then I recall my night at Marrow, where a young bar-back hovered just out of speaking range before coming up to Brooks with obvious deference, his head a little bowed. "Dude," he managed above the music, "I have to say: I love your trilobite tattoo."

It's on the back of Brooks's arm, the one I thought was a chubby ear of corn.

"Trilobite?" I asked.

"Eh," Brooks said. "It's kind of a Midwest thing."

On Chicken Tenders

By Helen Rosner

From *Guernica*

Like many food writers, Helen Rosner—a veteran of *New York* magazine, *Saveur,* and *Eater,* where's she now executive editor— has spent plenty of time in the temples of fine dining. But for the arts magazine *Guernica,* she voices a seldom-admitted truth: The kids' menu is where all perfect foods live.

I know this about you: you love chicken tenders. You *love* them. You might not ever eat them—you might be a vegetarian or a vegan, or not consume birds for whatever reason, or not want to deal with the carbs, or not think it's okay for adult humans with serious opinions about fracking to dip a toe into the children's menu—but that's a choice about ingesting them. It's not you not loving them. Because you do. You love chicken tenders. Everybody does.

This is because chicken tenders are perfect. They're perfect in flavor, perfect in aroma, perfect in shape, perfect in color. They're salty and savory, crisp and juicy, easy to eat with the hands but absolutely okay to go at with a knife and fork. Their ubiquity on kids' menus isn't a mark against their perfection, but rather proof of it: the kids' menu is where all perfect foods live. Pizza, hot dogs, spaghetti. But king of all perfect foods is the chicken tender.

Perfection is a precarious state. It occupies a narrow peak, the very pinnacle of the mountain. By its very nature, perfection leaves no room for wildness or risk. Perfection is passive, it's static, it verges on bland.

It's a circle. A cloudless sky. An unmarked page. It's everything and it's nothing, and it's glorious, and it usually comes with fries.

In 2009 I began eating professionally. This isn't as common among food writers as you might think. Food is a topic, not a practice. Researching and reporting on chefs and restaurants gives you access to an unending feast, but very few people in the food-writing world have jobs that *demand* the consumption and consideration of actual food. But when I began reviewing restaurants, I become one of them: eating became a job requirement.

This was very weird. Any leisure activity loses some appeal once it becomes mandatory, and eating dinner at New York's cool new restaurants isn't an exception to that. The civilian pleasures of dining out are largely connected to ideas of novelty and choice. At a restaurant, you're getting something you wouldn't normally get at home: a fully funkadelic dry-aged tomahawk ribeye, a soul-warming bowl of *bún bò huế*, or the undivided attention of a balletic thirteen-person service team. And you get to make a lot of decisions—what restaurant to go to, what food you want to eat, when and how often you want to go out at all.

When you're eating a meal for a paycheck, all of that is stripped away. And what remains? A miraculous adaptation, the inverse of the receptive adjustments we perform when faced with unpleasantness: just as we naturally tune out familiar noises or lingering foul smells, we can also become inured to delight. In a months-long barrage of sensory spectacle, enchantment rapidly gives way to tedium. Restaurant reviewing is a parade of the extraordinary, a half-dozen special-occasion meals each week. You hear a hundred explanations of how to order, smile your thanks at a thousand *amuse bouches*, read a million back-of-the-menu culinary manifestos. I texted to my boyfriend on my way from the office to a review dinner: *I'm so tired of foie gras.* He replied: *Read back to yourself what you just typed.* You can have too much of a good thing.

But the truly oddest part of being a restaurant critic was what happened to me when I was off the clock. You don't get into food writing without loving food, loving to eat. I'd always been an adventurous and ambitious eater, ordering the most outlandish things at restaurants and swinging for the fences with my kitchen experiments. And I still was—as long as I was working. But on my own time, ordering delivery or cooking dinner or out with friends, I reverted to the palate of a suburban six-year-old. All I ever wanted was toast with butter, pasta with the thinnest-possible coating of red sauce, or—my salvation, my obsession, the only thing I ever reliably wanted to eat—chicken tenders.

A true connoisseur of the chicken tender knows that there are three immutable rules.

The first is the rule of physical integrity. A tender has a proper shape: flattish, oblong, and gradually tapering from a wide front to a narrow end. Unlike nuggets, which are largely made from processed, re-formed scraps, the chicken tender takes its name from an actual piece of the chicken: the *pectoralis minor*, a muscle located under the breast, against the sternum. The tenderloin. It's rare nowadays to get actual tenders when you order them (hence the rise of "fingers" and "strips," terms of art that veil all manner of creative butchery), but integrity demands that a wedge of breast put at least some effort into mimicking the actual part of the chicken it is trying to be.

The second rule of chicken tenders is that, contra any advice your mother may have given you, what's on the outside matters infinitely more than anything on the inside. A chicken tender lives or dies by its exterior: batters, breadings, the disappointing faux-sophistication of panko. The subtlety or intensity of its spice and salt. The crispness of the exterior is what creates the tenderness of the interior, its structural cohesion when submerged in hot oil helps the chicken inside stay juicy and good. But it can't adhere only to itself: a good chicken tender's breading stays connected to the chicken inside once you take a bite, not slipping off like a silk stocking or the bullshit batter on an onion ring.

The third rule of chicken tenders is that sauce is a last resort. You shouldn't have to dip your chicken tenders in anything. If you want a vehicle for ranch dressing, order the crudités.

I wasn't a big-deal restaurant critic; you wouldn't know my byline. I was writing capsule reviews for the weekly magazine where my day job was covering restaurant news and gossip. But I brought up my curious change in palate with a friend who *is* a big deal, the kind of guy whose photo is pinned up in restaurant kitchens like a wanted sign, and he nodded with recognition.

"Why do you think every chef says his favorite food is roast chicken, or oysters, or a steak?" he asked. So much complexity makes simplicity appealing. Spending your days trying to one-up your own palate is exhausting. Stepping away from the wood-grilled matsutake mushrooms with nasturtium agrodolce, and towards an uncomplicated hunk of meat is the gastronomic equivalent of collapsing into your bed at the end of a long day.

It's true that ribeyes and oysters and even pizza and tacos share a soothing simplicity, but nothing is more *nothing* than a chicken tender. A roast chicken has a certain dinner-party elegance to it, and you know at least the sketch of an origin story for your pizza or your taco—but a chicken tender is a chicken tender is a chicken tender. Some restaurants might try to gussy them up, gently carve each tender from the breast of a bird that lived a happy life and lovingly dust them in a custom spice blend, but a true chicken tender comes out of a five-hundred-count freezer bag. They come from nowhere in particular—when you eat them, you could be anywhere.

Even the other kids' menu stalwarts have more history to them than the chicken tender, a relatively new addition to the gastronomic landscape that only reached deep-fryer ubiquity in the 1990s. (This itself is a fascinatingly rare phenomenon: when was the last time something truly novel hit the culinary zeitgeist that didn't have a trademark appended to it?) It takes more than one generation to develop the intricate root system of nostalgia that anchors the ballpark pastoral of hot dogs or nachos, the picket-fence vignette of fried bologna sandwiches, or the dusty-road Americana of a burger and an ice-cold Coke. Chicken tenders have no history, they have no metatext, they have no *terroir*.

This deliciousness without backstory was liberating for me when I was reviewing restaurants. I don't do much of that kind of writing anymore—for the most part, my meals are my own again—but I still need the kind of relief chicken tenders provide. It's exhilarating to be part of the food world as it rockets from fringe interest to massive cultural force, but there are times when I want to step off the ride, to make a food choice that doesn't double as a performance of my identity.

Food means more than it used to—what we do with it means more. Picking this restaurant or that bunch of carrots isn't just a decision of interest or appetite; it's telling a story, it's choosing a tribe. Instagram means that once-private pleasures can be even more pleasurable when they're broadcast to an audience of thousands. I may love the garlic scape pesto I whizzed up at home yesterday, or the peppery butter-milk *panna cotta* at Blackberry Farm in Tennessee, but more than that, I love broadcasting that love, a narcotic combination of "but it's my job" rationalization and the validating thrill of a push notification. Every picture of food is a selfie.

Not so with chicken tenders. There's no narrative to chicken tenders, there's no performance. That is the substance of their allure: If you're ordering them, you don't have to look at the menu. You don't have to think about whether you've been posting a lot of pasta lately or whether it's kind of passé at this point to go for a kale salad. Chicken tenders aren't cool. They're not retro. They're not funny. They ask nothing of you, and they don't say anything about you. They are two things, and two things only: perfect, and delicious. That's enough. That's everything.

In Praise of Ugly Food

By Kat Kinsman

From SeriousEats.com

Kat Kinsman's writing beat covers food and drink—at CNN, Tasting Table, Time Inc., etc.—as well as mental health. (Look for her new book *Hi, Anxiety: Life with a Bad Case of Nerves* this fall.) So she's got to wonder—what does the Instagram era's obsession with exquisite food shots say about our values?

Let's start with chicken and dumplings. Few dishes come closer to what I imagine the cafeteria rations in heaven will mercifully taste like than perfectly executed chicken and dumplings. Then again, perhaps no other dish looks quite so, well, *regurgitated*, either. So, at a recent Southern Foodways Alliance symposium in Oxford, Mississippi, when world-renowned chef Sean Brock served up a batch he'd cooked—with his very own mother—some of my fellow diners were in a visible tizzy about what to do.

Throughout the event, we'd all been posting hundreds of images of each course to our Instagram accounts. The slice of golden skillet cornbread, the glistening bowl of butter beans, and the Technicolor-green pickles were all objectively lovely. But chicken and dumplings, it seemed, was the whiz kid who couldn't find a date. And as people wavered and then lowered their cameras without snapping a shot, I found myself downright upset. I mean, this was a rare privilege: An A-list chef and the woman who'd pretty much taught him how to cook, putting their down-home dish on a pedestal in front of some of the biggest names in the food world. And we were shying away because it was homely? Screw that, I thought. This is honest food, and it should be honestly portrayed. I steadied my phone, clicked, and posted. The caption: "Some food isn't pretty and does not need to be."

As a food writer, I've found myself both annoyed and a bit mystified that the social-media value of our breakfasts, lunches, and dinners is considered almost as important as their gustatory properties. While the nose never lies—and neither do the taste buds—the eyes do, all the damn time.

I've been thinking about ugly food, and ugly things in general, for an awfully long time now. I still remember using my post as a high school yearbook editor to make sure the wallflower kids were just as well represented as the tall poppies in our class. Sure, they weren't the prettiest of the bunch, but I felt a certain solidarity with them. I knew we had a special value all our own. As a girl who figured I'd never measure up as lovely enough (mostly because so many people flat-out told me so), I had always identified with the ugly and the overlooked—the teddy bear with the wonky eye, the holey thrift store dress. I understood these things. I celebrated them.

The foods that pleased me the most were the objectively ugly ones: the stews, gravies, gumbos, curries, goulashes, mashes, braises, and sauces that were cooked long and low until they slumped and thickened. Maybe I knew that these foods, like all the ugly ducklings in this world, had to work harder to get their proper due. It takes time and effort to transubstantiate flour and fat into cocoa-dark roux, a rough hunk of muscle into sumptuous brisket, and raw, tough leaves and tops into sweet, savory greens. Time, it seems, can make some foods taste like heaven, and look like hell.

It's a good reminder that aesthetics are a poor predictor of goodness; that there are other qualities to consider—the most important of which, to me at least, is the olfactory. When presented with, say, a muddy bowl of beef stew, I'll sweep my nose down low over it and inhale, like Hawkeye Pierce over his powdered eggs in the M*A*S*H mess tent. For him, it was probably preventive. For me, it's a tease of impending pleasure. But before I take my first bite, I will lovingly snap a photo of it and post it to Instagram or Facebook, chronicling the dish the same way I did my dorky classmates back in high school.

I know it may seem foolish to use a visual medium to capture the way we eat, but until Smellstagram and Snaptaste technology appear, it's one of the best ways we have to celebrate the overlooked, while at the same time documenting our not-so-camera-ready colloquial chow for future generations. Unless, of course, we want them to think we were a civilization fueled entirely by green smoothies, avocado toasts, and baked goods tied up with red and white baker's twine alongside mini milk bottles. Such a twee vision of our culinary culture would be a tragic misrepresentation of the foods America does best. I fear that Instagram, blogs, and glossy mags continually bump my favorite foods from their collective menus in favor of eye candy. I'm terrified that the less-lovely and monumentally delicious ducklings will be lost to the ages, overshadowed by prettier dishes in this new era of visual gluttony. If they aren't beautifully documented, Pinterested, or posted, they must not be worth it.

When exactly did we start losing purchase on this slippery slope? I can't help but point a finger or two at Martha Stewart. Starting in the 1980s, she was the one who helped make clench-jawed perfection de rigueur for home cooks, rather than the bailiwick of restaurant chefs, caterers, and civilians with cash to burn on personal kitchen staffs. With beautifully packaged features and photographic technology in her arsenal (not to mention a team of food stylists who must have suffered from debilitating tweezer-hand cramps), she was a driving force in bringing food's physicality to the spotlight. And while I've never found myself under her sway (mostly out of self-preservation and, for a long time, personal brokeness), I have seen some of my favorite people—rational human beings whom I care about deeply—reduced almost to tears because their perfectly delicious *pâte à choux* didn't puff up as prettily as Martha's does.

Martha wasn't the first person to challenge us to such impossibly high standards, though. A paw through my collection of vintage magazines and home entertaining books—*The Art of Serving Food Attractively* (1951) and *The Perfect Host: A Husband's Guide to Home Entertaining* (1975) are particular favorites—underscores the importance of polished silver service and a wide array of molds from which to deploy aspics, meat rings, and unnerving desserts. (One chapter of the former provides detailed instructions on fashioning a lettuce skirt for a "lady China figurine," while another suggests crafting a clown from spiced peach halves, gumdrops, and wads of cream cheese!) Then again, those books were meant for entertaining company. With the launch of *Martha Stewart Living* magazine in 1990, however, such aesthetics were promoted as something we should incorporate into an everyday lifestyle that allows for—even insists upon—devoting time and energy to optics on a daily basis.

Until the age of Instagram and bloggers with DSLR cameras, it didn't occur to me that we mortals were on the hook to make our food look as good as Martha and her predecessors once did. But I was still taken aback when a commenter on my Instagram account took time out of her day to tell me how vomitous she found my wedding food—including my dad's goulash and my mother-in-law's chicken and dumplings— to be. She was, so far as I could recall, not on the guest list. I'm not the only one held to the task. Even Martha was hoisted with her own petard after she posted images of dishes (granted, from restaurants, not from her own kitchen, but still . . .) that commenters likened to all manner of bodily secretions ("spit," "poo," even "cat vomit"!).

Yes, Martha's images were poorly lit, blurry, and bizarrely framed. Yes, the fault was clearly the photographer's. But behind the big, steaming heaps of schadenfreude, there was plenty of condemnation of the food itself. And that freaked me out. Martha was partially responsible for taking food presentation and photography to an almost absurd level. And sure, she was contradicting everything she had taught us by taking some pretty terribly lit and unfocused photographs. But is French onion soup even supposed to be *très jolie*? Isn't the job of chicken liver pâté to simply taste good? Do they really need to strut through Instagram's version of a swimsuit round? Does every dish, no matter how unattractive it may be, need to aspire to the level of food porn? (And what is food porn, anyway? Did you ever find your grandfather's stash of food porn wedged behind the busted toaster and kidney bean cans in his basement workshop? When you were growing up, did your mom emerge flush-cheeked from the pantry with a fluted tart pan, some Demerara sugar, a hank of baker's twine, and a fancy-ass camera?)

So be forewarned: The next time someone trots out "You eat with your eyes" in my presence, I'll seriously consider testing that theory by flicking biscuit crumbs toward their tear ducts and spackling their sockets with room-temperature (I'm not a monster) cream gravy until their face is smoothed over from the cheekbones up.

I don't know your particular life. I hope that it's grand and delicious and satisfies all of your senses. I only know that when I'm hungry, my sight is the last thing that needs to be fed. And while I will continue to document my favorite dishes with a point and a click, there's no need for the perfect shot, no mandate to try to make it pretty. If I share a photo of a bowl of soup or a mess of greens with you, I'm sharing it because there's something more than meets the eye. An uncelebrated beauty. If you see an ugly duckling, look closer; imagine what it smells like, and how it tastes. Lo and behold, you might just see a swan.

How to Dupe a Moderately Ok Food Critic

By Luke Tsai

From *East Bay Express*

In the Bay Area food scene, Luke Tsai—restaurant critic for
the alt-weekly *East Bay Express*—has had to carve out his own
niche by scoping out the creative start-ups and storefront ethnic
joints of Oakland and Berkeley. But in a social-media-driven
foodscape, the grass-roots approach can backfire.

T he East Bay's most exclusive underground Chinese restaurant
can be found inside an unassuming bungalow on a residential
street nestled high in the El Cerrito hills. Chiu's Moderately Ok Chinese is a dining establishment that's so far under the radar it doesn't
have its phone number or hours of business listed anywhere on the
internet—but, according to Yelp user "Sung L.," it's so popular customers routinely have to wait in line, and it serves wonton soup and salt and
pepper spareribs that are, in the words of Yelp user "Shirell B.," where
"heaven can be found on earth."

Oh, and there's also this: Chiu's doesn't exist.

But I didn't figure that out until after I had driven 45 minutes along
winding backroads, fueled by a small number of enthusiastic online reviews and the prospect of a big scoop, to arrive at a cute little house
that most certainly didn't *look* like a restaurant. Still, I didn't give up
hope—not even after the middle-aged white lady who answered the
door (and who, I'll admit, didn't exactly fit the picture of the "Chiu" I'd
conjured up in my mind) politely explained that she'd been living in the

house for nineteen years, and, as far as she was aware, there had never been a restaurant there. Helpfully, she suggested that I check out Uncle Wong's around the corner.

I held onto that shred of hope even after circling the area several times to determine whether a slightly inaccurate street address might have been the culprit. And even days later, after I verified that the Contra Costa County health department had never inspected or issued a permit for any legitimate restaurant with the name "Chiu's Moderately Ok Chinese" (or anything remotely similar) in El Cerrito or any of the surrounding cities, I wondered if the place might be some kind of top-secret, unlicensed supper club. Did the woman who answered the door turn me away because I didn't know the password, or because she pegged me for a health inspector, or worse yet, a journalist?

In the end, after reaching out to the four Yelpers who wrote the reviews that first sent me on this misadventure, I figured out that the correct explanation was the simplest one: I'd been duped. And it's embarrassing how easy it was to fool me. The first step, if your goal is to prank a food critic, is to come up with a good name for your fake restaurant. Goofy and self-deprecating, "Chiu's Moderately Ok Chinese" is a *great* restaurant name; possible headlines for my intended review practically wrote themselves.

Step two: Make sure the photos look tasty. (Look at that steamed fish pictured above, and tell me, honestly, that you wouldn't drive an unreasonable distance to eat it.) Conveniently leave out the restaurant's hours and phone number, so there's no way for anyone—including Yelp—to confirm the existence of the place except by driving up into the hills. Finally, and this is the part that pains me to admit: Pepper your fake reviews with breathless exclamations about long lines and the gritty, off-the-beaten-path nature of a dining experience that you won't find in any normal restaurant. You might say, as Yelp user "Leah E." did, "This spot is for the person who wants an Anthony Bourdain-esque dining experience . . . i.e. no reservations."

What does it say about me—or about our food-obsessed culture, which places such a premium on discovering the latest and greatest obscure restaurant—that I fell for such obvious food-writer catnip? What significance is there to the fact that I read four reviews offering little to no actual information about the dishes served at Chiu's—except that they were, in "Amanda W.'s" words, "THE BOMB"—and considered that par for the course? What does it say about Yelp—a company dogged by accusations of unethical business practices—that, as of this printing, a completely fictitious restaurant entry that lists some innocent bystander's home address hasn't been taken down more than a month after it was created? (It was more than a little bit ironic to see, above a series of fake reviews, Yelp's disclaimer: "Your trust is our top concern, so businesses can't pay to alter or remove their reviews.")

Once I realized the whole thing was a joke, I wondered what the punchline was. If it was a prank, who was it a prank *on*? The typical foodie who'd be dumb enough (like me) to drive into the middle of a remote residential neighborhood just for the bragging rights of being one of the first to have some uniquely authentic food experience? It might be awfully self-absorbed of me to imagine so, but it occurred to me that the entire stunt might be an elaborate trap to ensnare *me* personally. Anyone who has read my columns for any length of time probably knows that if a sandwich shop opens in the back of a convenience store or a barbecue pitmaster sets up outside of a gas station, it's practically a guarantee that I'll find some way to write about it. An internet troll wouldn't have to think too far out of the box to realize that a secret homestyle Chinese restaurant is right in my wheelhouse.

The truth turned out to be somewhat more mundane. A group of friends decided to write "reviews" of a dinner party hosted by their friend Chiu, reportedly an excellent Chinese cook. Chiu's friends had long told him that he should open his own restaurant. "Maybe your misadventure will finally motivate him to try," "James T." wrote.

I hope it does. At the risk of playing to type, I have to admit: If Chiu ever really does open his "moderately ok," top-secret underground Chinese restaurant, I'll be one of the first in line.

Three-Ring Meal:
The Grasping Novelty of Modern Dining

By Jennifer Cockrall-King

From *Eighteen Bridges*

Canadian food journalist Jennifer Cockrall-King has enjoyed a front-row seat as the farm-to-table movement has transformed the food scene. (Her most recent book is *Food Artisans of the Okanagan*.) But at what point, she asks here, does trend-chasing become an end in itself?

I sat frozen, wanting to reach for my wine. My extremities had long ago been numbed by the cold but the syrah was icing over. With two layers of thermal underwear, a parka, and wearing my puffiest down-filled winter mittens, every manoeuvre required precision. I reached out, formed my hand into a claw, advanced it toward the glass. It was like dining using the Canadarm. I slowly brought it back towards me towards my lips, tipped it up, and took a generous glug. Mission accomplished.

There we were, a collection of extreme diners, doing our best to manipulate knives and forks in sub-zero weather. It was January and we were in a farmer's field, hours away from any city, near the aptly named town of Viking, Alberta. (Those who weren't dressed in Everest mountaineer outfits were swaddled in animal pelts.) Here, Blair Lebsack of Edmonton's RGE RD restaurant had built a walled enclosure with giant hay bales and was serving a six-course meal of hay-smoked pork hocks, beet "caviar" and local whisky hot toddies. We dined away under a Ted Harrison sky while coyotes yipped in the distance.

Dining outdoors in January on the Canadian prairies might be carrying things a bit far, but it demonstrates the lengths diners and chefs alike are going to in order to create alt-dining experiences. And rather than a one-off oddity, it's part of the growing enthusiasm that has been building for some time now for the anarchic category of plein air long-table dinners (albeit usually in the summer), pop-up restaurants, food truck rallies, and underground supper clubs. Epicureans in the new Experience Economy—the term coined by B. Joseph Pine and James H. Gilmore in 1998 to describe the shift from a service economy to an economy in which customers buy experiences rather than goods—are clearly chasing moments as much as flavours. Surprise and novelty are practically the main course. We want a tasting menu while skydiving. (Not a real thing). We want a twenty-course audio-visual extravaganza known as a gastro-opera. (Which is a real thing, courtesy of Ultraviolet by Paul Pairet, a restaurant in Shanghai.) We want to drink and dine on a Plexiglas platform, suspended above or beside a major world monument. (Real, as well, for a price, throughdinnerin thesky.com.)

Of course, dining suspended above a world monument and gastro-opera are clearly on the outer edges of this trend, but the gastronomical destination is changing. Even my dining calendar is studded with "one night only" chef collaborations, community hall culinary takeovers, and invitation-only dinners where the destination is revealed at the last moment. There has been enough of a trickle-down effect that I've been wondering whether tastemakers and taste-breakers are growing bored with brick and mortar, stationary, make-a-reservation-for-7-p.m.-on-a-Friday-night restaurants. And yes, I do acknowledge that this feeling might be confined to a jaded, mercurial lot of overfed food writers and globetrotting frequent diners. I have many friends who are still thrilled by a night away from the kids in a dimly lit restaurant.

I recently posed this question—whether fine dining has been replaced by extreme dining—to Irish restaurateur and chef J.P. McMahon. His restaurant, Aniar, in Galway, Ireland, has had a Michelin star since 2013, the very symbol of this tradition. Even so, McMahon trucks with a group of avant-garde chefs who are changing perceptions of what Europe's top dining experiences can and should be. Aniar's menus change daily, and are sourced from ingredients fished, grown or foraged from west Ireland land and sea. Burnt kale ash stands in for black pepper. Tea is steeped from wild plants.

"Fine dining is often not viable on its own," replied McMahon, reinforcing that the market is speaking loudly and clearly. He told me that his tapas bar, Cava Bodega, "pays for the fine dining [of Aniar]." He and his wife Drigìn Gaffey also own a gastropub called EAT. Without these two businesses, there would be no Michelin-starred Aniar. He told me about Bubbledogs, a popular Champagne and hotdog joint in London, the profit of which supports an adjacent nineteen-seat upscale space with a multi-course prix-fixe menu for £88 per person. "And the owner, Albert, just opened a fine dining restaurant and a taquería in the same space in Barcelona!"

Albert is Albert Adrià, of the Adrià brothers' culinary fame. At the turn of the millennium, their groundbreaking el Bulli restaurant in Spain pioneered molecular gastronomy, a culinary pursuit in which chefs doubled as scientists to reshape the presentation of ingredients. Until it closed down in 2014, it was untouchable as the world's most inventive restaurant. But even before closing el Bulli, the brothers were moving ahead, envisioning a collection of Barcelona-based restaurants in which nary a single white tablecloth would be spotted. Their stated objective from the outset was to create the world's first culinary amusement park.

Currently, their park includes Bodega 1900, a vermutería (a neighbourhood bar that specializes in vermouth-based drinks, cold cuts and potato chips). There's Tickets tapas bar, and 41° cocktail bar, both casual. Pakta is a Japanese-Peruvian fusion restaurant. Add to that the aforementioned taquería, Niño Viejo. Albert Adrià has been blunt in discussing the business model—the casual (and profitable) sites make the upscale restaurants possible.

I met Albert Adrià in October 2015, in Calgary of all places. He was travel-weary from weekly commutes between Barcelona and Ibiza (apparently, their culinary amusement park has an outpost on the Mediterranean island). It was an entirely new concept, he told me, switching between Spanish and English mid-sentence. Heart Ibiza wants to combine theatre, live music, dance performances and culinary experiences as you wander the various spaces of this hedonistic nightclub. You might be thinking that it's as if the Adrià brothers went into the restaurant business with Cirque du Soleil's founder Guy Laliberté. But wait, they did go into this business together. And who does experience better than Cirque du Soleil? That said, I'm not sure that I want an actual circus in my face while I'm trying to eat. It's enough to make me pre-nostalgic (in that I haven't visited Heart Ibiza yet) for those expansive, baroque dining rooms where waiters glide phantom-like between a sequestered kitchen and your very own table, at which you dine with your very own friends or family, and eat food that's actually about the food. Ah, the good old days.

I found myself wondering, not for the first or last time I suspect, where the fickle winds of food trends were blowing this past July as my skin prickled in 38-degree Okanagan heat. I was lined up with some friends, waiting to board a yellow school bus. We were schlepping our own chairs, our own small table, our own food. We were, as dictated by a set of rules, dressed hat-to-heels in white. Not beige. Not ivory. Not eggshell. But bright, stark, white. We didn't know where the bus would take us—that's part of the fun. More than a thousand of us arrived in concert and were herded into a public park overlooking a beach, an invasion of white that was probably visible from space. It was my third Diner en Blanc, a flashmob dining event that bills itself as a "secret posh picnic" in multiple locations around the world on a set day. Despite the hassle, the rules, the rigid dress code and that it's by invitation only, the event is wildly popular. In 2015, there were white dinners in 65 cities such as Kigali, Mexico City and Paris (where the registered trademark event originated).

Our group's leader marched us to our designated spot on the lawn. We were instructed to set up our chairs and tables. Dinner would commence in less than 10 minutes with the waving of our white cloth napkins above our heads. Soon enough, we uncorked our one allotted bottle of wine, ate our dinner (which we'd made ourselves earlier that day) and danced barefoot on the grass. On cue—and on schedule—we decamped as quickly as we came. It was fun, but it was an awful lot of effort.

The effort did make me begin to wonder what is there to do when both diners and chefs have moved, strange as it may seem, beyond the food and habits of traditional fine dining? Is "experience" the only thing left? Diners sweat through a regulation all-white outfit at a secret group picnic. Restaurateurs serve pub food and tapas to pay for their more creative impulses. And if you're the Adrià brothers, you literally send in the clowns. Sigh. Cheque please.

Sorry, Blue Apron, the Joys of Cooking Can't Fit in a Box

By Corby Kummer

From *The New Republic*

As *The Atlantic*'s long-time food columnist, Corby Kummer was a pioneer in helping food coverage win a place in mainstream magazines. He always offers an intelligent, entertaining perspective on new gastronomic issues and trends—like this year's sudden surge of meal-kit dining.

Really, why would anyone who loves food—discovering it, hunting for the elusive ingredient, researching how to treat it right—give up the pleasure of finding and fondling it? Why, that is, would anyone pay a premium for a large box filled with ice packs and little baggies and tiny shampoo-sized bottles whose contents will produce a few meals and a lot to recycle?

That's what I thought when I started reading about companies that packed up drops of hoisin and pinches of Aleppo pepper to ship the makings of one recipe to your kitchen. Who would put up with such waste? Who would let somebody else tell you how to follow a recipe, be the unseen hand constricting your every move in the most sacrosanct space of your kitchen? Companies kept opening to waves of publicity. Nuts, I thought. It'll never catch on.

I won't be marketing my services as an investment adviser, at least not soon. Friends and relatives are ordering these boxes—functional adults who know how to cook and have at least a passing familiarity with grocery stores and farmers' markets. More startlingly, one friend is putting money into "meal-kit" companies, as he informed me is the term of art. It seemed clear I couldn't keep dismissing Blue Apron, with its three million meals a month and almost $200 million in venture capital raised so far. Or its rival Plated, co-founded by two fresh-out-of-Harvard-Business-School entrepreneurs, Nick Taranto and Josh Hix, whose office I recently visited. On one wall was a huge drawing of the Plated world of the future, with employees dispensing Plated boxes as if from a CSA in a mini-grocery store run, of course, by Plated; vertical farms along the brick walls of a reclaimed factory neighborhood; cyclists bearing Plated boxes; and, my favorite touch, hovering drones dangling multiple boxes emblazoned with the bright red Plated logo. Both services deliver to all the Lower 48—or as Matt Salzberg, the founding CEO of Blue Apron, put it, "We reach 99.7 percent of the population."

Just Add Cooking, the Boston-area company my friend invested in, was co-founded by Jan Leife, who in his native Sweden witnessed the success of Middagsfrid, often referred to as the world's first meal-kit company (it dates to the dark ages of 2007). Purple Carrot, another Boston-area company but one that is all-vegan and ships to the Northeast and Mid-Atlantic, emphasizes the farm origins of its ingredients—like everybody else, now that the local, sustainable gloss is mandatory.

I spent an afternoon in the stunning Buckhead, Georgia, home of Hadi Irvani, the young founder of PeachDish, a meal-kit company that has already made it into the big leagues: It was featured alongside Plated in a recent *Today Show* segment. Once a week, Irvani's home serves as a test kitchen for recipes. I tasted and watched as the team—including Seth Freedman, a chef who spent time teaching cooking at a farmers' market in an underserved Atlanta neighborhood, and Judith Winfrey, a former leader of a local Slow Food chapter—worked on perfecting the instructions for a broccoli-scallion-egg stir-fry from *Root to Leaf: A Southern Chef Cooks Through the Seasons*, a new cookbook by Atlanta's most farmer-friendly chef, Steven Satterfield.

All meal-kit companies have teaching in their mission, or say they do, along with encouraging people to cook at home—against which no right-minded person can argue. At a price of about $9 to $12 per person per meal, they need somehow to make the experience they offer compelling and exciting. They're competing with prepared-meal sections in supermarkets; restaurants, particularly "fast casual"; and an ever-increasing number of grocery-and meal-delivery services, including UberEats and Google Express.

The companies are trying to give customers options to fill the at-home-on-a-weeknight gaps (generally three meals a week, one owner told me) with leftovers for one more meal and a lunch—portions are very large.

The advantages of meal kits are by now familiar: No more bottles of fenugreek that go stale once you've used a half-teaspoon for that Indian recipe. You can take a chance on a new and possibly scary ingredient, say fish sauce. Meal kits bring Slow Food Ark of Taste ingredients to the masses who have never heard of Slow Food, let alone the Ark of Taste, which are ingredients at risk of extinction—in the case of PeachDish's Halloween chili, merkén, a Chilean spice and pepper blend. Meal kits hold hope for the always-vexing problem of cooking for one, in which buying small amounts while maintaining a varied menu can seem discouraging, if not downright depressing.

Over three cook-a-thon evenings, one with only my spouse and the others with groups of six and ten people, I tried a variety of meals from four different companies. What all had in common was a lot of packaging. All of the companies are strenuously, and loudly, working to reduce this problem: Plated has moved to a compostable "Jutebox" bag that looks like woven brown grass in a dry-cleaner bag and can be recycled; Blue Apron says it is starting a packaging returns program. There's the unwrapping and laying out of *mise en place*; proteins are at the bottom, between ice packs, then the heavier produce, like potatoes, then the bits and bobs of spice and sauce packets, or "knickknacks," as Blue Apron somewhat too cutely calls them.

Certainly, there was fun in cooking together, and the reason corporations buy cooking-school time for team-building exercises kicked in: The teams I'd assembled had to learn to work together, figure out sometimes opaque or misleading instructions, sort and delegate chores, and try to be considerate but expedient, even when it was clear their cooking partner had no idea how to peel a clove of garlic, let alone identify and separate one from the full head. I could sternly tell teams, including one newlywed husband, that the first commandment of cooking is to clean up as you go. Too many recipes called for a profligate number of pots; only PeachDish admirably stuck to its pledge of no more than one pot and one pan per recipe. Every recipe from every company took longer than the instruction card promised.

Surprisingly for services that target total food novices, one thing not provided on most instruction cards was the basic information any decently written cookbook includes: exactly what equipment is necessary; the order of what to preheat and when; and which steps to do first and how long each step should take. Only one company said to wash all produce and herbs. One cooking team member sliced through a long, fresh green jalapeño lengthwise and immediately jumped back, her nose running and her hands tingling; soon everybody was wheezing. Nothing in the directions said gloves were essential and cold running water would quell the fumes.

As a longtime veteran of cooking classes and demonstrations, and as a pedant, I enjoyed showing the garlic neophyte how to smash the clove with the flat of a knife and then mash it with a bit of salt to release the flavor without releasing the strongest chemicals, a favorite trick Barbara Kafka shared in her cooking classes. What I didn't realize I needed to do was tell people to taste for seasoning: One card said to salt at three or four different stages, something a chef would do, but always tasting each time. One company sent a bag of pretty coral-colored seasoned salt without saying just how much should go in, resulting in inedible dishes when the teams logically assumed the right amount was all of it.

Who would put up with such waste? Who would let somebody else tell you how to follow a recipe?

Would I ever buy another meal kit? Nah. I appreciate the idea that a party in a box comes to your door, but for me half the party—all of it, really, in my version of cooking for one—comes from meeting the people who sell the food I'm looking for, the serendipity of discovering, say, a new kind of lobed winter squash, getting it home, and figuring out what to do with it. I see how meal kits can unlock these worlds—I admit I'd never made a daal, a huge and versatile category, and so of all the meals I tried, Just Add Cooking's simple daal with various Indian spices, peppers, and a base of sautéed onion was the most satisfying and memorable. But they don't offer depth.

The kits did make me slightly revise a longstanding criticism of myself as a cook: that I'm too slavish to recipes. I say it's because I'm so enraptured with the writer and want to experience their world, but it's really because I'm a timid and literal-minded cook. Yet the lack of notes from any of the companies encouraging—mandating—improvisation got to me. The instruction cards generally elicited presentable results. The dishes and platters my somewhat flustered and tired but content groups brought to the table were attractive enough. But they mostly had the homely, let's-ooh-and-aah-for-the-earnest-kids look of a small paint-by-numbers oil. The outlines were someone else's. The spaces were precisely mapped out. The coloring in was sometimes skilled, sometimes ungainly. But it was always a facsimile.

Recipes are blueprints, nothing more. The trouble with meal kits is if they achieve their goal of making people try and then embrace the exotic and new, and give them long-hoped-for confidence in cooking, they'll liberate the newly hatched cook from ever buying another meal kit. So they can't last as a viable business. Remember what I said about my investment advice?

Quitting Season

By Debbie Weingarten

From *Edible Baja Arizona*

Based in Tucson, Arizona, Debbie Weingarten doesn't just write about the local artisanal food culture—she's also a community activist on issues of food security and organic farming. These small-scale family farmers are her friends—so when one local star went belly-up, Weingarten could give the story extra nuance and depth.

This past February, Tina Bartsch, co-owner of Walking J Farm, sat cross-legged on the floor of my Tucson apartment. We ate lunch and watched my newly mobile baby move in curious circles around the room. For the last several years, Tina and I have provided each other with moral support as we navigated the precarious balance of farm and family. We've traded homeschooling curriculum and birthday party invitations; we've called each other in frustrated tears and celebrated yoga teacher certifications and new babies; we've cursed the glut of cheap redistributed produce at the farmers' markets and spent hours together in meetings trying to solve the food system gaps in our community.

On this particular day in February, Tina told me that she and her husband, Jim McManus, had decided to stop farming. Though many of our conversations had touched on this as a potential inevitability, this time it was real. After five years of solid recordkeeping, the numbers showed the farm operating at a net loss every single year.

A month prior, Tina and Jim had traveled from Amado to Clarkdale to present their agribusiness success story at the second annual Arizona

Food & Finance Forum. But over the course of a 20-minute presentation, McManus shared the farm's sobering financial reality, hoping to spotlight the disconnect between the local food craze and farmers being able to make a living.

"What I've determined is that I can't go on this way," McManus said to the forum attendees. He explained that after calculating the full cost associated with producing a single beef cow, the farm was losing $62 per animal selling by the quarter, and averaging a mere $214 profit per animal selling retail cuts at the market. McManus announced that they had no choice but to raise their retail prices by 40 percent; the week before, a pound of Walking J ground beef had cost $8, and this week it was going to cost $11.

"Every year we've gone up three percent, five percent to match inflation . . . but that hasn't been enough," he said, adding that, "we are running a big test here. We don't know if the market will bear it, or what our customers are going to say. A lot of folks are going to really swallow hard when they see that their filet went up $10 a pound. But that's what I have to do. That's what the numbers say."

A month later, the results of Walking J's experiment were in. The market was not willing to bear the increase in price, and Walking J's last effort to save the farm by charging prices based on the true cost of meat production was a flop. Since raising their prices, the farm had lost 30 to 70 percent of their client sales. The customers had spoken loud and clear.

"It's a no-brainer at this point," Tina told me, as we sat together in my living room. "We have to quit."

I have been that farmer who chose to step away from the farm, and though I chose it as surely as I chose the farm in the first place, it has been no less a loss. Barring a catastrophic event, the decision to stop farming is rarely made overnight. Depending on how you look at it, it is either a steady erosion or a slow coming-to. Farmers spend years crunching numbers, tweaking production methods, and trying to stay ahead of market trends. There may be second or third jobs, a clambering for creative financing, or a reliance on government assistance programs such as SNAP, the Supplemental Nutrition Assistance Program, or state health insurance. Year after year, the decision to quit can be kept at bay by a successful season or the hope that next season will be easier. But at some point, for some of us, the scale just tips. The moment comes when continuing feels too risky, the path forward too unsure—when it makes the most sense to quit.

In the beginning, Walking J hit the ground running with a smattering of products for the local marketplace, including chicken, turkey, pork, beef, eggs, and produce. Year after year, they ticked off the microenterprises that did not pay the bills. The heritage pork did not make money, nor did the Thanksgiving turkeys. The layer hens required too much outside feed, as did the broiler chickens. The farm's pastured poultry system demanded bimonthly slaughters of 150 birds, which required an immense amount of time, skilled labor, and freezer space.

Jim and Tina embraced a direct-market sales model, typical for a small-scale diversified operation. They started a CSA group, for community supported agriculture; built partnerships with high-end restaurants; and began vending at the Tucson farmers' markets. But as the number of those farmers' markets increased and the pool of customers became diluted as a result, they were forced to seek out new markets. They drove to Nogales with product, tried to establish a CSA in the nearby town of Tubac, opened up a Saturday farm stand, started an online store, and eventually made their way up to Phoenix markets. At one point, they were staffing six farmers' markets each week. In 2012, Walking J Farm received a USDA grant—which they had to match with a private loan from family members—to cover marketing costs, meat processing, and the purchase of butcher cattle.

Despite their exhaustive efforts to offer a variety of sales outlets, meet product demand, and create meaningful and profitable relationships with their customers, Tina says that it became clear that the business was not making money.

What followed Walking J's announcement was a flurry of bewilderment and a general sense of shock among friends and customers. Supporters took to social media to encourage their friends to flood Walking J's market booth with sales. Someone suggested an emergency Kickstarter. But urgent Facebook posts and new Twitter followers do not save a farm. Jim and Tina were financially, physically, and emotionally tapped.

No one wants to think about farmers calling it quits. It muddies the heroic glow cast around our food producers. It cuts through all of the feel-good chatter about food systems and local economies. Each time a farmer quits, a little piece of our new agrarian dream dies. But however hard it is to discuss, the rate at which farmers are walking away from their farms—whether by choice or by force—may be the most important measure for whether our food systems are actually working. Because although farmers' markets are springing up everywhere—and although heirloom kale has never been more popular—the average small-scale farmer is barely surviving.

For farmers like Jim and Tina, who believe in producing food by stewarding their land responsibly and supporting plant, animal, and microbe biodiversity, a direct-market relationship with customers who support those production values makes sense. But if our farmers cannot charge prices based on the cost of real production numbers, this model falls flat.

Consider these numbers from a 2011 study, which shows that southern Arizona farmers and ranchers on average sell a collective $300 million of food products per year, yet spend $320 million to raise those crops. The same study finds net farm income trends have been negative since 1989, which means that our farmers have consistently lost money producing food. According to the same study, southern Arizona farmers and ranchers reportedly lost $106 million in 2009, which equaled 39 percent of all sales that year. 2004 was the only recent year when southern Arizona farmers earned more than they spent producing food.

National numbers reflect our region's numbers. According to the 2012 Census of Agriculture, farmers earned just 10 percent of their income from farm sales, while approximately 90 percent of their income came from off-farm occupations. The projected median farm income for 2015 is negative $1,558.

We are better local food consumers when we remember that our farmers are not just growing our food—they are human beings, who are trying to refinance their mortgages, purchase dependable health insurance, fix their teeth, send their kids to college, and take a vacation once in a while. Behind the scenes, our farmers spend hours at the computer, wearily adding up market totals and expenditures. It is here in this solitary lamp-lit space that farmers visit some very dark emotional places. It is impossible to convey the deep anxiety for everything at stake, the fear that accompanies the risk, and the wounds that this stress inflicts upon a psyche or a family.

Although the choice to stop farming is a personal one, there is a familiar narrative that repeats in quiet reverberations across our country's farmscapes. Lisa and Ali Moussalli are the former owners of Frog Bottom Farm, a small-scale diversified farm in Appomattox County, Virginia. Having spent years apprenticing with other farmers, the Moussallis were firm in their resolve to build a business that could support their family without the reliance on off-farm income. This priority forced the couple to be absolutely diligent in their expenses and calculations.

"There was never a day when we weren't thinking about the financial soundness of our business," Lisa remembers. "Can we afford a second tractor? Are we charging enough for eggs? What's a reasonable debt burden? Should we drop this market? Are cherry tomatoes and green beans worth the labor?"

When the Moussallis purchased their land, they planned to continue farming there for many years. And while they fell deeply in love with their farm and the lifestyle that it afforded their family, Lisa says, "It was the relentlessness of our worry that eventually wore us down."

Though Frog Bottom Farm was never technically failing, they were always just scraping by. Lisa and Ali wanted to have a second child, and like any growing family, they craved financial stability. During a conversation in the fall of 2012, the couple made the heartbreaking decision to sell the farm.

"We were sitting in the kitchen discussing our finances . . . and suddenly everything seemed very clear," Lisa remembers. "Ali suddenly said, 'Our family is more important than our farm.' And there it was."

Two years after their last season at Frog Bottom Farm, Lisa, Ali, and their two young children live a block away from the Delaware Bay in southern New Jersey. Ali commutes to work as a full-time manager at Beach Plum Farm, where he and his crew work to provide produce, herbs, honey, eggs, and pork for three farm-to-table restaurants in the resort town of Cape May. With the support of Lisa and the kids, Ali is still farming, and as Lisa says, "His work is still full of the problem solving and tangible results he loves."

Though Lisa admits that the shift away from their life at Frog Bottom Farm has been hard at times, she says they don't regret their decision to leave. Beach Plum Farm offers an alternative model of food production—not only by truly walking the walk of farm-to-table, but prioritizing the stability of its farmers by providing a salary, health insurance, and a 401k.

In Iowa, Shanti Sellz, the owner of Iowa City's Muddy Miss Farm, considers farming her career and does not intend to quit. But she does question whether the small-scale direct-market model will provide her with long-term stability.

Sellz, who spent nearly a decade as an activist and farmer educator in Tucson, has been farming since she was 16 years old. In 2012, she moved back to her hometown of Iowa City, armed with a small amount of savings and a business plan for a small-scale diversified farming enterprise. Now in her fourth season of farming on her own, Sellz is cultivating a cooperative model with a fellow farmer. This model allows the farmers to share resources, such as labor, equipment, fuel, and marketing. Sellz and her cooperative partner then aggregate their products in order to create volume and to cater to a more diverse market. Like any farmer, Sellz constantly questions her farm's specific model, but she feels strongly that sharing the risk, instead of taking it on completely as a sole proprietor, has many benefits.

Sellz reiterates that finding the right model is as much about financial sustainability as it is about human sustainability. She says, "I want to farm, and there is no reason why I shouldn't be able to make a living if my profession is feeding people, which is one of our society's most basic needs."

And this is where all of the stories, told and untold, seem to collide. Like the Moussallis, like the farmers of Walking J Farm, like the hundreds of thousands of farmers producing food across our country, Sellz is simply trying to make a living by doing what she does best: feeding her community.

"I am a good farmer," Sellz says. "I successfully grow a lot of food for a lot of people, and in a time when most people have lost connection to where their food comes from. If I don't grow food, who will?"

Wendell Berry asks, "Why do farmers farm, given their economic adversities on top of the many frustrations and difficulties normal to farming? And always the answer is: love. They must do it for love."

I have an immense amount of respect for Wendell Berry, but I am growing tired of this answer. Certainly it would be a mistake to become a farmer if you did not enjoy being outside, if you were not fiercely independent, if you did not enjoy the physical labor involved in food production. But a farmer cannot survive simply by loving her profession. Love does not pay the mortgage, put diesel in the tractor, or make up lost revenue after a late freeze. Love does not fix hands spent from years of milking goats or resurrect the CSA vegetables when the walk-in refrigerator goes out in the middle of a summer night.

When farmers choose to transition to alternative models of farming, or to quit altogether, they are making decisions that best support their lives, families, and careers. As Sellz says, "Farmers are inherently practical people. We have to be. If something is working, we pursue it and give it everything we have. But if it's not working—if we are losing money, our health, or if it's just not sustainable—we have to try something different. We get creative, find alternatives, leave enterprises that are not valuable to us. We survive."

Although Tina and Jim can imagine Walking J's finances stabilizing in five to 10 years, Tina explains, "That's a long time to sit in the hole and work to get out of the red. And we just aren't willing to do that. It doesn't make sense."

Of the moment that she and Jim decided to quit, Tina says, "It was emotional, but it was a relief. We had all these questions. How do you shut a business down? How do you do it? And Jim's like, 'You just do it. You just stop.' He said, 'We've got to stop the bleeding.'"

There is no disputing the fact that communities love their farmers. Walking J Farm has been heralded as one of the most successful and beloved farms in the region. And here is the disturbing reality at the crux of this entire issue: the fact is that Walking J Farm is so beloved in the southern Arizona local food community, that its farmers are so intelligent, so conscientious, so good at what they do—but they still cannot make a living from the farm. And this is not because they have failed—it is because our archaic food and agriculture system has failed *them*. One thing remains certain: if, as a society, we don't prioritize the health, well-being, and financial solvency of our farmers, we will lose them by the droves—along with all of their precious resources, talent, and skill—and along with our food.

Down the Hatch

The True Story of Good Coffee

By Matt Buchanan

From TheAwl.com

Features editor of *Eater* and former co-editor of The Awl (motto: Be less stupid), Matt Buchanan has also worked at BuzzFeed and Gizmodo, so you might say that tongue-in-cheek is his second language. (Or maybe his first.) And it has not escaped his notice that coffee is having a big cultural moment.

There was a time not so long ago when all of the coffee in the entire United States of America was bad. It only came in giant cans and it was roasted and ground until it tasted like dirt and no one who drank it knew where any of it came from or even cared because it was very cheap and all of the coffee farmers were very sad. But then in 1966 there was a man, because of course it was a man, and he realized that if he made the coffee a little bit better by roasting it darker he could charge more for it, and his name was Alfred Peet. And then in 1971 there were some other men, and they talked to Alfred, and one of those men went by the name of Howard Schultz, and he made sure that everybody in America was awakened by the ancient Italian coffee known as the Frappuccino. A couple of decades later, in 1995, there was another, a man but also a woman, and their names were Doug Zell and Emily Mange, and they decided that they would buy coffee directly from coffee farmers and not blend it with coffee from other farmers and that also they wouldn't roast it all that dark, so you could taste the flavors of the actual farm where this "single-origin" coffee came from, sort of like wine, which costs a lot of money, and maybe coffee could cost that much too, and they called their coffee Intelligentsia. Other men, like a man in Portland named Duane Sorenson, thought that Good Coffee was a Good Idea, but he could make it Better, so in 1999, he went to the countries where they farm the coffee and took a lot of pictures and posted them online and said things like, "I don't want to sell my coffee to everyone . . . It's not for everyone. I don't have the fucking time for it, man." It was like a whole Wave of coffee, and I guess that is when the coffee became Good and many people in many cool cities drank it, or at least that is how the story goes.

Over the next few years, a lot of other foods, meat and vegetables and alcoholic beverages alike, became Good too—sustainably raised, ethically uprooted, hand-slaughtered, locally bartered—and a whole lot of people with a lot of money decided that they really liked Good Food, especially as a way to show how they were better than other people with a lot of money. This made the people who were making the Good Coffee think, "Wow, a lot more people could be drinking our Good Coffee, which is currently only a mediocre capitalist venture with marginal profits," even though they had three or six or ten stores and were selling a good amount of coffee to cafes and restaurants who wanted to serve their Good Coffee. Some people with money, mostly but not entirely men, called venture capitalists, or investors for short, agreed with them, and started giving some of the coffee men money to expand. In 2011, a company called TSG, which had previously given the world VitaminWater, bought most of Stumptown, which had realized that while it would be cool to open roasteries and cafes all over the country, it would be even cooler to sell its Good Coffee to a LOT more people, so they put it in retro-style glass bottles and in cute cartons with milk and sugar and, more recently, in nitro cans and giant kegs, which could be marketed as "cold brew on tap" and sold all over the place, so customers didn't have to bother with any of the things that make brewing Good Coffee so annoying. And things were Pretty Good.

At the same time, in San Francisco, another coffee man, named James Freeman, had started a Good Coffee company called Blue Bottle. One of things that made his coffee company different is that in addition to selling his Good Coffee out of beautiful shops, it was based in San Francisco at a time when there were a lot of men with a lot of money and a lot of taste—because they made apps, or gave money to other men to make apps, in order to change the entire world (which requires a lot of discernment). These tasteful app men loved Blue Bottle so much they gave it twenty million dollars, and then twenty-five million dollars, and finally seventy million dollars (that's over a hundred million dollars), so that their favorite coffee company could grow—"scale"—just like their favorite app companies, and acquire millions of users and change the world with Good Coffee. Blue Bottle took that money and acquired some other, smaller Good Coffee companies and a famous San Francisco bakery and it opened some more coffee shops and it sold lots and lots of cute Good Coffee cartons and it even acquired a company that will let it sell Good Coffee in every grocery store in every city in America. Wow. Every other Good Coffee company suddenly looked very small next to Blue Bottle's big pile of money. This made some of them decide to raise money too, and because venture capitalists do not want to miss a good opportunity to venture their capital in order to acquire more of it, they gave millions of dollars to other companies that they thought might have Good Coffee, like La Colombe Torrefaction, and even obviously not-so-good coffee companies like Philz Coffee.

Meanwhile, in a land far away, called Europe, there is a company called JAB Holding Company. It owns a lot of other companies, like Jimmy Choo, and many of its companies own companies of their own. A lot of these companies that its companies own are coffee companies with Fine Brands, like Caribou Coffee, Espresso House, Baresso Coffee, Tassimo, Senseo, Gevalia, and many others. In 2012, the year that the app men started giving money to Blue Bottle, one of JAB's companies bought Alfred Peet's Fine Coffee company, Peet's Coffee & Tea.

A few months ago, for reasons that are still not clear, but perhaps because Stumptown was not "scaling" fast enough to become the next VitaminWater (maybe because Duane Sorensen became a restaurant man, and not so much of a coffee man anymore, or at least that is what many other coffee men and women say, but who knows), TSG decided to sell its stake in Stumptown, and a few weeks ago, Peet's decided to buy it, because it was a Good Coffee Brand whose ready-made cold brew would be easy to scale. That same week, it became public that Intelligentsia, after twenty years in business—some of which were financially rocky, according to many coffee men and women, despite making it all the way to Los Angeles and New York from Chicago—put itself up for sale or a lot of investment, whatever. Peet's decided to buy it, too, because while it owned a lot of Fine Coffee Brands, it could always use another Good Coffee Brand.

There are perhaps some people who will be upset that their favorite Good Coffee Company is now just another Good Coffee Brand, revealing once again the insignificance of their person and the futility of their Brand Devotion when it is set against forces vastly larger than themselves, like capitalism, but they should take solace in the fact that even if the Good Coffee Brand becomes less Good as it becomes ever larger—which, FWIW, Blue Bottle has only gotten better as it has gotten bigger—it was never even Great to begin with. It was just coffee.

Getting Drunk on Tea Infusions with Montreal's Underground Connoisseurs

By Rowan Jacobsen

From *Vice Magazine*

In this piece for *Vice Magazine*, Rowan Jacobsen takes a break from his usual masterful journalism about food and the environment (*A Geography of Oysters*, *American Terroir*, and *Apples of Uncommon Character*, among other books) to attend a tea party. But definitely *not* your grandma's tea party.

Near dusk, once the last customers had been sent off clutching their sachets of Earl Grey and green jasmine, K closed the doors of his little shop in Montreal's Latin Quarter and lowered the blinds. A few of us had already gathered, and by dark a few more trickled in. We pushed six tables together, set two electric kettles to near boiling, and started to unload our haul—foil pouches with Hong Kong addresses, baggies of dried green herbs with scribbled notes. This select group of collectors had gathered in North America's best tea shop for the free-for-all that K officially calls "After Hours." When he described it to me, he said, "Think *Fight Club*." Everybody brings his or her best stuff and, under the guise of camaraderie, hopes to be pummeled into enlightenment.

We'd taste 15 to 20 teas, doing several infusions of each. K asked whether I'd ever been tea-drunk. A whole leaf releases caffeine more slowly than a pulverized bean, but the more players you add, the more it builds toward a kind of mental gamelan concert. "When you consume a lot of tea, like we're going to do tonight," K said, "it's quite a nice buzz, because you're getting very stimulated and very soothed at the same time."

Tea geeks eschew sugar. Milk is kryptonite to them. They seek out teas of consummate lightness, often coming from tiny "gardens" in places like Darjeeling, Taiwan, and southern China. These rare teas have always simmered on the back burner of caffeine culture, damned by association with Grandma's cuppa. To coffee people, tea is just dirty water. But lately, as more people have discovered *Camellia sinensis*'s 5,000-year pedigree and pharmaceutical charms, it has become an unlikely breakout.

I'd gotten to know K at a UC Davis conference on terroir, the French term for "taste of place," in 2012. He was the tea guy with the crisp English accent and diction so soft and precise that it could be taken for menace. We poured a legendary cabernet from one of Napa's best vineyards, and the Masters of Wine in the group expounded on its "powerful nose" and "essence of cassis." Then K set down his glass and said, "There's a hole right through the center of this one." And we all got quiet and stared at our glasses because, now that he mentioned it, there was a hole right through the center.

I stayed in touch, bought teas whenever I was in town, and every now and then he slid me stuff that was beyond my pay grade. It was exhilarating to get a glimpse of tea's heights, the ethereal aromatics that had no earthly analogues, and depressing to realize just how low on the mountain I'd been toiling. Then K let slip that he'd soon be returning from Asia with some ridiculously rare goodies. "I guarantee that a tasting of this caliber is not happening anywhere else in North America," he told me. I gave him the full puppy dog, and he said I could come, but he banned cameras and other obvious journalistic paraphernalia. The first rule of Tea Club is you do not talk about Tea Club. "Can I take notes?" I asked. "Everybody takes notes," he said.

At K's shop, the tables were scattered with notepads and packets of tea and an insane number of pots—some triangular, some heavy-bellied, some iron, some clay. All were tiny by Western standards. Serious tea is to Lipton as espresso is to Folgers. Fistfuls of leaves are stuffed into elfin pots for brief, intense infusions. After a few hits, your mind does somersaults.

For our first cup, we had a golden Bi Luo—"Snail Spring"—from Yunnan. We set the pots on boats—low wooden boxes with slatted tops—and filled them to the brim with water, then pushed down the lids so water cascaded over the sides and through the slats. It was nice and malty, but everyone withheld praise. It was just a warm-up.

We followed it with a Yiwu made from centuries-old wild tea trees, then white tea, oolong, Hei He Shan from the Vietnam border. The cups were coming every few minutes, and I began to feel my chest opening like a flower.

By the 20th cup, the heavy hitters came out. K staggered us with a chestnut-scented Thurbo Estate from Darjeeling. "So spacious," somebody murmured. Everything was hyper-sharp, like I'd been chewing coca leaves all day. I wondered whether I was tea-drunk.

The oolong specialist at the shop presented a velvety Da Hong Pao from China's Wuyi Mountains, some of the oldest tea turf on Earth. Good Wuyi costs more per ounce than gold. "It's the Holy Grail of tea," he said. "In Japan, Taiwan, and India, we know what the best teas are. We can find them. But China is different. Over a million producers, with the longest history and culture. Some old families still have the best plants and knowledge. There's always some double-black-belt master in the Wuyi Mountains making tea beyond what you've encountered."

The Tea Club usually ends with the Pu'ers. Most teas are best as fresh as possible, but Pu'ers get better with age, making them eminently collectible. In China, Pu'er "cakes"—compressed disks the size of small Frisbees—are bought and sold like masterpieces. This spring, a disk of ultra-rare 1910 Pu'er surfaced in Vancouver at a price of $600,000.

A Gérard Depardieu lookalike who writes the poetic descriptions for K's online catalogue brewed a 1996 Dayi full of musty cave energy. It drank like a Werner Herzog film. Like all Pu'ers, it's prized ($15 a gram, if you must know) as much for its chi as its flavor. "With great teas, I always look for that special feeling," he said. "Westerners taste from the neck up. But in Asia, they taste with their whole body."

"Nice bib on that one," said K, tracing the chi down his chest.

The Depardieu lookalike, who leads whiskey-tea-pairing seminars around Montreal, broke out a bottle of 2003 Evan Williams single-barrel bourbon and matched it with a 1976 Bai Hao roasted oolong that made us swoon. I was deep in the cave, free-associating like a schizophrenic, dots of meaning stippling my consciousness, and suddenly a theory of "The Leaf and the Bean" coalesced on the cave wall. Tea, I realized, doesn't work like coffee or wine, where flavor is an edifice built from blocks of compounds, like a cathedral, the more complex the more impressive. It's more like a reflecting pool, where you lean in closer and closer, seeing nothing, and then suddenly the wind stops and the ripples calm and you gasp as the whole sky blinks back at you.

I turned to communicate my revelation to my fellow clubbers, but the kettles were already burbling for another round. There were still a few hours of night, and there was so much more tea to drink. As the sun swung hard around Yunnan, firing a trillion chloroplasts on green terraced hillsides, K filled his pot with something rare and potent—I'd lost track of what—and wraiths of steam rose from the clay as we drained our cups and tested one another's limits. Sooner or later, we knew, the light would come.

The Great Bourbon Taste Test

By Wells Tower

From *Garden & Gun*

Short-story writer and journalist Wells Tower grew up in
North Carolina, which apparently was enough of a connection
to be allowed to hang out for a few hours in Nashville with chef
Sean Brock and a pack of other bourbon aficionados. Here's
his account of that gathering—at least, as much as he can
remember.

"I'm not sure we've got enough bourbon," said the chef Sean Brock
on the morning of the epic whiskey tasting. Brock was joking. The
quantity of bourbon in the room had turned the daylight brown.

Bourbon was not only the dominant decor in Brock's downtown
Nashville loft; it was, by volume, the primary occupant. Crowding
Brock's living room were geriatric gallons of Old Grand-Dad and Old
Fitzgerald, enthroned on their own miniature rocking chairs. Imp-scale
bottles peeped out from behind cured hams (another form of furniture
here). Against the near wall stood a four-shelf bookcase stacked three
deep with bottles that would make a bourbon fancier take out a second mortgage. Shelved there were delicious antiques including but not
limited to Old Rip Van Winkle, David Nicholson 1843, and Very Very
Old Fitzgerald, which Brock sells at his acclaimed restaurant Husk for
$240 per pour.

The business at hand, however, was not Brock's deep holdings but a
lately acquired army of fifths, pints, and handles crowding the kitchen
island. With the help of his girlfriend, Adi Noe, Brock—known for his

Charleston, South Carolina, restaurants McCrady's, Minero, and also Husk, whose Nashville branch opened in 2013—was draining the bottles into anonymously numbered flasks for the day's blind tasting.

The collection represented a twenty-four-year "vertical" of W. L. Weller Special Reserve containing a bottle from every year from 1987 to 2010. Vintage Weller is a substance direly coveted by bourbon fanatics. It is a close sibling of Pappy Van Winkle, a bourbon over which the whiskey world has lately gone insane. *Empty* bottles of Pappy can sell on eBay for upwards of a hundred dollars. A full bottle, when it can be found, will set you back thousands. The good news is that modern-day Weller is a lot easier to find than Pappy, and it is genetically identical to the celebrated stuff. Weller and Pappy enter the world in the same distillation. As they age, the most extraordinary barrels get set aside for the Van Winkle line. The unchosen ones are sent off to market under the Weller label at a bit north of twenty dollars a bottle, within reach of the common man.

In Chef Brock's unguarded opinion, vintage Weller is "the best damn whiskey ever made in the whole world. You taste it and you have to have it, no matter the cost. Then you become obsessed with different labels and expressions and years, and then you wake up one day and you have way too much whiskey in your apartment."

The loosely scientific purpose of today's gathering was to determine which bottlings and distilleries have produced the tastiest Weller. This advance in whiskey knowledge, Brock explained, had come at considerable inconvenience and strain. "This will only happen once," he said, topping off a taster's flask. "It's a pain in the ass and it's expensive as hell."

Assembling the twenty-four Wellers took him the better part of a year and the better part of ten thousand dollars. So where did he find all of these obscure bottlings? I asked Brock. He looked at me as though I'd demanded power of attorney. "It's a secret," replied the chef, a solid, low-built man of thirty-seven with plentiful tattoos. "If I tell you where I bought it, then you'll go buy it all, and then I'll kick your ass, and then we're not friends anymore."

Sampling all twenty-four bottles would be a full day's work running from noon to night in two shifts with a lunch break in between. Right around twelve o'clock Brock's team of connoisseurs arrived. There were twelve or so of them, I think (soon into the tasting, they became hard to count). Mostly from out of state, they were a disparate bunch of middle-aged men who had intersected over the Internet at a common node of bourbon obsession. There was Mike, a guy from Pennsylvania who, in addition to ransacking "dusties" from the storerooms of rural liquor stores, worked for a water quality bureau and also collected jeeps. There was a hulking man named Jared, the whiskey curator of the Washington, D.C., bar Jack Rose. Rampant peptic ulcers had forced Jared onto the wagon, but his commitment to bourbon was so intense that he had traveled more than five hundred miles merely to *smell* the Wellers. There were guys who worked in restaurants and residential construction and a guy who claimed to be the campus chaplain at a university in Florida. Beyond maleness, their only ostensible common thread was a nearly hazardous degree of whiskey expertise. To get into conversation with these fellows was to become a receptacle for information about tax stamps, the history of sour mash, Distilled Spirits Plants codes, and the chemistry of barrel char.

Elevating the gathering from an assembly of serious bourbon hobbyists to a conclave of the royal whiskey society was the arrival of Julian Van Winkle III and his son Preston. Julian III is the president of the Old Rip Van Winkle company. He is the grandson of Julian "Pappy" Van Winkle, Sr., the late co-owner of the Stitzel-Weller Distillery, which sits at the headwaters of the Weller/Van Winkle bourbon streams. It was Julian III who first bottled the Pappy Van Winkle line of whiskeys and who also made a bourbon extremist out of Sean Brock.

"I wasn't a bourbon fanatic until I drank Pappy Van Winkle, which wasn't until 2007," Brock recalled. At that point, he had been confining his culinary relentlessness to the meticulous sourcing of heritage rice strains, cowpeas, grits, and Ossabaw Island hogs. In 2008, Van Winkle collaborated with Brock on a Pappy Van Winkle dinner at McCrady's. After that, Brock fell into an obsession whose ferocity outstripped Van Winkle's own.

"Damn," said Van Winkle, taking in Brock's bourbon rack. "And I thought I had it bad." Then Van Winkle turned toward Brock, and in a coals-to-Newcastle gesture, presented the chef with a bottle of twelve-year-old Weller. "What do you want for it?" Brock asked.

"I don't know," said Van Winkle, musing. "Let me drink good whiskey all day, I guess."

By now, the connoisseurs were getting restless. They were up on their toes. They were ready to drink. A visiting journalist, however, was feeling pangs of concern. While the rudiments of bourbon drinking are not lost on me, twenty-four was more glasses of whiskey than I usually have in one go. Grateful though I was to be along for this once-in-a-lifetime binge, I did wonder how much of the vertical I would manage to blind-taste while remaining vertical with sight left in my eyes. The temptation was strong to batten down, to put leashes on my wallet, phone, and keys, to pin to my lapel the address of my hotel. Still, this was anxious expectancy of a pleasurable kind, like anticipating the onset of a sumptuous typhoon.

But in his wisdom Chef Brock had laid in a hospitable array of sobriety preservers: a fleet of deviled eggs, pimento cheese and crackers, ham biscuits with pickled cauliflower, and a saw-your-own hog leg over by the bourbon shelf, a saber jutting from the meat.

There was no spittoon in sight.

"Dig in, boys," Van Winkle said, and so it began. The tasters' sheets were handed out. The men approached the bottles and tipped brave quantities into Glencairn glasses. Each man then stole off to a chair or a corner to get into a communion with his portion. Moans were general.

Van Winkle sat on a pile of cookbooks (in Brock's apartment whiskey fills the bookshelves; books go on the floor) and put his nose into his glass. "This is from back in the day. A little oxidized," he said, when pressed for a description. "Not much oak, huge vanilla. Funky, basementy." He took a sip, tested his palate, and awaited the arrival of adjectives that did not come. "Aw, hell, I'm the worst whiskey writer. I like it or I don't. This, I like."

"Oh, my God," Chef Brock was saying to his glass. "That is so good. That's it right there. That's Stitzel-Weller. I'd know it anywhere."

Without straying too far down connoisseurial rabbit holes, it must be noted that within the general mania for Weller bourbons is the submania for the Stitzel-Weller vintages that has claimed Sean Brock. Opened in Shively, Kentucky, outside Louisville, in 1935, the Stitzel-Weller Distillery churned out W. L. Weller, Old Fitzgerald, Old Cabin Still, and Rebel Yell until 1992, when the business shut down. The W. L. Weller label was then sold to the Bernheim Distillery and resold, in 1999, to the Sazerac Company, whose Buffalo Trace operation produces the Weller and Van Winkle bourbons today. The general consensus in Brock's living room was that Buffalo Trace Wellers are unlikely to recover the glory of the Stitzel-Weller years. Though the mash bill remains the same (using sweeter wheat instead of spicy rye), distilling is an occult business, dependent on the idiosyncrasies of the oak in the barrels, the method of grain milling, the distiller himself, and the thermal felicities of the warehouse where the whiskey is aged.

Stitzel-Weller bourbons, Brock said, still sniffing his sample, could be identified by aromas of maple, butterscotch, basements, and other quiddities that are hard to pin down. "You know when you're in the room with your girlfriend or your wife and you know her smell, her perfume? Stitzel-Weller's like that for me. I'll be surprised if I miss any. It's all I drink."

But what if, God forbid, Brock should find himself far from home at cocktail hour, with no Stitzel-Weller in reach? Which commonly available label would he resort to in a pinch? "Easy: none. It doesn't exist" was his discouraging reply.

By two o'clock, having sampled and rated the first twelve whiskeys, the connoisseurs gathered around the kitchen island to announce their findings. Most eyelids in the room were sagging redly at half mast, but no one yet had fallen down or begun to speak in tongues. As far as the connoisseurship went, green apples, cooked apples, cellars, peanuts, damp periodicals, cardboard, cough drops, Goo Goo Clusters, cocoa, and maple were the notes most commonly cited. After each bottle was commented upon, Adi Noe (who was abstaining and still perfectly literate) would read its vintage from her code sheet, confirming a glum fact: Tasted blind, the bygone Stitzel-Weller bourbons rated the highest.

Nevertheless, Chef Brock was happy. Brock was exuberant. "Who wants to have a push-up contest?" was a question he put before the group. This challenge went unanswered. "All right, all right, who wants to go eat lunch at the greatest restaurant in the entire goddamn world?" At this invitation, the group, in serious need of solid food, perked up.

The greatest restaurant in the world was a place called Arnold's Country Kitchen, a cafeteria-style Southern joint between the Nashville neighborhoods of Pie Town and the Gulch. Arnold's standard bill of fare is a meat and three. But the manager on duty was a sympathetic friend of Chef Brock's, and she had her own prescription for our group's condition. "Just give 'em everything," she told the servers at the steam tables. After a solid ballasting of roast beef, chicken, fried catfish, succotash, potatoes, green beans, stewed okra, black-eyed peas, turnip greens, baked squash, mac and cheese, and peach and chocolate pies, we were once again prepared to look a glass of whiskey in the eye.

Back at Brock's apartment, the restorative feed notwithstanding, tasting the next twelve bottles of the best goddamn whiskey ever made in the whole world began to feel like work. Jotting taster's comments became not quite possible. The bourbon began to seem like an attractive but querulous girlfriend demanding confessions of "feelings" one was unable to articulate. Reports of failing faculties came in from around the room.

"I can't feel my legs," said a guy named Quintin. "Is that a good thing?"

"I don't know where I am, but I'm having fun," said Mike.

The effects of our researches had ripened to a point where a rash of fistfights, weeping fits, or embraces seemed both possible and imminent. "Hey, do you know karate?" Brock asked me in a tone that did not put me at my ease.

Across the room, Beau, a builder from New Orleans, was leaning into the personal space of Julian Van Winkle III. "Julian, we are brothers from another mother," he informed the bourbon king.

"As long as you don't ask me for a bottle of whiskey, I'm your buddy," said Van Winkle, turning toward a tabletop teeming with unsampled bottles. "Man," he said wearily, "a *cold* beer would be good right about now."

Close to 5:00 p.m., with the light fading in the windows, Brock roved the room like the coxswain on a rowing galley, urging the exhausted tasters to press on. "Hey, come on, let's finish this thing so we can go ahead and get f**ked up." (By the chef's standards, apparently, there was still work to be done on that score.)

In due course, the tasters' congress got to its feet and congregated, bespattered tasting sheets in hand. Opinions were ventured, profanely contested, and sheepishly disavowed. Over the course of twenty-four whiskeys, the differences between Stitzel-Weller, Bernheim, and Buffalo Trace bourbons had grown markedly less profound. Vintages and distilleries were wildly misguessed, which wounded the aficionados' pride. Round two of the tasting was pronounced "a disaster," "a crap-shoot," and "amateur hour." Nevertheless, Brock carried everybody's tasting sheet off to a back room, where something statistical was going to happen. "Well, the important thing," said Mike, pouring a fresh glass, "is at least everybody got drunk."

Though not to the point of calling it quits. With the program of scientific drinking concluded, the connoisseurs were now at liberty to drink whiskey for fun. Brock's shelves of priceless bourbons were set upon. A 1949 Old Fitzgerald in a gold brocaded bottle got passed around. Someone broke the seal on a '41. Julian Van Winkle III was seen slugging Very Very Old Fitz straight from the bottle. This phase of the spree was both thrilling and worrisome. It was like watching a greenhouse of priceless orchids under siege by discerning but hungry goats.

Fortunately for Brock's collection, by nine o'clock everyone had drunk as much bourbon as he cared to. The idea of stepping out for a cold beer was proposed to unanimous approval. Out into the Nashville night we lumbered. Music came from the saloons. The bouncer at Robert's Western World saw fit to take us in. On the stage a grimacing guitarist rolfed a Telecaster to wring from it that drunken Nashville sound. Some cunning, generous member of our group figured out where the bar was. And just in the nick of time, we were each of us handed a coldly perspiring can of Pabst Blue Ribbon, which we drank like the water of life.

The Case for Bad Coffee

By Keith Pandolfi

From SeriousEats.com

While Keith Pandolfi has sterling food-writing credentials—he's a senior features editor at *Serious Eats* and a former senior editor at *Saveur*—he's also an ex-Starbucks manager. So when he noticed he was bucking coffee-snob orthodoxy to drink instant Maxwell House, he had to puzzle out why.

Standing at my kitchen counter, I measure out two teaspoons of Maxwell House instant coffee into my favorite mug, pour in 12 ounces of hot water from a tea kettle, and stir for a moment. I look toward the automatic drip maker to my left and feel a pang of sympathy for its cold carafe that once gurgled and steamed each morning with the best coffee money could buy. On top of the refrigerator, my old friend the French press has gathered dust. When I notice a dead housefly decomposing inside it, I wonder what the hell has happened to me.

I wasn't always like this. I used to spend silly amounts of money on sturdy brown bags of whole-bean, single origin, locally roasted coffee at the gourmet market down the street. I would scowl after sipping an inadequately poured espresso shot pulled by an inexperienced barista if the taste was a little too bitter, the crema a little too thin. I waited fifteen minutes in the morning for a pour-over at a coffee house in my old neighborhood of Fort Greene, Brooklyn. When I spent a semester in Italy during my senior year in college, I made sure to follow local customs—to never order a cappuccino after 10 a.m., to stand with confidence at the local cafe counter as I downed my umpteenth espresso of the day, perfectly paired with a rum-soaked baba or, in most cases, a cigarette.

For a time, coffee wasn't just my passion, it was my livelihood. In my 20s, I managed a coffee shop in a tony Cincinnati neighborhood where we played Yo La Tengo on the stereo in the morning and Miles Davis at night. When Starbucks came to town in the mid '90s, I signed on as an assistant manager, and remained in that position until I was 28 years old. I watched with little shame as my friends became lawyers and business owners, journalists and chemists. I was proud of the fact that I knew my ginger-bready Ethiopian Sidamos from my rummy Ethiopian Harrars. I knew that it took 19 seconds to pull the perfect espresso shot. For a while, I considered entering a Starbucks training program that would allow me to open a location of my own. I wanted coffee—really good coffee—to be my life.

But lately, something has changed. Lately, I've been reacting to fancy coffee the same way a child reacts to an accidental sip of red wine mistaken for grape juice. I don't know when it happened, but I've devolved into an unexpected love affair with bad coffee. It's not just instant coffee that I hanker for each morning, either, it's any subpar coffee I can get my hands on. (As I write this, I am a sipping a watery cup of java from an old pancake house down the street from my office in Little Italy.) Instead of that gourmet market in my neighborhood, I've begun perusing the coffee aisle of my local Ideal Supermarket like I once did the cereal aisles of my youth. I'm delighted by the big, red jars of Folgers, the yellow Chock-full-o-Nuts, the sky blue cans of Maxwell House.

The worst part of this newfound obsession is that it isn't even an affectation. I don't drink cheap coffee to be different. I don't boast of my love for Cafe Bustelo, which has become the PBR of the bearded Brooklyn set. I usually buy Maxwell House. There is nothing cool about Maxwell House.

Maybe it all started a few months ago when I found myself paying $18 for a pound of what turned out to be so-so coffee beans from a new roaster in my neighborhood. It was one of those moments when I could actually imagine my cranky diner-coffee-swilling Irish grandfather rising from the grave and saying, "You know what, kid? You're an idiot."

It's more than just money, though. I'm as tired of waiting 15 minutes for my morning caffeine fix as I am waiting the same amount of time for my whiskey, cardamom, and pimento bitters cocktail at my local bar. I am tired of pour-overs and French presses, Chemexes and Aeropresses. "How would you like that brewed?" is a question I never want to hear again.

But perhaps my newfound allegiance to the House of Maxwell is that I simply prefer it over the expensive stuff (which, don't get me wrong, I still occasionally enjoy). Cheap coffee is one of America's most unsung comfort foods. It's as warming and familiar as a homemade lasagna or a 6-hour stew. It tastes of midnight diners and Tom Waits songs; ice cream and cigarettes with a dash of Swiss Miss. It makes me remember the best cup of coffee I ever had. Even though there was never just one best cup: there were hundreds.

The best cup of coffee I ever had was the leftover swig of overly cream-and-sugared Taster's Choice my father would always leave in his mug when he departed for work each morning (I would come downstairs in my pajamas and down it like a shot when I was just nine years old). It was the Folgers my father and I drank out of Styrofoam cups five years later while attending his Alcoholics Anonymous meetings in a church basement off a suburban commercial strip.

The best cup of coffee I ever had was the dirty Viennese blend my teenage friends and I would sip out of chipped ceramic mugs at a cafe near the University of Cincinnati while smoking clove cigarettes and listening to Sisters of Mercy records, imagining what it would be like to be older than we were. The best cup of coffee was the one I enjoyed alone each morning during my freshman year at Ohio State, huddled in the back of a Rax restaurant reading the college paper and dealing with the onset of an anxiety disorder that would never quite be cured.

Then again, maybe the best cup of coffee I ever had was the one I drank in high school, right after my mother married a man named Ted.

Ted was short and portly and vulgar and gruff. Unlike my father, a dapper Italian and gifted home-cook who had a fondness for Strauss waltzes and old Platters records, Ted preferred polyester shirts, chain restaurants, Conway Twitty and Loretta Lynn. He was a coffee and cigarettes kind of guy who liked to sit in window seats and watch the world go by. He grew up in a rough neighborhood, had an eighth-grade education, was a Korean War vet, and owned the largest blueprint company in Ohio. He wore a big gold bracelet with the word "Ted" spelled out in diamonds.

The two of us had nothing in common, but my mother would often send us out to pick up food for dinner at the local Perkins or Frisch's Big Boy. "Let's get a cup of coffee while we wait," he would always say with a sparkle in his eye as we arrived at our chain of choice. "We'll sit back and relax. Sure, just relax a little bit." But it was never just "a cup" of coffee—it was always three, and sometimes four. The idea of being stuck with Ted at a booth or a counter stool made my head spin. We would be there for at least an hour as he talked about things I couldn't even pretend to understand—the blueprint industry, the stock market, the wisdom of the Republican party.

Ted drank his coffee black and I remember being self-conscious as I peeled the lids off at least three plastic containers of half-and-half and stirred a second packet of Domino sugar into my mug. Eventually, though, I started to enjoy those little coffee sessions of ours. I learned that Blue Chip stocks were always a better bet; that you should pay for everything with cash; that Loretta Lynn's voice was the stuff of heaven; that George H.W. Bush wasn't as bad as he seemed.

Sitting at Ted's funeral a few years ago, I remembered the little phrases he would use every time we went out on those suburban hunting and gathering missions. When a waitress asked us how we were doing, his response was always, "If I was any better I'd be twins." His parting words to the cashier were always, "Take no wooden nickels and buy your own Cokes." After we buried him with full military honors, I honored him by going alone to one of the old Perkins we used to frequent and drank not one, but three cups of coffee.

I don't have memories of such bonding experiences taking place over a flat white at a Manhattan coffee shop or a $5 cup of nitro iced coffee at a Brooklyn cafe. High-end coffee doesn't usually lend itself to such moments. Instead, it's something to be fussed over and praised; you talk more about its origin and its roaster, its flavor notes and its brewing method than you talk to the person you're enjoying it with. Bad coffee is the stuff you make a full pot of on the weekends just in case some friends stop by. It's what you sip when you're alone at the mechanic's shop getting your oil change, thinking about where your life has taken you; what you nurse as you wait for a loved one to get through a tough surgery. It's the Sanka you share with an elderly great aunt while listening to her tell stories you've heard a thousand times before. Bad coffee is there for you. It is bottomless. It is perfect.

Blending In

BY STEVE HOFFMAN

From *Food & Wine*

Food writer Steve Hoffman wears many hats—tax preparer, real-estate broker, beekeeper—so why not give wine-making a whirl? After all, he and his wife had transplanted the family from Minnesota for a year to a rural village in the Languedoc. If crushing grapes with the locals was the way to fit in....

Our backs hurt, our brains sagged, our mouths were sore. We had just spent a hardworking shift on our feet in the slightly headachy fluorescent glare of a laboratory. Outside, all morning, the Mediterranean sun had bathed the beaches and vineyards of this corner of the Languedoc in late-autumn warmth.

Mary Jo got in the car, shut the door and looked over at me. "Was that possibly the best morning we've ever spent in France?" I asked her.

"Holy crap," she said, with a grin that displayed some very pretty blue teeth.

For most of our years together, wine had been liquid in a glass, a minor life enhancer. This morning, in an obscure and insular fold of deep rural France, wine was the ring that held the keys to the kingdom.

Almost three months before, my wife, Mary Jo, and I had arrived at a rented stone house in Autignac—population 900 or so—in the Faugères wine region, where the last slopes of the Massif Central meet the coastal plain running out to the Mediterranean. Our hopes, as a Francophone American family, had been, in roughly this order: Send the kids to the local schools—which we had done—and integrate into the life of the village, which we had not.

The villages of southern France know just what foreign visitors want. What they want is to get sunburned on beaches, view pretty landscapes from elevated vistas, shop at markets and boutiques, and drink too much wine on terraces with other visitors who speak their language. That we did not want any of those things appeared to have come as a vast surprise to our fellow villagers. It wasn't really until we volunteered to pick grapes, and then persisted throughout the harvest, that our neighbors began to see us, with a wary *humph* of respect, for the very strange species of tourist we were.

One hot fall afternoon, late in the harvest, we were unloading crates of perfect grapes from the back of a cargo van when a man working alongside us asked, in a soft Midi accent, if we would like to join him for the *assemblage,* or blending, of a local wine called Mas Gabinèle. Our co-worker, as it turned out, was Thierry Rodriguez; Mas Gabinèle is his wine, and we were unloading his grapes.

It would be hard to overstate the thrill of this invitation. We'd flirted with the region. We'd enticed it into conversation. We had even sweatily held hands a few times. But getting invited to something as intimate as an *assemblage* felt like the first fluttery intimation that things might be getting serious.

So it was that we found ourselves, in late November, in a laboratory, surrounded by perhaps 70 years of winemaking experience divided among three of the attendees—Rodriguez, his enologist Jean Natoli, and Claire, Natoli's assistant. The two remaining participants, Mary Jo and I, representing the great state of Minnesota, boasted wine careers spanning roughly 70 days apiece.

Across the room waited our day's labor, arrayed along a countertop: 27 bottles with sloped, Burgundy-shaped shoulders and handwritten labels.

Thierry was speaking softly to Jean, in an improbably high tenor for such a big man. He looked concerned. Thierry often looked concerned. He was a finicky aesthete, we'd learned, who had placed an enormous career wager, in middle age, on a substance subject to the vagaries of weather, disease and hired help. There was much to be concerned about.

But today was an especially excruciating day to be Thierry Rodriguez, because today he would find out whether the 2011 vintage of his Mas Gabinèle wines would live up to his extremely high hopes for it.

Thierry produces three Mas Gabinèle reds—a traditional Faugères, using the appellation's blend of Syrah, Grenache, Mourvèdre, Carignan and Cinsaut; Rarissime, heavy on Syrah and a worthy rival to most Châteauneuf-du-Papes; and, finally, what you could call his folly, Inaccessible, mostly made from Mourvèdre and which sells for $100 a bottle in a region known for wines a tenth that price.

Jean described Inaccessible as *un monstre*: huge alcohol, huge tannin, huge fruit, all held in perfect balance. It was the kind of wine—demanding absolutely top-quality grapes—that couldn't be produced every year. It was the kind of wine that could make a reputation, or sit unsold on wine store shelves and destroy a career. And it was precisely the kind of wine that Thierry needed to sell, he explained, if he was going to pay for the brand-new winery, under construction when we were there, that he had designed to his own exacting and expensive specifications.

Jean made a pouting face meant to be reassuring. The 2011 vintage promised an adequate amount of monstrosity, he felt. Thierry looked over at him with hopeful, and somewhat anxious, professional deference.

And then it was time to blend some wine.

Each of the 27 bottles was a sample of the contents of a vat, or a row of oak casks, back at the winery. Each was made from a single grape variety, often from a single vineyard, and was the culmination of several dozen decisions—how to prune, how much growth to allow, when to harvest, which fermentation method to use, how long to macerate, whether to age in oak and for how long. Our job over the next three hours would be to sip from each bottle, assess and track our favorites by sliding the best bottles forward. Based on those ratings, we would attempt to assemble three costly and complex wines, in descending order of quality and price, in hopes that Jean could deliver, at day's end, the recipes for Thierry's 2011 wines.

We began marching down the row of bottles. Claire would pour two fingers from each and announce what it was: "Syrah, Carbonic Maceration, Casks 1–6." The five of us would swirl, sip, suck, consider and spit into a sink—in a tight, elegant stream if the spitter was, say, a winemaker or enologist, and sometimes in a flaccid, splashing cascade. Then we would discuss.

Occasionally, if a wine merited it, we would move a bottle forward a few inches. More rarely, we would come across one of the monsters, or a slightly less powerful *bébé monstre*. That bottle would take two or sometimes three steps forward.

" . . . Mourvèdre, Barrels 45–57 . . . "

It sounds like a joke to claim that a morning spent tasting wine was hard work. But around wine number 20, Mary Jo and I were rubber-legged. Our backs hurt. Our brains sagged. Our mouths felt chalky and sore. "I'm going to pass out," I said, "and I haven't swallowed a drop."

We sat out a few rounds, marveling at the stamina of our crewmates. And then, a little heroically, Mary Jo and I grabbed our picks and shovels and headed back down into the mine that is wine tasting and *assemblage*. We worked until the whistle blew at bottle 27: Cinsaut, no oak.

At this point, Jean began acting very much like a scientist in a lab, which, of course, he was. He poured winning bottles into glass beakers, and beakers into other beakers, until he had concocted one complete imaginary bottle of wine, a bottle he then offered to us to taste.

I don't pretend to have access to all the reasons the blend accomplished what it did. Earlier, sipping from the row of samples, I had thought to myself several times, OK, stop right here. Here's your wine. No need to blend anything. But a mouthful of Jean's prototype made most of the individual bottles seem a little simplistic or exaggerated. The peppery spikiness of the Syrah got smoothed out. The hard tannic darkness of the young Mourvèdre softened. The blend had more flavor. It filled your mouth differently.

We're used to varietal wines in the US: Cabernet Sauvignon, Pinot Noir, Zinfandel. But winemakers in southern France talk about blending as lying very close to the heart of what they do. There is a refreshingly blue-collar dimension to much of a French winemaker's year, a lot of pruning and spraying and pumping and shoveling. The French winemakers we met didn't often use the word *art*, but when they did, they were usually talking about blending. Our morning in the lab made clear what they meant in a way I could never have understood until I'd sipped down a row of single varietals and then tasted, minutes later, their individual contributions to the blended whole.

Jean found this first effort "pleasing enough," but he wanted to deepen the color with more Syrah and use one particularly luscious Grenache to add a bit of silkiness. This was what he could do that the rest of us could not. He was not reacting to what was there, but building something that wasn't. Even Thierry spent a good deal of time nodding to the beat of Jean's improvisations, rather than contributing his own riffs.

Four permutations later, we all agreed that the 2011 Inaccessible had found itself. It spilled over with excess as it was supposed to, but—and here Jean got to use one of his favorite words—the final blend was nevertheless remarkably "consensual." We had just witnessed the birth of a vintage, and 2011 was going to be a very good year at Mas Gabinèle. And we had the privilege of watching a man of almost courtly reserve spend 10 minutes quietly corking his baby monsters, with a smile of the purest fatherly delight.

Later, in the parking lot, as a kind of exclamation point, or possibly just intoxicated by the general felicity, Thierry kissed Mary Jo and me on both cheeks and thanked us for being there with him, as one might thank a supportive friend post-crisis. Then he grabbed a mostly full bottle of the last vintage of Inaccessible, the 2010, and recommended that we enjoy its remaining $80 or $90 worth of wine with dinner.

Back in the car, Mary Jo and I wound homeward along the familiar curves of the D13, richer by a bottle of wine, among other things. Ahead of us waited a tiny village, a stone house and two kids to pick up at school.

Cooking the Books

The Servant Problem

By Toni Tipton-Martin

From *The Jemima Code*

Pioneering food editor, cookbook collector, and community
activist Toni Tipton-Martin fills a crucial gap in culinary history
with her beautiful, scholarly 2015 book *The Jemima Code: Two
Centuries of African American Cookbooks*. At last, the black cooks
whose recipes have long fed America get their due respect.

When I first encountered *The Picayune Creole Cook Book*, I
thought it masterfully illustrated the sentiments expressed
by this young, eighteen-year-old poet living in Washington, D.C., in
post–World War I America.

This popular catalogue remained in print through fourteen editions,
many with the same frontispiece, a photographic illustration of an antebellum hearth kitchen and romanticized recipes that "your mother
used, and her mother and her grandmother, and the grandmother
caught [them] from the old-time 'Mammy' who could work all kinds of
magic in that black-raftered kitchen of the long ago."

The Picayune Creole Cook Book was created "to assist the good house-
wives of the present day and to preserve to future generations the many
excellent and matchless recipes of the New Orleans cuisine by gathering up from the old Creole cooks and the old housekeepers the best
of Creole cookery." It presented an amalgamated cuisine, created when
French chefs and the best cooks of Spain shared ideas that New World
cooks adapted "to their needs and to the materials they had at hand," for
a result that was "beyond speech."

The book perpetuated the stilted reasoning that she who owns the cook owns the recipes, yet simultaneously imparted a measure of visibility to ignored cooks. It exposed the frustration felt by a growing number of white employers who found it impossible to separate their contempt for black servants from their dependence upon them, and it forecast a coming practice by mainstream cookbook authors—one that opened a crack in what David M. Katzman described as "southern caste etiquette," which dictated that blacks not appear to be in control. Ever.

In *Seven Days a Week: Women and Domestic Service in Industrializing America* (1978), a pioneering study of domestic relationships, Katzman tells the story of a northern mistress, Antoinette Hervey, trying to follow a delicious cookie recipe as told by her servant, "big black Katherine." Hervey recorded Katherine's recipe in vernacular language that was hard to follow. Katherine's mouth-watering treat "came from experience, not from any cooking manual . . . handed down from her mother or a close relative," Katzman explained. "Creativity in cooking was part of a folk tradition shared by many black women. And cooking was part of an oral or practical tradition, not a written one. Rather than reflecting ignorance—the point of Hervey's retelling the story—the anecdote [sic] revealed Katherine's mastery of the kitchen arts. . . . But her Northern mistress had little understanding of this Southern folk system."

No matter; the door opened.

Although Katherine possessed the knowledge of a specialist, Hervey and a generation of southern ladies set in place a harsh and false impression that misled the public: the black cook may have cooked excellently, but she was too ignorant to translate that experience into scientific formulas, much less into print.

While the *Better Homes and Gardens Cook Book* (1st ed., 1930) and *The Boston Cooking-School Cook Book* (1st ed., 1896) offered wordy details and sometimes lengthy cooking instructions for inexperienced cooks, southern cookbook authors representing the plantation style asserted their authority racially—by repeatedly resorting to condescending language and disparaging images when mentioning black women, whom previous designers had simply ignored.

Everywhere I looked—Nathalie Scott's composite cook, Mandy; Mary Moore Bremer's "negro woman"; the "colored cooks" described by Harriet Ross Colquitt; and the bandana-headed women whose faces graced the covers of manufacturers' recipe pamphlets and brochures—mid-twentieth-century mainstream cookbook authors in both the North and the South froze black food workers in trophy-like portraits of antebellum characters: the fruit vendor, the potato man, the groundnut vendor, and the honey man. In commentary that both praised and ridiculed the cook, these authors inadvertently introduced us to black cooks who understood the nuances of regional cooking.

As late as 1941, respected writers such as Marion Flexner exaggerated their "scientific approach to cooking" by juxtaposing illustrations of elegant plantation scenes against cabin hearth cooking done by black women in head rags. And she was far from the only one. *The Southern Cookbook: 322 Old Dixie Recipes* (1939), compiled by Lillie S. Lustig, S. Claire Sondheim, and Sarah Rensel, has become a perennial favorite with Internet booksellers on eBay. It mingles classic southern recipes, demoralizing etchings of slaves at work, vernacular language, and lyrics from spirituals and hymns.

In their lavishly illustrated *200 Years of Charleston Cooking* (1931), Blanche S. Rhett and Lettie Gay applaud black cooks for their "famed" regional dishes. Crab Soup, Shrimp and Hominy (Grits), Fish Soufflé, Stuffed Crabs and Mushrooms, Fried Chicken with Corn Cakes, and Sweet Potato Croquettes are attributed to a butler named William Deas, "one of the great cooks of the world." Sally Washington, whose "cooking was of a kind to make one speculate as to whether she was a genius in her own right or whether Charleston was gifted by the gods," is credited for her recipe for Red Rice.

Harriet Ross Colquitt made her confused prejudices known through plantation sketches laced with bitter complaints about the near impossibility of procuring recipes for her *Savannah Cook Book: A Collection of Old Fashioned Receipts from Colonial Kitchens* (1933).

> We have had so many request for receipts for rice dishes, and for shrimp and crab concoctions which are peculiar to our locality, that I have concentrated on those indigenous to our soil, as it were, begging them from housekeepers, and trying to tack our elusive cooks down to some definite idea of what goes into the making of the good dishes they turn out. Getting directions from colored cooks is rather like trying to write down the music to the

spirituals which they sing—for all good old-timers . . . cook "by ear" and it is hard to bring them down to earth when they begin to improvise.

Eleanor Ott's hyperbolic recipe collection, *Plantation Cookery of Old Louisiana*, boasts wistful reminiscences of the charm of antebellum cuisine and wows readers with the vast number of servants on her grandmother's "culinary plant." At the same time, she revered the cooks for their "Intelligence, Industry, and Art." Kitty Mammy, the plantation doctor and nurse who supervised the herb garden, and Becky Mammy, the high priestess of the milk house, both were honored simply: "Genius, sheer, breathtaking Genius."

A few African American authors manage to self-publish remarkable recipe collections of their own between World War I and the dawning of the civil rights movement. Their collections stand in the gap for the mammy, the Cream of Wheat Man, and the procession of colored maids in Hollywood films. But more than that, these writers can be seen as predecessors of modern celebrity chefs who press through publishing favoritism and prejudice, boost spirits, and cheer on the next generation, all while championing middle-class American cooking.

The delicacies and grace rendered by *Eliza's Cook Book: Favorite Recipes Compiled by Negro Culinary Art Club of Los Angeles*, Lena Richard's wise entrepreneurship, Lucille Bishop Smith's empowering spirit, and Freda DeKnight's global kitchen existed in the shadows of pervasive and perverse debasements. These authors understood the work of the kitchen, and they used that knowledge to untether their foodways from distorted representations.

In the same way, Idella Parker stared down jocular characterizations of domestic servitude and ushered in an era of culinary liberation with her account of life in the household of the Pulitzer Prize–winning novelist Marjorie Kinnan Rawlings. Though little was written elsewhere to accurately credit black cooks as experts, this former domestic, teacher, and cook accepts her life of service as the renowned author's "Perfect Maid," without drowning in that murky dishwater. Her memoir does not contain recipes in the traditional sense, and it wasn't published until fifty years after Rawlings wrote *Cross Creek Cookery*, a book of classic southern dishes. Parker does, however, present an insightful look into the complex relations between a black cook and her white employer. "Marjorie Kinnan Rawlings called me 'the perfect maid' in her book *Cross Creek*," Parker writes in the preface to *Idella: Marjorie Rawlings' Perfect Maid*. "I am not perfect and neither was Mrs. Rawlings, and this book will make that clear to anyone who reads it."

As the story of their life together unfolds, Parker provides a believable, poised, and fair account of how it felt to be underpaid and overworked. Naturally, she was frustrated. After months spent together in the kitchen testing recipes for *Cross Creek Cookery*, including many that Parker claimed were hers, such as the chocolate pie, Rawlings credits her on just three. Still, Parker's courage accomplishes something unique and wonderful: it draws everyone into the kitchen, inviting folks to cook for one another and to persevere through awkward race conversations.

This truth would have been a sight for the sore eyes of Cuney's domestics and the authors on the following pages, who invented regional, cultural, and ethnic specialties when they left their own kitchens to manage someone else's.

Chained to the Stove: What It's Really Like to Write a Cookbook

By Jessica Battilana

From SeriousEats.com

Jessica Battilana—a cheesemonger turned caterer turned food writer—has already coauthored cookbooks, with chef Charles Phan, master baker Chad Robertson, and butcher Ryan Farr, all Bay Area food stars. Writing her own cookbook, however, offered a different kind of challenge altogether.

For the last several years, while I've coauthored five cookbooks with five different chefs, my professional role has been Full-Time Pain in the Ass. As any of the chefs with whom I've collaborated can tell you, I'm well suited for the position.

It's been my job to badger them with questions about pan dimensions; to hound them for plausible substitutions for dried wood ear mushrooms; to rush at them, measuring spoons in hand, to ensure that a pinch is only a pinch. Behind their backs, I've rolled my eyes when their recipes casually called for a Vitamix, a chinois, or any other of a dozen tools that the average home cook most likely doesn't have.

So I naively thought that when it finally came time to write my own book—a long-held dream—it would be a breeze. After all, I know how to write a book proposal. I know how to draft and retest recipes. I know what it's like to cook in a home kitchen, and I know how many rounds of edits come between a manuscript and a finished copy.

And now I know how wrong I was.

As the deadline for my first solo cookbook, *Repertoire*, draws near, I have been to the grocery store every day—sometimes twice a day. My home kitchen, once used to make tidy dinners for two adults and two children, is now in constant chaos. I've made gingerbread six times, tweaking the recipe with each iteration, until the sight of it cooling on the counter fills me with rage and despair. I have cursed over trays of burned nuts, left toasting in the oven too long while I tended to beef browning on the stove and ice cream churning on the counter. I've delivered impossibly crispy potato pancakes to neighbors, foisted not-quite-right cookies on the UPS man; I've frozen half-eaten chickens with plans to return to them later, unable to waste the birds by tossing them into the compost, unable to stomach the thought of another bite.

The premise of my cookbook is that it contains dishes that I cook all the time, or, as I promised in my proposal, the "infallible recipes that form the backbone of my cooking life." The proposal I submitted introduced the project and included a table of contents plus a complete recipe list; I labored over the proposal for over a year before my agent sent it out to publishers to review. Because I'd done such a comprehensive outline, and because the recipes I'm including are my favorite dishes— the ones I've been making for years—I thought the recipe development process would be relatively easy. Or, at least, it would be easier than fixing a laser eye on a chef who attempts to drizzle in an unmeasured amount of heavy cream at the last minute, or decides on a whim to grill rather than roast the chicken.

But, through the process of writing my own book, I've learned that codifying something I do intuitively is frustrating as hell. I've also realized that part of what makes a good cook is the ability to riff on a recipe, to alter it based on his or her own taste and the ingredients on hand. Did I make the last batch of tortilla soup with Early Girl tomatoes I froze in the summer, and does that explain why this batch, made with store-bought canned tomatoes, isn't quite as good? Is it possible I tossed some long-frozen oxtail into the stockpot the last time I made chicken stock, making it especially silky and gelatinous? What did I do last time? What should I do next time? I'm balancing my commitment to providing foolproof recipes with my own desire as a home cook to add that last browning bit of fennel to the soup pot, to use cheddar in this batch of *gougères* because I've run out of Gruyère. It all matters, and it all doesn't: Part of my goal with *Repertoire* is to inspire home cooks to think and taste while they're cooking, to use the book as a jumping-off point but have the confidence to make a recipe their own, to riff on it until it feels like it's part of their own repertoire as much as it is mine.

I think about the chefs I worked with on their cookbooks, and I can finally appreciate the exasperation with which they met my questions—how long should I cook it? (Until it's done, they replied.) How much salt should I add? (To taste, they said, shrugging.) Writing a recipe that will work for every cook in every kitchen is a tedious task, one that clips the wings of a freewheeling cook.

But this is the real work and the real magic of a cookbook: to distill one's perspective and experience, one's trials and errors, into a spectacular recipe that readers can use as a roadmap to a great meal. When I think of it like that, I'm sure I've got the best job in the world.

But oh, how there have been setbacks along the way. Last week, I tested a recipe for spatchcocked chicken. I've made dozens and dozens of spatchcocked chickens over the years, so, in my mind, I'd already checked the writing of this recipe off my to-do list. I love this method—removing the backbone so the chicken can be opened like a book and flattened slightly—because the bird cooks quickly and has a broad expanse of crispy skin. On an ordinary night, when I'm just making this chicken and not testing *how* I make it, I cut out the backbone with a pair of kitchen shears, arrange the chicken on a baking sheet, and toss it into a cranked oven. I fold a load of laundry, administer justice in a quarrel between my two boys, make a salad. I don't set a timer—I just pull it out when it seems done. But on the evening I tested this recipe for the book, I slavishly measured the ingredients for the spice rub, carefully minded the oven temperature (starting it high and then lowering it), and set a timer.

When the timer chirped, I transferred the chicken to a cutting board as my hungry children circled around me like vultures. As I began to carve, I discovered that the bird was totally raw at the bone, and spilling pink juices all over the board. The chicken was mocking me. "Did I mention I'm writing a cookbook?" I said to my wife, Sarah, who was already reaching into the freezer for some tamales to placate our ravenous brood while I returned the chicken to the oven. I hate moments like this, of course, when my confidence is temporarily shattered. But I also love them because they remind me why it's so important to write recipes that work, and to test them until they're perfect. We ate three more spatchcocked chickens that week, until what emerged from the oven was ready for prime time: golden brown, crisp-skinned, and, yes, cooked all the way through.

When I'm cooking for work, sometimes it just feels like *work*, not the relaxing, fun hobby that got me into this in the first place. To keep pace with my deadline, I have to make meals count, so dinner is often less about what I feel like eating and more about whatever recipe I need to refine. Like a lot of people, I want to braise in winter and eat the hell out of spring's first asparagus, so I'm trying to align my testing schedule so that I'm cooking and eating seasonally, rather than trying to make my favorite corn salad with the starchy ears now available at my local grocery store or simmering cauldrons of French onion soup on days when it feels too hot to turn on the stove.

When I worked on other people's cookbooks, I was able to maintain an objectivity that was helpful in the recipe-testing process. A dish either worked the way the recipe said it would, or it didn't. It was delicious, or it wasn't. When it comes to my own recipes, it has been hard to know when it's as good as it can be. I might make a dish once, or twice, and still feel like something's not right. I'll tweak the recipe, adding an ingredient or changing the cooking method. My friends may love the third and fourth iterations, though they may grow tired of me standing nearby as they take the first forkful, quizzing them, "Does it *need* something?" A friend asked for my gingerbread recipe after tasting version two (out of six). "It's perfect," she enthused. It's hard not to sound like a jerk when you tell someone that the sugar-dusted square they just tasted and loved is far from perfect, that it's just a work in progress.

What would happen, I wonder at night, if I swapped the all-purpose flour for bread flour in my calzone dough recipe? Could I reduce the number of egg yolks in that chocolate ice cream custard and still get the same creamy result? There are a million ways to alter a recipe, and so there are a million ways to drive yourself crazy considering the possibilities. So I don't dwell—instead, I concede success when my wife cuts a fat wedge of the cake I made the night before and eats it for breakfast, or when a friend tries something I've cooked and says, pleadingly, "That's going in the book, right?" And sometimes, after I've tested a recipe many times, I have to admit that it's not going to make the cut—I want every one of the 75 recipes in my cookbook to be absolute slam dunks, which means some are going to hit the cutting room floor.

I thought it impossible that I'd end up being harder on myself than I'd been on the chefs I've worked with, the ones I'd cajoled and badgered with questions. Turns out I was wrong about that, too.

The Epiphany That Turned Me into a Good Baker

By Kathy Gunst

From the *Washington Post*

Author of fourteen cookbooks (including *Notes from a Maine Kitchen* and *Soup Swap*) and resident chef of the NPR radio show *Here and Now,* Kathy Gunst certainly knows her own way around a kitchen. Baking was never her natural forte, though—until she gleaned wisdom from other writer's recipes.

When I attended the Cordon Bleu School of Cookery in London in the late 1970s, I learned the foundations of French cuisine. But even as Ms. Cadbury was teaching us the proper way to fold butter into puff pastry and the technique for making silky béarnaise sauce, I made a silent vow to myself: I would follow the rules, and then I would break them. I would be a jazz musician, riffing on the classics, creating my own dissonant, experimental compositions in the kitchen. And for years, that has been my approach to cooking.

For the most part, it has worked. Except for when I bake.

I've always believed that great bakers are good at following rules. And so, for someone who prides herself on being a bit of a rebel—in the kitchen and out—baking has been a challenge. Being a really good baker requires understanding what makes bread dough rise and why some cakes are light and fluffy, and that is a matter of working within the lines. Isn't it?

Then, a few years ago, I was asked to judge a prestigious cookbook competition—in the baking category. I tried to decline, explaining what an honor it was but telling the organizers that they had picked the wrong person for the job. I lobbied to switch categories. "Why would you want someone who isn't proficient in a subject to judge the experts?" I asked.

"Think of it as a challenge," the head judge said. "Call me if you get into trouble."

Within a week, I had three enormous boxes of books: close to 50 devoted to cakes, cookies, pies, French pastry, ice cream sandwiches and more. I tucked myself into bed each night with a dozen or so titles and made my way through the pile. Eventually, as instructed, I narrowed the field to the five that made me believe I could become a better baker.

Then came the scary step. I needed to test two or three recipes from my top choices. Because this was baking, I would have to follow the recipes to the letter. And that was going to be tough.

I spent 10 days testing recipes: baking pies and fancy pastry, icing cakes and generally feeling bad about myself. Honestly, who likes spending time doing something they're not good at? I started having nightmares about my tyrannical fifth-grade math teacher, who insisted we write all our math equations in ink.

Instead of calling my therapist, I dug in deeper. I started weighing everything, and I learned there was a big difference between what I called 1½ packed cups of brown sugar and the generally accepted 330 grams that 1½ cups of packed brown sugar is supposed to weigh. Expert bakers could have predicted that: My eyeball-it approach was a big part of the problem. When I scooped out 1 cup of flour that should have weighed 128 grams, my scale showed close to a 20-gram discrepancy. When I actually measured the spices called for in a gingerbread cake, I was amazed: My practice of filling the spice cap up to what I'd assumed was ½ teaspoon was way off.

I had a major aha! moment. From then on, when a recipe told me to take the eggs or butter out of the refrigerator an hour before I used them, I did what I was told. If a recipe called for a 9-inch cake pan, that's what I used. If it said to whip eggs and sugar at high speed in a mixer for a full 10 minutes, until light and fluffy, I didn't call it quits after five. I was a soldier, following the commands of my superior. I didn't cut a single corner or question the requirements.

My first (typically rushed) attempt to make French tuilles (delicate, buttery cookies that resemble the roof tiles on French houses) resulted in cookies too fragile to hold their shape. But when I retested them, measuring the ingredients and nailing every detail, they came out perfectly. Every failure led to deeper inquiry. I looked through each book for answers. The books that made the cut answered my questions about what to do if the dough fell apart when you rolled it out, or if the cake didn't rise properly, or if the crème anglaise separated.

When my three-layer chocolate cake with mocha-chocolate buttercream came out looking like it could be sold in a real bakery (or at least would be the first thing to go at a bake sale), I felt victorious. I'd gone into the experiment kicking and screaming, and many cakes, cookies, puddings and pastries later, I'd emerged a much better baker.

Then, one fall, several months after I judged the competition, a friend brought me a basket of apples from her orchard. Time to make a pie. I didn't want to follow someone else's recipe. I wanted to try something different, something I could call my own. I also didn't want to slip back into my old sloppy baking behavior. For the crust, I decided to substitute nut flour for half of the wheat flour.

I whirled the flours with butter and ice water, and it became a wet, sticky mess. But something told me to forge ahead: I placed the dough in plastic wrap and chilled it for several hours. It was way moister than what I was used to, and when I tried to roll it out, it was almost impossible to work with. So I draped it into a French tart pan with a removable bottom, pressing it together like a kid molding Play Doh.

I peeled the apples and tossed them with brown sugar, ground ginger and cinnamon, then overlapped the fruit slices. It was pretty, but it looked dry. So I boiled down apple cider with ground ginger and a touch of cinnamon. I waited until it was almost thick enough to coat the back of a spoon. I poured that glaze over the apples and placed it in the hot oven, and soon the kitchen smelled like some kind of autumnal fantasy. The tart was a perfect balance of nutty crust, juicy, sweet apples and fragrant spices.

At Thanksgiving, when my youngest daughter asked for pumpkin cheesecake, I went a little off-script again. I studied several recipes and made a plan: Rather than blend pumpkin puree into a cream-cheese base, I swirled it in by the tablespoon. I was patient in the baking, nestling the cake in a water bath for its oven time and letting it rest and cool before refrigerating. The rewards were huge: a perfectly creamy, smooth-topped cheesecake with a stunning marbled effect.

Another revelation came this past Valentine's Day, when I planned to serve my husband a chocolate dessert. I used the same nut pastry I had discovered when baking the apple tart and filled it with a simple dark chocolate batter. Feeling the need to be creative without veering off-course too wildly, I sprinkled coarse sea salt and toasted unsweetened coconut on top of the still-warm tart. The white flakes set against the dark chocolate tart looked, and tasted, pretty impressive.

This spring, when I visited San Francisco, the season's first locally grown strawberries appeared at the farmers market. I wanted to bake fluffy biscuits that would showcase them, and I kept fantasizing that Mary Berry of "The Great British Baking Show," in her clipped British voice, would taste them and say: "Nice bake! Very nice bake, indeed." In the past, my biscuits have fallen ... short. I didn't have my baking books with me at the time, but I remembered that one had advised folding finished dough over itself several times to create layers. That's what I did, without overworking it, and the results were light, layered and truly spectacular. (A ginger butter took them right over the top.)

The winning baking books from the competition now line my shelves. When I pull them out to bake, I feel a weird sense of pride, as if I wrote them myself. During my two weeks as a full-time "baker," I gained a few pounds and got jazzed up on sugar. But I also learned that if you follow the rules and understand why they are there, you can go ahead and start to break them, a little at a time. My crash course in baking taught me plenty of techniques, and it taught me a few things about myself: namely, that I needn't fight my urge to experiment. I just needed to learn how to do it right.

Even a rebel, it turns out, is capable of restraint.

Chocolate Tart with Sea Salt and Toasted Coconut

You might say this tart combines several popular flavors. The pastry is made from almond flour and all-purpose flour and is very buttery and crisp. The filling is like a chocolate mousse: good bittersweet chocolate, cream, eggs, vanilla and sea salt. It's topped with toasted coconut flakes and more sea salt. The tart filling has no sugar; it's all about honoring the chocolate and the balance of the salt.

If you serve the tart the day you bake it, it's like chocolate pie. But if you refrigerate it overnight, the filling becomes dense and almost fudgy. It's delicious either way.

You will need an 8-inch round tart pan with a removable bottom.

Make Ahead: The pastry dough needs to rest in the refrigerator for at least 1 hour. Plan on letting the tart cool for at least 1 hour, or cover and refrigerate it for up to 12 hours.

For the crust and topping

1 cup (120 grams) all-purpose flour
½ cup (60 grams) almond flour
Pinch sea salt, plus more for sprinkling
2 tablespoons (28 grams) sugar
12 tablespoons (1½ sticks) unsalted butter, well chilled, cut into small pieces
About ¼ cup ice-cold water, or as needed
⅓ cup (20 grams) unsweetened flaked coconut

For the filling

1½ cups heavy cream
9 ounces (255 grams) bittersweet chocolate, finely chopped (may substitute 5 ounces 65 percent bittersweet chocolate plus 4 ounces milk chocolate)
2 large eggs
½ teaspoon vanilla extract
½ teaspoon (3 grams) good sea salt

Directions

For the crust and topping: Whisk together the all-purpose and almond flours, the salt and sugar in a large bowl. Add the butter; use your hands and a light touch, work the butter into the flours until it resembles coarse cornmeal. Add a few tablespoons of water and mix, using a soft spatula or wooden spoon, until the mixture just comes together. Add more water as needed, using only enough to keep the dough together.

(Alternatively, pulse the flours, salt and sugar in a food processor just until blended. Add the butter and pulse about 15 times, until the mixture resembles coarse cornmeal. Add only enough water so that the dough begins to pull away from the sides of the bowl.)

Place the dough in a sheet of plastic wrap and form it into a ball. Refrigerate for at least 1 hour and up to overnight.

Unwrap the dough and roll it out on a clean work surface into a 10-inch round. Drape the dough into the tart pan, covering the bottom and up the sides of the pan; trim the edges (you'll have scraps left over), but make sure there's enough to fit just over the rim. Cover with plastic wrap and refrigerate for 20 minutes.

Preheat the oven to 350 degrees. Remove the tart shell from the refrigerator; use a fork to dock the pastry in several spots. (This will keep the pastry from puffing up.) Place the tart pan on a baking sheet; bake (middle rack) for 10 minutes, then let it cool on a rack for 10 minutes. Keep the oven on; spread the coconut on the baking sheet and bake for about 5 minutes, watching closely, until the coconut begins to turn golden brown. Let cool; keep the oven on.

For the filling: Heat the cream in a medium saucepan over medium-low heat until it is gently bubbling at the edges.

Place the chocolate in a large mixing bowl. Pour the hot cream on top and stir steadily until the chocolate is completely melted and the mixture is smooth.

Whisk together the eggs, vanilla extract and ½ teaspoon of sea salt in a separate mixing bowl until frothy. Add the egg mixture to the chocolate mixture and stir until fully incorporated and smooth. Pour the filling into the cooled crust and bake (middle rack) for 25 to 28 minutes. To test for doneness, gently shake the tart; if the middle wobbles just a little (and still appears undercooked) but the sides seem solid, it is done. The tart will continue to cook once it's removed from the oven, and it will firm up when cooling.

While the tart is still warm, sprinkle it with the coconut and about ½ teaspoon of the coarse sea salt; press the salt and coconut very gently into the tart to make sure they adhere. Let the tart cool for 1 hour before serving, or refrigerate (see headnote).

Zahav vs. The Food Lab

By Phyllis Grant

From Food52.com

*

Dancer-turned-pastry chef Phyllis Grant lives in Berkeley, where she writes the culinary/parenting blog Dash and Bella (named for her children) and the Food52 column Cooking What I Want. As a judge in Food52's annual Piglet cookbook tournament, Grant made a shrewd call—to enlist her kids as sous-judges.

To J. Kenji López-Alt and Michael Solomonov:
I love cookbooks. I have stacks of them in my kitchen, my hallway, next to my bed. They are towering columns of comfort. They bring color and light to each room. I flip through them for inspiration. I'm writing one. But unless I'm making pastries, I don't follow recipes. And my kids don't either: For thirteen years, I have been teaching them the importance of playing in the kitchen. Tweaking, adjusting, rejiggering. Listening to their guts.

Then The Piglet came along.

My daughter thought it was unfair to compare your books. *They're too different, mom. It's just not right.*

I couldn't agree more. Cerebral, meticulous, scientific treatise on sous vide cooking and burgers and sticky buns versus Israeli food?

And then I went into a tailspin trying to define what makes a good cookbook.

My kids weren't very helpful. *That's easy,* said my son, *a good cookbook has photos that make you want to lick the pages.* He puts Aleppo pepper on everything and eats pickles for breakfast while my daughter is all about mug cakes and freakshakes. So, of course, from my daughter: *Mom, a good cookbook has a nice balance of everything. Especially desserts.*

Unlike novels and memoirs, cookbooks are often judged by their looks. Here's what I might have said about these two at first glance:

The Food Lab has a serene and inviting cover. Almost 1000 pages. Your head will spin. You will need a martini. Or a sherpa. So. Many. Words. So much exciting science to dive into. So many awkwardly composed and poorly-lit photos screaming out for some natural light.

Zahav is 373 pages of Israeli home cooking inspired by Michael Solomonov's Philadelphia restaurant of the same name. It is filled with stories of tragedy and triumph and reconnecting with his Israeli heritage. It's uncomfortably styled. Overly lit. Looks a bit nineties.

But how could I possibly know if your books were good unless I cooked from them? Would I forgive some of these foibles? Or would they become more glaring?

We put colorful Post-its next to every single recipe we wanted to make.

I was very strict.

I didn't let my son put Sriracha in your Caesar dressing, López-Alt. And Solomonov, no Nutella in your babka, even though we wanted to.

No improvisation allowed.

I am proud to say that my kids and I managed to cook over 20 recipes from each of your books.

Before I continue, I would like to lodge a formal complaint against you, J. Kenji López-Alt, for the overuse of the following words: AWESOME, ULTIMATE, BEST, PERFECT, FOOLPROOF, EASY.

But here is why I forgive you:

You taught me how to spatchcock a chicken.

You explained why my scrambled eggs weep. I now add salt to the eggs 15 minutes before I cook them.

You got me to throw three generations of egg-poaching technique out the window. We no longer add salt and vinegar to the boiling water and create a whirlpool with a butter knife. We now strain the loose whites away and slide the egg into the boiling water. No stray tentacles of whites. No murky acidic water. Just a tight white exterior hugging a just-firmed yolk.

You introduced us to light and fluffy buttermilk pancakes, immersion blender mayonnaise, Peruvian-style jalapeño sauce, steak with red wine pan sauce (that my son is still talking about), 3-ingredient blue cheese dressing, cheesy Hasselback potato gratin, sticky buns (six batches, bitches).

Just yesterday, I was slicing cheese and buttering bread and my son said, *Stop, I hope you're doing that the Food Lab way*. Because, thanks to you, regular old grilled cheese just won't do. They now want melted cheddar inside and crunchy Parmesan outside.

Thank you for explaining everything to me. Wait. Except for one thing: Why did the sickly sweet orange cream cheese glaze for your sticky buns keep splitting?

Solomonov: Your first chapter in *Zahav*, "Tehina: The Secret Sauce," should win a James Beard award. I got so caught up in your magic that I overnighted two jars of Soom, your favorite tehina, from Amazon. I wanted to make amba tehina, harissa tehina, black garlic tehina.

And, dude, I will never buy hummus again. I will always do as you do. I will pulverize a head of garlic with lemon juice, pass it through a fine strainer, and slowly whisk in tehina, water, salt, and cumin until it resembles a shiny pourable icing and tastes like a savory, nutty mousse. I will store this gloriousness in my fridge and mix it with puréed chickpeas for hummus, eggplant for babaganoush. I will use it as a salad dressing base. I will place it on top, under, around, and in between meat and vegetables.

My friend Margi offered to help me test recipes. She took one look at *The Food Lab* and said: *I don't even know what I would do with this*. But *Zahav* inspired her to host a Middle Eastern feast. Her main dish was your *pargiyot* (baby chicken) three ways with harissa, amba, and onion marinades. She and I agreed that on the page, they all looked and sounded quite different, but once grilled—while delicious—they all looked a similar greenish-orange and tasted virtually the same.

I made your chocolate babka. Such a solid recipe all the way through to the end. And so fun for the kids. But I think it needs more salt. Maybe some brown butter?

We need to talk about the fried eggplant with tehina and pomegranate seeds: The recipe said to cook the ¾-inch rounds in ½-inch of shimmering oil, five minutes per side. I've never experienced slices of eggplant cooking in ten minutes and, sadly, by the time they were creamy and soft inside, they tasted like oily hockey pucks. They went out with the compost.

But thank you for your beautiful tehina cookies. I kept several batches in my freezer and ate them all while binge-watching the second season of *Transparent*. Did you know they're even better with vanilla, a bit of salt, and rolled in sugar? And it helps to slightly undercook them. And you should try them with hazelnut butter. See? I tweak.

I make a lamb pie with about 20 ingredients in the filling, so I was psyched for the simplicity of your beef pie. I loved adding that field of sesame seeds to the top that sinks down into the buttery pastry. But it was missing excitement (maybe 15 ingredients?).

Until a month ago, if you'd looked in the back of my fridge, you would have found a jar of your pickled persimmons and dates with dried limes. Texture: mealy. Flavor: medicinal. I couldn't even give them away.

I really thought your book would win. *Zahav* is more my kind of food: Hella flavor. Nothing precious. My biggest criticism is that there is too much emphasis on your personal journey and not enough attention given to the recipes. People have raved to me about your restaurant. What got lost in translation? What didn't get onto the page? Why do too many of your dishes fall flat?

There are some shots of you eating at home with your family. These are the meals that intrigue me. These are the stories I want to hear. The foods I want to taste. I want to sit at that table; I wish more of the book felt this way. But I'm not giving your cookbook away. This month, I'm going to make your shakshouka, Turkish coffee ice cream, twice-cooked eggplant, fluke crudo, coffee-braised brisket, lachuch, and borekas.

López-Alt, your book is as intimidating as shit. It is oddly structured and filled with so many details that often it's hard to find the gems. But part of the joy I got from this book was discovering something new every time I flipped it open; and it was only because of the Piglet that I forced myself to excavate. I would like to thank you from the bottom of my heart for testing the fuck out of these recipes. I have never seen anything like it.

What It's Like to Cook with Dominique Crenn

By Daniel Duane

From *Food & Wine*

A contributing editor at both *Food & Wine* and *Men's Journal*, Daniel Duane writes equally well about food and adventure sports (hence his 2012 memoir *How to Cook Like a Man*). Here's his version of a kitchen smackdown, challenging star chef Dominique Crenn to prove her recipes could work in his home kitchen.

I am not sure what I expected when I challenged chef Dominique Crenn to cook from her new book in my home kitchen using only my knives and pans. But I do know why it seemed like a fine idea. I taught myself to cook by slavishly following recipes in compendiums by Alice Waters and Thomas Keller, but that approach floundered with newer books from modernist restaurants like Noma, Mugaritz and Manresa. Time and again, I swooned over the photos and then read a few recipes and concluded that a single dinner party would cost me a week and a thousand dollars. I began to wonder what these ultra-luxe cookbooks were even for—who was meant to buy them, and why?

Crenn's book was the one that put me over the edge. She grew up in France, won *Iron Chef America* in 2010 and became the first female cook in the U.S. to receive two Michelin stars. Her cuisine blends classical French technique and high technology to create dishes of magical lyricism—poetic culinaria, as Crenn calls it—and if you're picturing foams and gels and billowing mist and forest moss, you're getting the right idea. I had one of the greatest meals of my life at San Francisco's Atelier Crenn, and I came away desperate to know how she did it. So when I got my copy of *Atelier Crenn: Metamorphosis of Taste* and saw those wildly complex recipes, I thought, *Enough already! Let's see you do this in my kitchen, and without all those helpers.*

"Of course," said Crenn, when I phoned to ask if she would consider such a demonstration. "Monday—I come at two o'clock, we can eat at six."

Perhaps she had misunderstood. I told her, "That's only four hours. You have to cook everything yourself."

"Let's pick a menu," Crenn continued in her lovely French accent. "Maybe start with The Sea, and then Lobster Bisque and . . . Summer Squab? You can find all the ingredients? For everything? How about dessert?"

"No need for dessert," I told her. "This isn't a dinner party. It's just about you cooking this stuff in a regular home, alone."

"But food is to be eaten and shared. It does not make sense otherwise. Maybe the dessert also called The Sea. You can find all the ingredients? For everything?"

Off the phone, I fell into a state of confusion. The savory version of The Sea transforms the seafood platters made by Crenn's mother in Brittany into a kind of hyperrealist evocation of a tide pool, with mussels and clams and raw fish on edible white sand, with edible sea foam and beachcomber's flotsam that includes squid-ink meringues, fennel puree, candied lemon peel, smoked trout roe and saffron aioli. Similar deal with Lobster Bisque: inspired by Mom but reconceived as a tiny bowl covered with seaweed, through which a diner's spoon must plunge to find the broth bearing hidden treasures like lobster tail, fried sweetbreads, gelled plankton, lobster brain and pickled pearl onions. And, Summer Squab: fermented kumquats surrounding a little gift package on a plate, so that you cut through raspberry wrapping paper to find seared squab breast with onion soubise, daikon-sake puree and squab-reduction sauce.

Throw in the aforementioned dessert and Crenn had chosen a menu involving 34 distinct sub-recipes and multiple pieces of equipment that I do not own, like an immersion circulator, a vacuum sealer and a dehydrator.

As for the ingredients, they fell into three categories: first, the expensive and time-consuming to procure, like Maine lobster, marrow bones and sweetbreads, for which I drove all over San Francisco with an ice chest; second, the still-more-expensive, dangerous-sounding and unavailable, even in San Francisco, such as sodium hexametaphosphate, for which I placed a $250 Amazon order; and, third, the hyper-esoteric-even-on-the-Internet, such as sake lees. I finally gave up on this last category of ingredients and decided their absence would have to be part of the challenge to Crenn.

On the day in question, 2 p.m. came and went—then 2:30, 2:45. As my wife left to run errands, I told her there was no chance we'd be eating at 6.

Then, at 3 p.m., Crenn breezed into my kitchen wearing impeccable French casual—sailor shirt, faded jeans, white Comme des Garçons Converse—and trailing her pastry chef and *Iron Chef America* teammate, Juan Contreras.

Smiling a movie star smile and radiating confident control, Crenn tied on my favorite blue apron and asked, "You can read the recipe to me, for Lobster Bisque?"

"What do you mean?"

"Just the ingredients for the broth. Tell me what they are?"

I did, and then Crenn got to work: She sliced vegetables for the broth, then put them in a pot to sweat. Meanwhile, Contreras killed and poached the lobsters, pulled out their brains, cut off their tails and threw the carcasses into the pot for the broth—a step not in the cookbook. Crenn then cut the legs and wings off the squab and, in another departure from her own recipe, seared them in a Lodge cast-iron Dutch oven.

Over the next few hours, I gave up trying to count all the ways in which Crenn and Contreras were diverging from her cookbook. Instead, I just enjoyed the sight of pots simmering on every burner, knives flying and conversation remaining always friendly and off-topic.

At 5:45 p.m., my daughter Audrey waltzed in from basketball practice. She barged into Crenn's work space, made a peanut-butter-and-jelly sandwich and asked, "What's up?"

Crenn smiled, then offered a spoonful of a mysterious orange liquid. Audrey slurped and said, "Yummy! What's that?"

"Lobster brains and tomatoes," Crenn replied. Turning to me, she asked, "Six o'clock still good to eat?"

"Are you kidding?" I asked.

I texted my wife, and she texted back that she could be home by 6:10.

I told Crenn, and she paused as if to let time pass. Then she began multiple operations simultaneously: deep-frying sweetbreads, adjusting the seasoning of her sauce, searing squab breast and, in yet another adaptation, squab liver.

At 6:08 p.m., my wife walked through the door. At 6:10, Crenn set down four plates of The Sea stripped to its essence: mussels, clams, nearly raw fish, edible sand and sea foam and absolutely none of that beachcomber's flotsam. Precisely 15 minutes later, she delivered a bisque without pickled onions or that seaweed veil over the top of the bowls, followed by squab wrapped in a raspberry veil but without fermented kumquats or daikon-sake puree.

But here's the thing: The Sea still evoked a shoreline stroll, the bisque remained an unctuous dream. As for the squab, suffice it to say that my daughters still talk about Crenn's onion soubise as if it did not accompany pigeon liver.

Crenn petted our cat until we finished eating. Then she ran off to the soft opening of her new restaurant, Petit Crenn.

I felt like a dolt. Of course it was not possible for a single person—or even two— to cook a menu from Atelier Crenn in a home kitchen in a few hours. If it were, Atelier Crenn would not have its Michelin stars. Crenn was too classy to say that to me, so she found a polite way to communicate it by coming into my home, cooking a lovely meal for my family and showing me that her cuisine is more about poetics—beach walks, hidden treasures, gifts—than ingredients and technique, which must remain flexible in response to availability and context.

Throwing a dinner party from *Atelier Crenn: Metamorphosis of Taste* would therefore seem to involve the borrowing of ideas: identifying the essential vision in a few dishes, stripping out superfluous components, trusting everything to come out fine. I might even try this myself someday, though I doubt the results will be the same.

Pile of Goop

By Kathleen Purvis

From the *Charlotte Observer*

One of the deans of Southern food writing, long-time
Observer food editor and columnist Kathleen Purvis is a savvy,
no-nonsense expert on barbecue, bourbon, pecan pie, and
the like. Still, she was willing to give Gwyneth Paltrow's new
"lifestyle" cookbook a fair try....

Gwyneth Paltrow eats furikake with her fingers.
A Japanese seasoning made from crumbled dried seaweed, sesame and coconut sugar, it tastes a little fishy, and black crumbs flutter all over you when you eat it. But Gwyneth loves it so, she apparently sprinkles it on everything. She doesn't worry about the flakes—she probably has people to whisk seaweed off cashmere.

A hunger for furikake (it sounds a little like "fee-ur-cake") is just one of the ways Gwyneth is different from you and me. She has her own fab-lifestyle website, Goop.com. Her staff calls her "GP" (and I am just now realizing where the name Goop came from, so yes, Gwyneth is smarter than me). She sells $27-an-ounce Moon Dusts to sprinkle in smoothies. (Yes, she's much, much smarter than me.)

But does Gwyneth Paltrow really live better than you and I? When her new cookbook, "It's All Easy: Delicious Weekday Recipes for the Super-Busy Home Cook" (Goop Press, $35), landed on my desk, I had to find out:

Just how easy is it to be Gwyneth?

A Window to Her Soul

The book, co-written by Goop.com food editor Thea Baumann, includes many pictures of Gwyneth's life—winsomely gazing out of windows in gauzy light, wandering through Parisian parks, lingering over glasses of wine. While she's gluten-free and sort-of vegetarian (no red meat, but lots of chicken, eggs and even pancetta—pork apparently is white meat in her world), she loves wine, snacks and big dinners.

There are even a couple of pictures of Gwyneth cooking, although, oddly, no pictures of Gwyneth putting food in her mouth. Furikake crumbs in very white teeth aren't a good look on anyone.

The book's pantry list includes ketchup, kimchi (Gwyneth loves kimchi), nori seaweed sheets, kuzu root, Vegenaise (vegan mayonnaise) and manuka honey. It also includes more things than I knew could be made from coconut. (Sugar! Flour! Lingerie! No, wait, that last one was "South Pacific." Sorry, Gwyneth.)

The equipment list includes a bamboo matcha whisk for green tea, a spiralizer for turning zucchini into pasta, and a Vitamix blender, $329 to $600 at Amazon.com.

For a cookbook that promises easy weekday recipes, you have to pick carefully. I skipped the Bo Bun Salad with four sets of ingredients (eight for the chicken, three for the crispy shallots, six for the dressing and eight to finish the dish, including Armenian cucumbers). Bo Bun Salad could send you straight to the drive-through for a Bo biscuit.

I settled on a day's worth of dishes: Asian Avocado Toast, Bibimbap Salad (only 19 ingredients, plus the furikake makings), Beet Chips, Tikka Masala Roast Chicken with Indian Creamed Spinach and Roasted Cauliflower with Curry and Lime, and avocado-based Chocolate Mousse with Cashew Cream.

Breakfast was a hurdle. I wanted to start with the Pitaya Bowl, made with frozen dragonfruit. While frozen dragonfruit may be common in Southern California, it apparently doesn't exist in south Charlotte. I picked Ginger Chia Pudding and forged ahead.

Honey, That's a Lot

First stop: Whole Foods. Now, my pantry is more eclectically stocked than most: I already had Korean gochujang (a pepper paste), coconut oil, rice vinegar and the spice blend called garam masala. I still had a 28-item shopping list, including brown rice syrup, Vegenaise, chia seeds, liquid stevia and tandoori spice.

Shopping took 1 hour 20 minutes, including five requests for help from employees. (Tip: Vegenaise is in the refrigerator section, not on the shelf with the other vegan mayos. Luckily, it's right above the kimchi.)

Even hitting store brands and sales, my bill for a single day of food came to $129.16. Good thing I skipped that manuka honey at $26 to $44 a jar.

Back home, I was ready for a pick-me-up, so I started the Asian Avocado Toast at 9:55 a.m. I quickly discovered the times given on recipes are a bit of a cheat. Many claim "less than 30 minutes," but involve things that take separate cooking, like poaching eggs and making furikake. "Under-30 minute" toast took closer to 40 minutes.

Still, it was tasty, even the sweet/salty/fishy furikake. I ate it and took a break to stand at the window, gazing winsomely while I picked seaweed off my shirt.

Is It Time to Wine?

Lunch was Bibimbap Salad. Again, it involves cooking rice, prepping a blender sauce (7 minutes 50 seconds), cooking mushrooms, mung beans and spinach separately, poaching another egg and shredding carrots. My score: 36 minutes, 40 seconds.

It was tasty, though. Even my vegetarian-averse spouse loaded up a bowl, easy on the kimchi. We're still consciously coupled because I don't make him eat much kimchi.

By 2 p.m., I started the Chocolate Mousse. Apparently, you do need a $350 blender to make cashew cream. In my Breville, no slouch at high speeds, it came out more gritty than creamy, and weirdly salty. But the chocolate mousse chilled up with a dense, smooth texture and only a hint of avocado.

Beet chips, shaved thin on my mandoline, had mixed results. Some got crispy, others stayed leathery. The crisp ones were tasty if you don't mind potato chips with a beet aftertaste. Then again, Gywneth advocates snacking with wine. After a glass or three, you might be fooled.

On to dinner: The chicken involved spatchcocking—cutting out the backbone, and don't we do that every day?—so add poultry shears to that equipment list. With the side dishes, it took 1 hour, 53 minutes. Not short by "super-busy weeknight" standards, but for a Saturday night, it's doable.

The cauliflower was tasty and I'd make it again. But the Indian creamed spinach was more Cincinnati than Calcutta—nice but underseasoned.

The best dish of the day turned out to be breakfast. If you like the soft pop of things like bubble tea and caviar, you'll love chia pudding. You just put seeds in a jar with coconut water, coconut milk and coconut sugar and refrigerate overnight. It gets a creamy/crunchy texture, perfect for a morning commute.

From shopping to cooking, my day as Gwyneth was occasionally tasty. But it was often more work than promised, and it takes a hefty amount of money.

It's all easy? Sorry, Gwyneth: That's a load of goop.

The Family Table

Moving Kitchen

By Laura Donohue

From CrumbsontheTable.co.uk

At Cottage Garden Cookery in Cambridgeshire, England,
American-born food writer Laura Donohue bakes, caters, blogs,
and gives cooking lessons that distill all she's absorbed from years
of globe-trotting. In this blog post, she invites us all to visit the
kitchen where her love of food was first born.

We are helping our parents to move house after forty years—
New Jersey to North Carolina. We are down to the wire, the
moving van scheduled for two days' time after months of planning. My
share in this project has been small: two flying visits. It has been easy for
me, until today, when we sorted the kitchen.

Amy is asking, "keep or chuck?," but every object has its story. My
mother hesitates. She speaks softly. I am hearing for the first time that
this bowl, with its discoloured glaze and chipped lip, belonged to my
mother's grandmother, and my mother ate green beans from that bowl
when she was a child. The glass bowl with stripes belonged to the original mixer my mother got in Tripoli at the base exchange when my father
was stationed in Libya back in the fifties, long before this kitchen. The
measuring spoons, no longer their original shape because I once used
the tablespoon to open a tin of paint, were bought at Woolworth's in a
small town in Texas when my mother was a girl collecting things for her
trousseau, longer ago still.

It's not possible to rush this. These stories need to be told. I'm
stunned that I've never heard them before, or if I have, that I don't

remember. My mother's quiet voice is not insistent. She speaks without drama. Her stories are subtle. Sometimes they get lost in the noise, in the demands of others. A family.

I've had meals in that kitchen. I sat in that corner at the aquamarine formica table, long since gone, doing my homework, eating peanut butter sandwiches and Kraft macaroni and cheese. I was sitting there as a teenager when Nixon resigned in shame, and always associate Watergate with that kitchen table.

When my parents redesigned the kitchen to fit more with the turn-of-the-century house, they got rid of the aqua formica and replaced it with a robust butcher block: the Female Eunuch table, we girls called it, its sharp corners exactly the right height to catch every one of us in the pubic bone. It's staying for the house staging to cripple the next generation of women—or maybe they will be taller than we are.

A kitchen. The heart of the house. The place of labour, of needs satisfied or disappointed, of sharing and arguments. This room is the one I used most and I am not sure I want to part with it, not because it's easy to work in, or because I love it, but because I'm not sure what I'll do now to remember the details of those times—the details that make all the difference to memory. I'm glad I have photos that catch my family in the context of this space: serving up the pork roast, the tomatoes and corn, the most recent birthday cake . . .

I take home with me the wooden rolling pin with the red handles and the battered colander that are now back in fashion because they're retro. And the dented angel food cake pan because it has those little feet, although I have a newer one in England and won't get this one in my suitcase. These are my transitional objects. They will remind me of this house, and incongruously of the Vietnam War, Germaine Greer, of oreos and milk, my own formative cooking sessions, shouting matches, pecan pies, and my mother's hands.

My mother-in-law, Joy, has also begun to give me pieces of her *batterie de cuisine*: a sponge tin, a tart ring, the bowl she used for mixing Christmas cake. She tells me she'll never use them again. She's matter of fact, practical, glad to have found a home for them. I am touched, sad, glad to have them. I can't let these moments pass so perfunctorily. Keep or chuck.

I want to honour all that cooking, all that time, all the effort: the planning, shopping, measuring, chopping, creaming, stirring, mixing, folding, browning, watching, turning out, cooling, tasting, serving, critiquing.

Do we appreciate enough? Of course we don't. We are too busy getting on with it. It takes the big moments to make us stop.

How did we get here? How do we make sense of time?

I settle on gratitude. All the being taken care of. The immense effort it takes to satisfy our needs, and wants, so many of them met in the kitchen by those who cook. All those days, and meals, and washings up. The pleasures and fulfilment they represent, the endeavour and sacrifice.

The Meaning of Mangoes

By Dianne Jacob

From *Lucky Peach*

Cookbook editor, food writer, and writing coach Dianne Jacob
is the author of the award-winning book (and blog) *Will Write
for Food*. Perhaps she was fated to grow up to write about food,
judging from the exotic mix of childhood food memories she
shares here.

In the 1960s, when I was a kid, the only tropical fruits in Vancouver
supermarkets were bananas, pineapples, and coconuts. My immigrant dad bought them all, but longed for the bright yellow mangoes he
had grown up with in Shanghai.

He'd tried growing his own Asian produce in our cold and rainy climate, with small successes. The melons and chilies didn't take, Chinese
chives did. On snowy winter mornings, I ventured into our backyard
to pick them for scrambled eggs. In summer my dad peeled long, pale-
green stalks of celtuce and left them in the fridge, bobbing in ice water,
for a snack that was sweet like tender lettuce and juicy like celery, without the stringiness. But there was no mango anywhere.

My parents came to Canada in 1949, refugees escaping the coming
Communist revolution, which didn't look kindly upon foreigners or the
bourgeoisie. Born in Shanghai to Iraqi Jews who had moved there from
India, they'd lived a privileged life, with servants, parties, and Paris fash-
ions. They were married in 1947, and Mao's army advanced a couple
years later. My parents got out fast, on the USS *General W. H. Gordon*,
bound for North America. They managed to bring an entire household

with them, including bolts of fabric, furniture, clothing, and a silver Art Deco tea set decorated with bamboo leaves.

They were surrounded by their stuff, but not by their family. Every day in Vancouver, my parents grieved for their past. One of Dad's brothers and his wife had settled in an apartment nearby. The rest of the family—their mothers and thirteen siblings—emigrated to California, New York, London, and Israel.

My parents balanced their new life while clinging to the old one. On weekend mornings, they wore floor-length brocade dressing gowns with Chinese slippers. They used chopsticks and ate on their twenty-four-piece phoenix- and dragon-patterned dinnerware. My mother made sticky rice wrapped in lotus leaves (*zong zi*), star anise-scented broth with vermicelli noodles and shiitake mushrooms, and sautéed tofu puffs (*da woo*, in the Shanghai dialect) with soybean and mung bean sprouts.

While they liked Vancouver's Chinatown, my parents could not communicate with the people there, who hailed from South China and mostly spoke Cantonese. Mom and Dad knew only the Shanghai dialect, a different language. The foods were different, too. Longing for the *da ping* flatbread she loved, my mom contented herself with *you tiao*, Chinese crullers she could find locally. Once a month we went to the Marco Polo, a fancy restaurant in Chinatown, for dinner, and ordered dishes my parents had never eaten in Shanghai—like crab with garlic and black bean sauce, and sweet and sour spareribs. On those evenings, we were just another white family in a Chinese restaurant.

And just as they were not the right kind of Chinese, neither were my parents the right kind of Jews. At that time, Vancouver's community of around seven thousand Jews was mostly Eastern European, with their own customs, dialects, and foods like brisket and gefilte fish, unknown to my parents. The other Jews spoke English and Yiddish, while my parents peppered their English with words in Arabic and Shanghai dialect. At the synagogues, the prayers were different, too. Life was never going to be like it was in Shanghai.

One day when I was eight or nine years old, my dad and his brother burst in the front door with a wooden crate hoisted above their shoulders. They had convinced the owner of a produce store in Chinatown to import a box of mangoes at great expense—the sweet, soft Philippine variety (aka Carabao, Manila Super, Champagne, or Honey mango), the sweetest mango in the world. My younger sister and I followed my dad and uncle as they carried the crate to the basement, long overcoats flapping. They pried off the wooden top with a crowbar, and then dug through flurries of crinkly foreign newsprint, checking each fruit for ripeness or damage. My sister and I craned our necks and tiptoed closer, but dad told us to stand back.

"Don't touch these," he told us sternly, holding up a pale yellow fruit he had unwrapped to inspect. "The mangoes will ripen, and only I can check to see when they are ready. If I find out you've handled them, you'll get it."

My sister and I waited for this miracle of ripening fruit. Every day, we opened the door to the basement, turning the squeaky brass knob quietly to avoid my father's wrath. We sniffed the scented air, dazzled by the increasingly fragrant cloud of tropical musk. We crept down the stairs and inched up to the box in the dark, fearful of arousing suspicion by turning on the lights. I dug through the paper, picking up a mango to admire its smooth, shiny skin. It might have been solid gold, for all we knew. I inhaled its scent, trying to anticipate its taste and texture. I was stuck on the literalness of it, too young to understand what this taste memory would mean to my parents.

After a week of anticipation, dad called my aunt and uncle to say that enough mangoes were ripe. My mother covered the dining room table with sheets of newspaper. As soon as our relatives arrived, we all sat down. My father came in with armfuls of the fruit and spread them on the table. Kidney-shaped, wrinkled, and some dotted with black spots, the mangos filled the room with a scent that drove us all mad with desire.

While my sister and I watched, my parents and aunt and uncle sliced the mangoes on either side of the pits, exposing their golden-orange flesh and handing halves to my sister and me. We dipped in with our teaspoons and ate the silky fruits one after another, the flesh like a tangy, honeyed pineapple. Following my elders, I sucked the buttery meat from around the pits, wasting nothing. My parents allowed my sister and me to eat as many as we wanted.

Finally, we all leaned back contentedly, covered with sticky juice. The adults lit cigarettes: Craven A for my parents, and unfiltered Player's Navy Cut for my aunt and uncle. Life was not full of perfect moments when I was a child, but this was one of them, eating blazing yellow fruit against the backdrop of gray and overcast Vancouver.

The Millionaire's Turkey: A Father-Daughter Story

BY BETSY ANDREWS

From SeriousEats.com

Prize-winning poet Betsy Andrews, the former executive editor of *Saveur,* is now editor-at-large for Rodale's *Organic Life.* Here's her bracing antidote to the annual flood of Norman-Rockwellish Thanksgiving fantasies: an unflinchingly honest essay about the ruined turkeys of her past.

I'm cooking the turkey again this year, and I hope I don't screw it up. I have a checkered history with the holiday bird, so it wouldn't be the first time things have gone awry. I blame my father.

Joseph John Andrews, my dad, was a Roman-nosed womanizer and an ill-tempered drunk. He grew up dirt-poor, the son of a Czech-born coal miner, in the Pocono Mountains. My father just wanted to get the heck out of there, and he did it by way of war. He got himself all shot up in Korea and earned a Purple Heart. The shrapnel remained in the form of dark, hard splotches beneath the skin on his thighs and neck. Occasionally, it fell out in the shower.

The experiences of going to war and growing up impoverished and ashamed spilled out of him all the time, though, ping-ponging him from self-aggrandizement to rage. He married my mother, a pretty girl in his math class at Penn State, where he went on the G.I. Bill. He wore combat boots to the ceremony because he couldn't afford shoes.

My father became an engineer and made a good life for himself while acting very, very bad. He wasn't home much, but when he was, he wreaked havoc in every corner of the house, starting with the kitchen, where he fancied himself a gourmet cook.

Rocks glass in hand at the yellow enamel stove, he would order me around, intermittently hollering his guts out. "Get me a spatula!" he would yell. "Quickly! QUICKLY!" My father would extract collusion in his conceit. "Betsy, your daddy makes the best turkey ever! Doesn't your daddy make the best turkey ever? Tell me your daddy makes the best turkey ever." Then, a beat later: "Your daddy is a millionaire!"

Eager to prove himself on both counts, he spent far too much money stocking the holiday bar with Almaden, Mateus Rosé, Crown Royal, and Canadian Club, and got too early a start on the booze and the cooking. The turkey was invariably over-roasted, and it was my mother's extended Philadelphia family's duty to eat the desiccated bird. Some years they indulged my father's boasting, other years they comforted my mother after my father had, say, chased her around the yard with a tire iron. But, either way, the cousins all agreed that, yes, his turkey was the best.

I was having none of it. At 16 years old, I became a vegetarian. At 27, I came out. The first turkey I ever roasted was for a lesbian Thanksgiving party in Brooklyn. I was so worried that it would end up like my father's dry bird that I basted the bejeezus out of it. To my surprise, it turned out amazingly moist and, so I was told, amazingly good—so good, in fact, that it landed me in bed with a woman I had, up until then, been fruitlessly pursuing. Yes, we were drunk, but it wasn't the booze that persuaded her. "I think it was the bird," she said.

The following Thanksgiving, at my mother's house—the first for which my father wasn't cooking, a ritual that had outlasted my parents' marriage, until we finally decided we'd had enough of him showing up from his man-apartment with 25 pounds of dry poultry—I volunteered to cook the turkey. The plan was to repeat the previous year's method, but I started too early, and I was drinking too much. Who knew you could over-baste it? The whole thing fell apart when my brother tried to carve it. It was like turkey soup.

After dinner, my father, older now, slightly deflated, stopped by en route to the country club bar. I sat drinking with him in the living room. I was a writer by then, and my father had been bugging me to write about him. Okay, I thought, he's asking for it. I turned on the tape.

"You know, Dad," I said, "it was brutal growing up with you."

"Really?" he said. "I don't remember." His mismatched eyes—one blue, one hazel—bulged slightly over a spreading smile. "I don't remember a thing. Maybe it's a gift to me. Maybe it's a gift from the gods."

"I think," I said, "it's the alcohol."

"Could be!" he said cheerfully, and took another sip.

Of all my father's bad behaviors I had repeated—cheating on girlfriends, crashing about in a drunken rage, tooting my own battered horn—I hadn't overestimated my own cooking. Or at least I thought I hadn't until then; it was years before I made the holiday bird again. But eventually, I got a job writing about food and drink. It was inevitable—a coming-to-terms for a daughter whose sense of survival was tied to how quickly she could fetch a spatula. Because I had to write about meat, I started eating and cooking it anew, and last year, again, I offered to roast the Thanksgiving turkey. Maybe I'd bring some leftovers the next day when I made my brief visit to my father's nursing-home bed—if the bird turned out well. If I were to feed him, it would have to be better than what he had fed me.

I bought a beautiful organic turkey from my local food co-op and trundled it to Philadelphia, where I was planning a magnificent sage-and-butter-basted roast. Wine glass in one hand, already tipsy, I reached into the cavity of the turkey with the other hand, fishing around for the giblets bag, and came up empty.

"Huh," I thought. "Where is it?" I shrugged, stuffed the bird, and shoved it into my sister's oven. I switched from wine to Scotch. Hours passed. The cousins arrived. The turkey's skin was nearing charcoal-black, but it was still dripping red juice. Finally, I carved the thing; the meat was dry as dust. The cousins all agreed it was the best they had eaten in years. In its overheated cavity, surrounded by stuffing, I found the source of all that dark juice: the cooked giblets bag.

My father yelled his guts out while preparing his Thanksgiving turkey. I, in turn, had left the guts inside—a metaphor, I suppose, for all the ways he had gotten under my skin. The next day, I stood at his bed, empty-handed, aching to get the heck out of there; aching, too, with guilt because of it. I couldn't bring myself to express any of my feelings. He managed one of the few words remaining in his stroke-damaged brain to describe his. "Embarrassed," he said.

This week, when I try to roast my next turkey, it will have been six months since my father died. I imagine that his drunken spirit will be in the kitchen, Canadian Club on ice in hand, hollering at me in a way so unnerving that I'll over-roast the bird (or over-baste it, or undercook it, or just throw it out the window in a middle-aged act of rebellion). No matter what happens, I have told myself, I'll make the damned thing on my own terms, keeping the wine glasses and the rocks glasses at bay until the skin is nicely burnished and the juices run almost clear. The cousins will say it's the best turkey they have ever eaten, really. As I cook, I'll ask little of my kid; I'll be gentle with my girlfriend. I will feel, I swear, like a million bucks.

Goodnight, Mrs. Calabash

By Besha Rodell

From *Gravy*

Besha Rodell has lived a peripatetic life—born in Australia, raised in the United States, she's been a food editor and restaurant critic on both coasts (first for Atlanta's *Creative Loafing* magazine, and since 2012 at *LA Weekly*). Yet if anything says "home" to her, it's the fried seafood of the Carolina coast. Here's why.

When I was three years old, my maternal grandmother was very sick with cancer of the everything. My mother and father and I were living in Boston, but her brother, my uncle, was in medical school at the University of North Carolina, and as a result my grandmother was transferred to the hospital in Chapel Hill for her last months of care. It was her final wish to be taken to the ocean, and, because of this, my earliest memories of the seaside are of the Atlantic coast of North Carolina. I remember playing in the sand with cousins a few years older than me, I remember the small beach shacks that lined the coast in the 1970s, and I remember my uncle carrying my grandmother out into the water in his arms because she didn't have the strength to walk.

I was born into a nomadic family of sorts, one that has split and fractured and regrouped and moved, over and over again. By the time I was 18, I had lived in 5 cities, in 16 houses, and on two opposite ends of the world. There were and are very few constants in my life, locational or otherwise, but the land between Wilmington, North Carolina, and Myrtle Beach, South Carolina, is an exception. It is the coastline to which I belong.

When I'm far away from this part of the world, as I usually am, three things tug at my heart the hardest. There are the beaches themselves, their old fishing piers and warm water and periwinkle-strewn sand. There's the thrumming, intense greenness of the marshes, a kind of green that doesn't exist anywhere else, that hits you when you cross the Intracoastal Waterway to the beach islands, an almost mossy green that's different from the green of a forest or field or pasture, a green that is basically the color of my soul. And there are the hushpuppies and fried seafood of Calabash, North Carolina.

Calabash is a small fishing town on the border of North and South Carolina, just on the north side, on an off-shoot of the Intracoastal Waterway called the Calabash River. In the early 1800s, Calabash was called Pea Landing, but when they got a post office another name was needed. Pea Landing was already taken. "Calabash" comes from the French and Spanish words for "gourd." The town likely got its name from the gourd-shaped river it sits upon.

The town comprises a few roads, most notably Highway 179, which runs the length of the town. A small waterfront overlooks the marshy river. It's not close enough to the beach or to the bawdy wonder of Myrtle Beach to be a true tourist trap. For people who have been coming to this coastline year after year, as I have, Calabash is beloved for two things.

The first is a 35,000-square-foot gift shop called Callahan's. About two thirds of that labyrinthine sprawl is run-of-the-mill beach stuff: shells, T-shirts, large sculptures of mermaids; the stuff you would use to tastefully (or not so tastefully) decorate the beach condo you just bought and named "Dune Nothin.'"

The back third of the store is Saint Nick Nack's, a year-round Christmas shop dazzling in its breadth of sparkle. There are rooms and rooms of lights and snowmen, dinnerware and Christmas-themed electronic miniature train sets, ornaments for hunters and bakers and bikers.

My husband, who was born and raised in North Carolina and who vacationed at nearby Cherry Grove Beach his entire childhood, still has a visceral horror-faced reaction when I say "Saint Nick Nack's," remembering summer days wasted while his mother dragged the family around the store, cooing over Christmas decorations in July. Fate is cruel: I do the same thing to him now.

Then there's the fried seafood. On the town's website and logo and elsewhere, Calabash declares itself the Seafood Capital of the World, and has done so for many decades, since back when the population was in the low hundreds. *The New York Times* reported in 1983 that Calabash had 180 people and 32 restaurants.

"Calabash-style" is a term used to describe breaded and fried seafood, usually served with hushpuppies and coleslaw. The term is ubiquitous up and down the North and South Carolina coasts and especially along the gaudy stretch of Highway 17 that runs through Myrtle Beach, one of the South's most popular destinations for spring break and summer vacation debauchery. True Calabash seafood is lightly breaded and lightly fried, and if you ask anyone who knows they'll tell you it's not really Calabash seafood unless you're eating it in Calabash.

Even so, more people know the term than the town itself. You can find restaurants advertising Calabash-style seafood throughout the Carolinas, and into Virginia and land-locked West Virginia. In Battle Creek, Michigan, there's a restaurant called Captain Luey's Calabash Seafood.

The mythology of how Calabash came to be famous for its seafood goes like this: In the 1930s, people would wait at the docks in the early evening for fishermen to drop anchor with the day's catch. Families began to set up tubs of hot oil and fry the fish along the riverbank, and these fish camps became so popular that they eventually attracted locals, and then visitors. In the 1940s, two sisters decided to turn their family fish fries into brick-and-mortar restaurants. Ruth Beck and Lucy Coleman each opened a restaurant: Coleman's Original in 1940, and soon after, Beck's. In 1950, their brother, Lawrence High, and his wife, Ella, opened Ella's.

As with any large family in any small town, different folks tell different stories of who came first and who invented what. But it's accepted that these three siblings are the originators of Calabash seafood restaurants. Descendants of those siblings still own all three establishments. Lawrence High's daughter, Sheryl Ann Hardee, took over Ella's after her parents died. When the owners of Beck's decided to sell in 2004, Hardee bought that restaurant to keep it in the family. Hardee's children, Kurt Hardee and Shaun Bellamy, now own and operate both Ella's and Beck's.

While the addictive quality of the seafood cemented the town's fame, it also got a boost from Jimmy Durante. Beginning in the 1950s, Durante began closing all his performances, which included television, radio, and live theater, with the words, "Goodnight, Mrs. Calabash, wherever you are."

Contested theories posit how and why Durante came to use that sign-off. (Was Mrs. Calabash Lucy Coleman, who fried the fish? Or did Durante's first wife love Calabash-style seafood so much that "Mrs. Calabash" became his pet name for her?) There's no doubt that Durante ate in Calabash at some point, and that it made such an impression that the town earned a prominent place in showbiz history.

My first consumer obsession was not food but junk, and it was junk that first brought me to Calabash. When I was a teenager, my family often drove down from the Northeast for a week or two in the summer to share a North Carolina beachfront home with my uncle. The summer after I graduated from high school, my mother bought a house in Tarrytown, New York, and the closing got pushed back until a couple of weeks after the lease expired on our previous house. We decided to turn temporary homelessness into a vacation. My mom and my three siblings and I piled into our station wagon and headed south to a beach house on Emerald Isle, North Carolina.

Within a few days, Hurricane Bertha had pushed us off the island, and that hiccup began a summer odyssey. The closing on the new house was pushed back again and again, and the five of us ended up driving around the South crammed into that wagon for what turned out to be months. We sat out the hurricane at a bed and breakfast in New Bern, my 14-year-old brother and I drinking the cheap complimentary port as we watched Bertha blow trees down the street. We drove to the mountains and then back to the beach, this time settling on Sunset Beach, our preferred beach, just to the north of Calabash.

Seeing as we had no time constraints and nothing to do, I insisted we stop at every thrift store, junk store, and flea market we passed. On the winding back roads around Sunset Beach, we found a junkyard owned by a craggy guy named Mr. Varnum and spent hours exploring the bombed-out cars and mysterious twisted metal on his swampy property. And I learned that Calabash, North Carolina, is one of the best towns in America for thrift stores. In the Calabash EMS thrift store, which was located in a falling-down house and run by a 97-year-old woman and was only open on Saturdays, I found a Miss Teen Pageant USA T-shirt that read: "The Quality Pageant for Quality Girls." It cost 10 cents. I still think of this as one of the shopping highlights of my life.

From there we stumbled upon Saint Nick Nack's. And from there, across the street, we discovered Ella's of Calabash.

Of the three earliest Calabash restaurants, only Ella's still operates in its original building. Ella's is built in the typical style of casual Southern coastal restaurants: There are wooden booths, brusque waitresses in pastel Ella's T-shirts, and a short salad bar (one trip: $3, all-u-can-eat: $5.99) with canned beets and cottage cheese and green olives and six kinds of dressing, all of them creamy. The walls are festooned with 65 years' worth of memorabilia, including a giant mounted fish that Ella herself is said to have caught.

The menu at Ella's is the same as the menus at almost every other restaurant in town: small or large plates of fried shrimp, oysters, flounder, scallops, or deviled crabs. Or combos with two or three of these items. You can get side orders of them, platters of them, sandwiches stuffed with them. Or, "for land lovers," there's a spaghetti dinner.

The original locations of Beck's and and Coleman's burned down. In October of 2012, Beck's caught fire due to some old wiring in the roof. It reopened six months later, in April 2013. The new, nautical-themed interior feels antiseptic compared to its former worn and homey building, which stood for 72 years.

Losing the original Beck's was heartbreaking for Shaun Bellamy, the granddaughter of Ella and daughter of Sheryl Ann Hardee, who grew up working in both restaurants. "My mom was so passionate about keeping Beck's in the family," Bellamy says. "She passed away just a few years ago, and that was her project. To see the old building go was just so hard. I love the new building, but it's not the same." Bellamy's father, who served as Calabash's mayor for 20 years and helped build the new Beck's building, passed away last January.

Lots of restaurants have burned in Calabash over the years. Last year, Coleman's Original went up in flames, for similar reasons, and it wasn't the first time: Coleman's had burned once before, in the 1970s. They are planning a comeback similar to Beck's—a new building to house all that old history. Captain John's, on the west side of Coleman's, burned in November 2010. Captain Nance's, next door to the east, burned down in July 1999.

Even before the fires, my family always gravitated toward Ella's. When I married into a North Carolina family, I was relieved that their loyalty lay with Ella's, too.

I don't know if there's much of a difference between Ella's and the other restaurants in Calabash. Bellamy says the recipes are all similar, but that doesn't stop people from arguing over whose is better, or greasier, or fresher. I do know that Ella's serves the kind of hushpuppies that are long and squiggly and lighter than the cornmeal spheres served at Beck's and most other spots. And I know that the fried oysters at Ella's taste the crispest and creamiest, probably because I ate there as a kid and I ate there during that crazy homeless summer and I ate there the day before my wedding. We said our vows under Spanish moss looking out over the marshes of the Intracoastal Waterway at a house about a mile and a half north of Calabash.

In the 32 years since that *New York Times* article, the population of Calabash has grown to just over 2,000, which is a lot of people to fit into 3.7 square miles. The largest restaurant in town is a newer place called Boundary House that sits behind (and is owned by the same folks as) Callahan's gift shop. In a dining room that looks like it belongs to a fancy mall restaurant, they serve frozen drinks and "oriental chicken salad" and spinach-artichoke dip in addition to fried seafood.

But according to Bellamy, not much has changed, despite the town's massive population growth. "There aren't nearly as many restaurants as there used to be. It's mainly just the ones with a long history," she says. "Someone came in here and tried to open one of those Myrtle Beach–style buffets that call themselves Calabash, but they didn't last long."

The remaining restaurants still have long waits for dinner many nights, but the shrimp trade that built Calabash isn't what it used to be. In the last 30 years, a combination of golf-course gentrification, declining shrimp hauls, and the glut of imported frozen shrimp have killed much of the business that was left. The two main shrimping companies in town now make most of their money from the charter fishing business. In the early mornings, a group of shrimpers gathers at the Calabash riverfront to drink coffee, tell stories, and reminisce. They're mainly retired.

Bellamy admits that because of the demand they face and the small supply, they often use frozen shrimp, though not when they can get fresh. On some things she stands firm. "At Ella's we have oyster roasts during the winter, and it's one of our most popular items." Those oysters, different from the variety she fries, come in huge metal tubs, still fused together. You have to wrestle them apart and open to get to the briny-hot goodness inside. "We want our food to represent this town, this part of the country," Bellamy says.

I've never eaten at Captain Luey's Calabash Seafood in Battle Creek, Michigan. I'm sure there's plenty about it to love, but I've come to the conclusion that some food isn't meant to transplant particularly well. It's okay if I can't get proper North Carolina or Texas barbecue in Los Angeles, where I live now, and it's okay if Calabash seafood is only truly possible in Calabash. If you want to try it, you'll just have to go there yourself.

To that end, I'm now teaching my son the exquisite torture of a trip to Saint Nick Nack's to buy Christmas ornaments in July, followed by a plate of fried seafood at Ella's. Despite the influx of residents, despite the fires, Bellamy is right that not much has changed here, which is maybe why I'm so attracted to this odd little town. The EMS thrift store has moved twice and is now open six days a week. I'd look stupid in a Miss Teen Pageant USA T-shirt these days. But the fried shrimp at Ella's still taste like history, and that mossy green marsh along the Calabash River is as close to a home as anywhere else I'll ever be.

Mom's Meatballs

By Victoria Pesce Elliott

From the *Miami Herald*

Born-and-bred Miamian Victoria Pesce Elliott—the *Miami Herald* restaurant critic—has spent years chronicling her city's vibrant, polyglot dining scene. In this piece, though, a phone call from her father sets off a very different—and poignant— culinary quest.

"Babe? Do you know where to find the cookbook with Mom's meatball recipe?"

It is my Dad's voice. I look at the numbers on the caller ID box on my kitchen counter. He is at home. Where I grew up. Where he and Mom still live after 42 years.

But the words don't make sense to me.

Cookbook? Meatballs? Recipe? My mom has been making the same meatballs forever. I've never seen a recipe. There is no recipe.

She taught me to mix the ingredients by hand, tearing the crusty hunks of leftover bread into milk to soften, then tearing them even smaller as we smush them into three kinds of ground meat, adding tiny cubes of diced garlic, plus parsley, loads of just-grated cheese, and lots of salt and pepper. A scoop of seasoned breadcrumbs and an egg or two, enough to hold it all together.

With the help of the old wood-handle ice cream scooper we form them about the size of billiard balls, digging into the huge metal bowl then rolling them with hands dipped in water.

Now Dad—who has never, ever picked up the phone to call me or anyone else that I can recall—is ringing me in the middle of a summer morning, while I am scrambling eggs and trying to get the girls off to Montessori.

I stare at my shelves of cookbooks, about to seize one. As if I were to find Mom's recipe inside. I have hundreds. No doubt I could have found a recipe for meatballs. In fact, I have written hers down often to give to friends who ask.

Has my old, macho, Italian Dad decided to start cooking in his old age? He had never cooked a thing in his life. Besides some truly unfortunate experiments with mango breads that turned black and watery the day after baking, his only forays in the kitchen involved fermenting anything he could make into wine or beer.

"Mom was planning to make them for some friends coming to town, but she can't remember the ingredients."

His voice was furtive. It was as if he spoke quickly enough I wouldn't question his motive.

10 Ingredients

Beef, veal, pork, garlic, parsley, cheese, bread, breadcrumbs, milk, eggs makes 10. There are 10 ingredients, not counting a healthy handful of salt and pepper. And, of course, the olive oil for frying.

No onion. No basil. Somehow I always had to remind myself about leaving out those two.

Twice as much beef as veal and pork.

Ten. Like the number of generations our family has been said to have been cursed. The curse of the bastard son.

Ten. Like a decade on the rosary. How many Hail Marys you have to say for each small bead between the Our Father and Glory Be.

The meatballs are the color of the rosewood rosaries that Grandma used to carry from Italy and keep in her bra. Ah, the things she pulled out of that soft, wide ledge, as big as a watermelon and padded with medals of St. Anthony, letters, tissues, a zippered change purse filled with real silver dollars, a key on a circle of yarn.

She was not much of a cook, but she married men who could cook. Men, one after another, who beat her, she said, until she looked like a *melanzana*, the deep purple color of an eggplant.

Mom doesn't cook from recipes. Well, there was that phase in the

'70s where she took a string of gourmet cooking classes and made French onion soup, Chinese stir-fry and baklava. She owned some lovely Italian cookbooks, but they always seemed more like guidebooks with pretty pictures. No stains or penciled-in notes.

Meatballs? She could make them in her sleep. Couldn't she?

A Slip

I remember one Christmas, my brothers and I were all home from college. We must have had 20 people for dinner. We had cooked for three days.

Lasagne, roast pork, meatball, caprese salad showered in basil from the yard, broccoli di rabe loaded with garlic diced so small it might have been coarse sea salt, stalks of asparagus with shavings of fresh parmigiano cheese. A platter of prosciutto as thin as petals wrapped around smiles of melon the color of a sunset.

As she carried the bowl of meatballs to the table, Mom slipped and dropped the whole bowl, crashing onto the golden-brown tile floor.

Quick as can be, she slid the wooden door shut, shielding us from the eyes of the guests at the dining room table. One by one she picked up the balls and put them in a colander. I got down to help, sweeping the remaining debris with a foxtail into the dustpan.

I noticed with surprise—shock, really—that she was not heading to the garbage with the colander but rather to the sink. Mom separated the glass from the meat, rinsing the balls, dozens of them, until they were clean. No more thick tomato sauce clinging to them. They are bald but for the flecks of white cheese and green parsley revealed beneath irregular sketches of a perfectly browned umber char from the cast-iron skillet.

She pulled a clean serving bowl from the closet and ladled out fresh sauce. They were ready, again.

Mom Is Sick

It turns out Dad had found Mom rummaging through her cookbook collection desperately searching for her meatball recipe. She asked him if he remembered the ingredients.

Why had she not called me?

Mom and I talked most every day. We talked about boys, and later men. We talked about school and stress, and real estate. She complained about my Dad. We laughed. We talked about travel and the weather and sometimes shopping, but always food.

"Don't make appetizers," she said once as she got older and more cynical—or maybe just more practical. "People fill up on them and then don't eat dinner." From then on it was a bowl of olives, some cheese or nuts, but not the colorful antipasti platters we knew from years before.

All at once I see, like a Christmas tree lighting up. Or the weatherman's map filling the screen.

Mom is sick. This is Dad's way of telling me he is scared. That he has known for a long time but could not say. She has the same thing that took Grandma.

There will be no more meatballs. Not hers, anyway. No matter how many times I make them, they cannot be as good as hers. Or, so I think. I taste only a trace of her in there. That is all that is left of her. A trace.

Though she sits at the table and eats, a small bite on the fork that the strong Jamaican nurse lifts to her lips. She stares out at something that none of us can see.

She does not remember the ingredients anymore, but she tastes them and nods. I cannot eat them. They taste of metal and tears, and I worry about the glass shards.

"Mangia, mangia," says Eric, my husband.

She laughs.

Mom's Meatballs

Yield: About 18–24 meatballs

1 pound ground beef
½ pound ground veal
½ pound ground pork
5 cloves minced garlic
1½ cups freshly grated parmesan cheese
¼ bunch Italian flat-leaf parsley (about ¼ cup chopped)
2 large eggs
½ loaf (about 1 cup) day-old Italian bread

¾ cup milk for soaking bread
½ cup seasoned Italian breadcrumbs
Salt and pepper
Bowl of clean water for dipping hands while forming meatballs
Enough olive oil for frying (at least 1 cup)

If you have a butcher who will grind the meat for you, have him combine the beef, veal and pork in the grinder. If not, mix the meats together in a large bowl. Add the garlic, cheese and parsley. Beat the eggs and add them to the mix. Gently mix with your hands. Break the bread into bite-size pieces and let soak in the milk until soft. Add the softened bread and milk to the mix. Add breadcrumbs. Salt and pepper aggressively. With an ice cream scooper or a large spoon dunked in water, form meatballs dipping hands into the water each time so the meat is smooth and wet as you roll it.

Heat ½ cup of the olive oil in a large skillet, preferably a cast iron one. Fry one marble-size meatball to taste for seasoning. Add more cheese, salt or pepper as needed. Fry meatballs four or five at a time. Do not crowd the pan. Turn them gently so that all sides brown to a nice golden color. They will still be pink in the center. Do not overcook them. They will continue to cook in tomato sauce. Let them drain on layers of paper towels until they are ready to go for a swim in sauce.

Kummerspecks

By Michael Procopio

From FoodForTheThoughtless.com

Devoted readers (and there are many) of Michael Procopio's award-winning blog, Food for the Thoughtless, know he can be wry, snarky, and downright hilarious. But his voice is so authentic, he can just as powerfully strike an elegiac note, going for the heart of what makes us all human.

My phone was being x-rayed by airport security when I got the call. There was a voicemail from my sister Lori. I didn't need to listen to the message—I knew what she had to say. I imagined the best thing to do under the circumstances was to get to my gate and find a quiet spot to sit down before I played the recording back. But I didn't need to. My sister phoned again.

She was calling from the hospice. Our mother was dead. The mortuary people were already there. Death may sometimes be a slow affair, but the business of death is always alarmingly swift. My father and stepmother would pick me up at the airport and take the two of us to the funeral home to make the arrangements for mom.

I wasn't hungry or thirsty, but I knew it was going to be a long day. I wandered over to the Peet's coffee kiosk for a medium regular and the first muffin I saw.

When I returned to the gate, I sat down and picked at my pastry for a minute before I noticed on the receipt that it was called a "Morning Muffin." I thought to myself, "They forgot the 'u' in mourning." I thought about my mother again. She couldn't have eaten that muffin—it had sunflower seeds on it. She couldn't eat seeds. In fact, there were a lot of things she couldn't eat. But she didn't have to worry about that anymore. I threw the muffin away, sat back down, and played a little game with myself where I pretend that everything is just fine.

I debated exchanging my free drink coupon for a tiny bottle of whiskey on the short plane trip home, but thought better of it. I worried I'd get emotional and become "that guy who cries on planes." It wasn't the right moment for self-medication—there were caskets and flower arrangements to select and such things are best done with as clear a head as possible under the circumstances. Besides, whiskey was one more thing my mother couldn't have. It would have been her 40th sober birthday in February. I asked for a water. No ice.

At the mortuary, we discovered that the only time we could book the church for our mother's funeral services was the day before Thanksgiving. We knew a lot of people would not be able to attend. There was no other choice—waiting almost two weeks was not a possibility we were willing to face. And at the end of the meeting with the funeral director, my father looked directly at me and said, "*You're* doing the eulogy," which sent a ripple of horror through my body. He was right, of course. There was no one else to do it. I'm "the writer" in the family. I'm the one who's supposed to have a way with words.

But how does one go about writing a eulogy for one's own mother? How do you compress 82 years of a person's life into a few minutes? How do you distill an ocean's worth of information into a cube of essence the size of the cardboard box we'd soon be storing her keepsakes in? I stared at my computer screen for days trying to come up with something worthy. My sister had been there for her every single day for the past two years during her decline. I worried that I would fail in the one important thing I was asked to do.

I also worried that I was no longer a writer.

Over the past several months as my mother withdrew deeper and deeper into her dementia, I found myself withdrawing more and more from writing. My desire for composition directly correlated with my mother's declining desire to eat. Perhaps we no longer saw the point in doing that which sustained us.

She had always been so proud of my writing. "You know where you got *that* gene from," she'd say. She was the editor-in-chief of her high school paper and was studying journalism in college when she met my father. She was always asking when my first book was coming out. Later, when she started getting confused, she thought it had already been published. I didn't have the heart to tell her that no publisher wanted it. I felt like even more of a failure that I never got to show her one. Not that it would have bothered her. Not too much.

But as I sat in bed in my brother's old bedroom on the day before the funeral, I realized there was something that really would have bothered her—that I was sitting in the dark feeling sorry for myself. Or worse, that I wanted to stop writing. She'd frequently told me how proud of me she was for never giving up. It must have been true, because she kept on saying it even after her mind began to go. The idea that I would use her death as an excuse to give up on writing would have really made her angry.

And she was a woman you definitely didn't want to piss off.

So I moved out to the family room, which is the one bright spot in the incredibly dark house of my childhood, and took to heart the most writerly of clichés—write what you know.

I understood that there was a lot I didn't know about the woman we were about to bury. She shared different parts of herself with different people—she was a friend, a coworker, a counselor, a wife, a neighbor and, in my case, a mother. So I started to write a list of all the things I could think of about her life and used that list as the basis for my eulogy:

Like how she turned down being a stewardess because the airline wouldn't let her wear her engagement ring on the job. And how, instead, she wound up taking a top-secret position at North American Aviation working on the X-15—the first thing the US technically got into outer space—where she had to model Chuck Yeager's flight suit (because they were the same size) and got to fly in a bomber plane with a briefcase handcuffed to her wrist like a Cold War spy.

Like how she was one of the first people to use a primitive form of the internet working for the Anaheim Convention Center, but still found it nearly impossible to send a damned email.

Or how everyone was so convinced she would die when I was six years old that a priest was called in to the hospital room to perform her last rites. And how she was somehow given a second chance at life and grabbed it with both hands.

That she managed to work two jobs, raise three children, and finally get her university degree at the same time.

That she fought like mad to keep my brother alive and healthy for years after he was diagnosed with AIDS. How she did so at the cost of her own health.

And how she still never lost her sense of humor.

That she was smart and loving, loyal, protective, beautiful and giving. That she could also be stubborn and hard and unforgiving at times. That she was as complicated as the next person. That she was wonderfully flawed and beautifully human.

And that, when I hear someone say that people are incapable of change, I always use her as an example to prove them wrong.

I was strangely relaxed when I delivered the eulogy. As much as anyone on the verge of burying one's mother could be. I think my mom would have enjoyed my speech because it was as free of bullshit and white-washing as I could make it. It was a small turn out, as predicted, but the people who were there were all important to her. My sister and I were pleased.

There were only eight of us who drove out to Pacific View Memorial Park. It was windy on the hill and the clouds had blown sufficiently apart to give us all an eyeful of the ocean promised in the name of the cemetery—so much so that we could see Catalina as we lowered her into the ground next to my brother. I took a flower off the casket before she was lowered. And then my father offered to take everyone present out to eat.

We lunched at another place with a view, appropriately named The Summit House. When our server commented on how dressed up we all looked and asked what we were celebrating, I responded, "My mother died," rather bluntly. My father's best friend Don suggested that the next time I might say something like, "We're celebrating my mother's life today." I took his advice to heart. Our server was unfazed. Without missing a beat, she suggested that under the circumstances we might need a round of drinks as soon as possible. She was marvelous.

The restaurant was festive and even more dressed up than we were—they were ready for The Holidays. We placed our orders, most of us choosing the prime rib of beef for which the place was famous. For starters, seven of us ordered the iceberg wedge salad with bleu cheese dressing. It's a dish I'd never ordered before in my life, but I remember how mom loved it—at least, in the days before my brother's death when she could actually eat salads without getting sick.

I thought about my menu choices and realized that my mother not only couldn't have eaten the salad, but she could eat neither the prime rib nor the creamed spinach nor the creamed corn. She certainly couldn't have had the martini I was drinking. Nor the second one I was planning on ordering. The only item she could have consumed in relative safety was the top of the Yorkshire pudding, which was the lone disappointing bit of food in front of me that afternoon. But she would have sat there with her iced tea and dried-out suet pudding and not complained. She'd just have had a little sandwich and potato chips when she got home later—it's what she liked.

And then it struck me that I would never share a meal with her again when the salad arrived.

The wedge of lettuce placed in front of me was dotted with crumbled bacon. "Kummerspecks," I thought to myself, playing with words to make such an awful moment seem less so. I knew the day I learned the word *kummerspeck* that I would always remember it, because my brain would never forgive me if I forgot such a marvelously specific German term for the weight gained from grief eating. "Grief bacon." My wedge was literally flecked with specks of grief. I didn't know whether to laugh at that or to cry.

I chose to do neither. I kept that little joke to myself. Instead, I decided to eat and drink all the things my mother couldn't when she was alive. I lifted the martini glass to my lips, finished off its contents, and gave a subtle nod in the direction I'd like to think she headed when she left her body. I hoped that she was now in a place like heaven where she could order whatever the hell she wanted to, knowing that in doing so she would be finally free from all pain.

Then I ordered a second martini to help dull my own.

Foodways

Butchering London

BY CHRIS NEWENS

From *Roads & Kingdoms*

Born in Surrey, England, Chris Newens now lives in Paris, where
he's a co-founder of the arts collective FourPlay and the theater
festival Montmartre Dionysia. (By day, he edits erotic literature.)
Heading back to London for Christmas dinner, he just had to
put an extravagant spin on the main dish.

There are four days until Christmas. It has just gone six in the
morning, I'm in the heart of the City of London, and I'm wondering: How do you tell a good quality pig's head from a bad one?

There are three left in the display cabinet, their dead eyes judging me
judging them. I look to the butcher, a balled fist of a man clutching a
vicious blade. I want to ask him which head he would recommend, but
worry that would mark me as even weirder than I already feel. Likely
one pig's head's as good as another.

"So, who will it be then?" he asks.

His voice is full of impatience, which doubtless builds in the couple
of seconds it takes me to realize that when he said "who" he meant the
heads. I point to the least misshapen, least hairy of the three, i.e., the
one that looks most like a pig.

"That one, please."

"So you want the pretty boy, then?" the butcher grins and reaches
into the cabinet to withdraw said "pretty boy." He drops the pink-grey
head into a plastic bag: "Anything else?"

This is Smithfield Market, the biggest wholesale meat market in the UK, a supermarket of animal parts impossibly located amid some of the most expensive real estate in the world. Every night it is a factory of cutting and blood. It is too grotesque for modern London to put up with in the daylight; for the general public to shop here, they must arrive before dawn.

Needless to say I did not drag myself out of bed for a pig's head alone, even a pretty one. I am hunting Cockentrice. The idea to attempt this medieval dish (delicacy is too fine a word) was born out of a desire to reinvigorate our Christmas roast. My friends and I had been discussing how easily the festive season can beget turkey fatigue and decided that this year our traditional pre-Christmas Christmas dinner needed a more inspiring, not to say, unusual main event.

With the head of a pig, the body of a capon (a castrated rooster) and a tail of goodness-knows-what, a Cockentrice was certainly that. This unlikely combination of fine dining and rogue taxidermy originated in the English cookbooks of the 14th century, and was roasted as the centerpiece of kingly banquets, delivered to the dining hall like some slain mythical creature amid fire and song. There was, though, only one place in London where I was sure that all of the beast's constituent parts could be found.

Smithfield Market has a pedigree even older than the Cockentrice. While its current butchers' incarnation dates back only as far as the mid-19th century, livestock has been traded here for almost 1,000 years. Originally named for being a "smooth field" outside London's walls, the area played host to city entertainments—jousts, dances, hangings (William Wallace, latterly of *Braveheart* fame, was put to death here in 1305)—then began to double as a livestock market sometime in the 1100s.

While over time the city expanded, the market remained. In fact, Smithfield was a livestock market right up until the mid-1800s. At its peak in the Victorian era over 220,000 head of cattle and 1.5 million sheep changed hands here every year. In the heyday of the industrial revolution, the heart of London resembled a manic farmyard.

Even today, the absurdity of the market's squeezed location is immediately apparent. A coronary of white vans clog the roads surrounding its elegant 19th-century colonnades (designed by the architect who built Tower Bridge, Sir Horace Jones) and closer still, there tussles a claustrophobic frenzy of forklifts, people, and meat.

The soundscape is of idling engines, bleeping industry, and coarse shouts. The smell is of cold blood. As I walk closer I am put in mind of a motorway pileup, or the aftermath of a battle. This is not meant for tourists.

It is though, a place where the spirit of London runs strong. For despite the excess of modern development that surrounds it—the chain shops, the glass and the chrome—there is something that feels very old about this part of the city. While many other European towns, particularly in the continent's south, may have their heritage better preserved than London, they can often feel like museums.

In London, in the central square mile that forms the City of London in particular, history has been bludgeoned so hard it has become a ghost, and thus so much more affecting. It haunts the street signs, the banks of the river Thames and the very early dawn. It is the ideal location to search for a medieval meal.

Long plastic flaps curtain across the entrance to the market's main arcade. Shouldering through them I walk into the biggest butcher's shop I have ever seen. In fact, it is many different butchers' shops, all selling slightly different produce, the variety of meats is remarkable. The uniforms of the butchers, though, are the same: white, with many spattered in blood.

Primarily a wholesale market, there are few concessions to more squeamish shoppers, and none of the hashtags or slogans of modern commerce. Most counters back directly onto their storage facilities, and are separated from them only by glass. It is a rarely offered backstage reveal of the butchery theatre, with whole hanging carcasses displayed like pink coats in an over-stuffed wardrobe. The blood smell is stronger too. It is a raw steak raised up close to your face: a clean smell but one that has the potential for decay. You feel it at the top of your nose.

A Cockentrice does not require that many ingredients (I settle on trying to find a beef rib for its tail). Nevertheless, it becomes apparent that I won't be able to find them all at the same cabinet. So I move on from the pork specialist, taking the head with me.

Smithfield is not all offal and off-cuts, but I am drawn to the unusual, to the counters that look more like medical anatomy displays than offerings of things to eat. I talk to a young butcher who tells me his name is Justin. In the counter, beneath his folded arms is a pile—literally a pile—of hearts (which animal they belong to, I have no idea, if I didn't know better I'd say they were human.)

I ask Justin if he sells many. "Course," he says, "'round this time of year 'specially. We sell bundles of hearts."

Later, I talk to another, more senior butcher: his position marked by the fact that his overalls are not covered in blood. His name is Oliver Absalom, director at Absalom & Tribe. I ask him the question that has been plaguing me all morning: how does it work? How does a wholesale market continue to function in the very heart of an area given over to finance? Don't the banks want it to leave?

Absalom admits that Smithfield's continued success remains a mystery, and that there's often talk about moving the market to a less central location.

"But, then, this place does have a sort of magnetism to it," he says. "And because we're right in the middle of everything it means buyers can come from all directions, from every corner of London, and even beyond. So there is a kind of practical reason to it."

But a central location does not come cheap. The rent on Absalom & Tribe's counter space is £100,000 a year, and buying it is not an option. Fortunately the meat trade does not show any signs of slowing.

Absalom & Tribe cannot sell me the meat that I'm looking for. Their trade is in more traditional cuts—a lot to kebab shops, Absalom tells me. I am directed to more specialist butchers, and in the smorgasbord of Smithfield my hunt for the other parts of my Cockentrice does not last long.

I leave the market building clutching the pig's head, a decent sized capon rooster, and a rib of beef. I step back into modern London, where an orange dawn is just cresting the surrounding skyscrapers. Then I go for a beer.

As well as warping one's sense of which century it is, Smithfield plays havoc with your perception of the time of day. The expertly carved and displayed meats that pile the pre-dawn counters are the product of an entire night's work. And like workers the world over, come the end of their shift, the butchers of Smithfield go in search of a drink.

A pub on Cowcross Street, with its morning opening hours, has been obliging them for generations. Its name, perfectly inappropriate for an establishment that specializes in dawn drinking, is "The Hope."

I enter with my bag of disparate animal parts clutched innocently in one hand, and walk to the bar feeling uncomfortably like a serial killer. My awkwardness must show, as before I know it, I'm being heckled from a nearby table; a group of punters are inviting me to join them for a drink. Keen to talk to more people who work at the market, I accept.

But these are not butchers; they are construction workers, fresh from a nightshift in the tunnels of Crossrail, London's new multi-billion pound subway expansion. The project, scheduled for completion in 2017, will link the West side of the city with the East.

It is an emblem of modern London: representative of progress at any cost, drilling blindly through layers of the city's history. At Smithfield, there were fears that that history may fight back, that Crossrail's tunnels may break into a famed 14th-century mass grave of victims of the Black Death. That it would release the anthrax spoors buried in the plague pit into the outside world.

Yet despite this potential for the area's history to bite back, the Crossrail project is set to leave the main market largely intact. And so Smithfield's unlikely success story continues. Indeed, the new train line may bring more customers to the area. Might the future of this wholesale meat market involve accommodating tourists after all?

When I ask the workers, though, if they are aware of any negative effects Crossrail may have had on the Smithfield area, they are fast to come to its defense.

"It's the biggest construction project going on anywhere in Europe," one tells me, proud to be a part of such an event. "An 'all the men workin' this part of it, they buy their meat from the market."

"Yeah, the butcher boys love us," says another. "I've got fifty-two steaks in my freezer at home."

"Fifty-two?" I echo; this seems like an unnecessarily high number.

"You tell me if I could afford fifty-two steaks from a plain supermarket." I shrug. "I couldn't," he says.

I am already feeling carried away, thinking how these men, hard at work on one of London's ultra-modern businesses, are connected with Smithfield, one of its oldest.

"And Dave here, he even buys a couple of pigs heads every week from the market, don't you Dave?"

I look to Dave. He has been silent since my arrival at the table. He's one of Crossrail's designated 'black hats,' a foreman on the project. He is broad and middle-aged, has a raised scar on his cheek, and arms that are intimidatingly crossed over his chest.

"Really?" I ask him, excited now. The centuries feel like they're cramming into each other: I've met a Crossrail worker with medieval tastes! Also, it occurs to me that I can perhaps I can get an answer to my question about how to judge the quality of a pig's head.

"No," Dave growls. "Sydenham Nick's having you on. But I do buy a lot of sausages."

Outside The Hope, time somersaults back the right way again. Dawn has broken now, and London is revealed in its gleaming modernity. A flow of cyclists and suited commuters are rolling past me, ignorant of all the blood so recently spilt nearby. The activity at the market has almost ceased.

The only butchers left are the younger ones, and rather than heading for The Hope, they are queuing to get into a Pret a Manger—a trendy, somewhat health-focused sandwich chain. After a night tussling with meat, perhaps I'd want a whole-grain super greens sandwich too.

With daylight, the ghosts of London's history depart. So, I too head home with the Cockentrice, thinking how this evening I will again cook up the past.

Charred and Feathered

By Brian Kevin

From *Audubon*

Managing editor of Maine's *Down East* magazine, Brian Kevin partakes of the free-wheeling style of Hunter Thompson (the subject of his 2015 book *The Footloose American*) in his sports writing, travel writing, and feature writing. Here, he travels to Iceland on a sort of environmental and culinary inquest.

L et's just get this out of the way: No, it does not taste like chicken. Soaked in salt water, smoked with wood chips and dried sheep dung, then boiled for two hours in a sweet malt beverage before being refrigerated and finally served, bone-in and cold, alongside a packet of butter, smoked puffin tastes briny and a bit fishy and musky-sweet in the manner of mesquite barbecue. In life, an Atlantic Puffin stands just 10 inches tall, its wings stubby and narrow; when its tiny torso is served in a paper tray, it's difficult even to recognize as having belonged to a bird. It looks vaguely insectoid, its wings all but meatless, thin bones curving out like antennae. The breast meat is a deep mahogany and pulls apart fibrous-but-tender, like the flesh of a medium-ripe peach.

The venue that sells this ostensible delicacy is a center-pole big top tent erected in a long-extinct volcanic crater on Heimaey, the largest island in an archipelago called Vestmannaeyjar, or the Westman Islands, seven miles off Iceland's southern coast. The crater valley is on the outskirts of the Westmans' only town—itself called Vestmannaeyjar, population 4,400ish—and is surrounded by steep, green cliffs. On their seaward-facing slopes, hidden in the short grass and soft volcanic soil, are some 100,000 puffin burrows, a fraction of the 1.1 million burrows found in more than 20 colonies scattered across the Westmans' 18 islands. From May until September, about 20 percent of the world's Atlantic Puffins—some 830,000 nesting pairs—breed on the archipelago, along with similarly impressive numbers of murres, guillemots, fulmars, gannets, razorbills, and kittiwakes.

But the puffin in my tray didn't come from the Westmans. It was harvested 225 miles away, off Iceland's northern coast, then imported to Vestmannaeyjar to be smoked and eaten during a 141-year-old festival called, in its anglicized form, Thjodhatid (pronounced thoth-ha-TEETH). The word literally means "people's feast," and for most of its history, that feast's main dish has been smoked puffin, served alongside pastries, lamb, flatcakes, and other delectables in some 300 white tents that locals erect in the valley each year. This tent city is Thjodhatid's base camp, and as recently as a decade ago you couldn't poke your head into a stranger's tent (which is encouraged) without being handed a plate of smoked puffin and a strong drink to wash it down.

These days, though, the only place to reliably find smoked puffin at Thjodhatid is in the concession tent, where, alongside cheeseburgers and chicken fingers, it's sold for 1,500 krona, or about $12, per bird. That's three times what it cost 20 years ago, making one little puffin an expensive snack; it'd take three birds to make a modest meal. So it isn't a popular menu item—the concession tent has stocked just 600 birds for a three-day fest that regularly draws 16,000 people. Still, the puffin has its devotees.

"I ate it twice yesterday," declares Anna Kristin Sigurdardottir, the concession employee who rings me up. "And I'll eat it again tomorrow. I look forward to it all year."

"People here used to eat it year-round," adds Kristina Goremykina, Sigurdardottir's coworker. But that was before it got expensive, back when Westman islanders still hunted puffins, before they started noticing alarmingly fewer young birds. Now that it's imported from up north, smoked puffin is only a special treat.

So what happened? Goremykina tosses a butter packet into a puffin tray and shrugs. "They all flew away or something," she says.

The Westman Islands' puffins haven't flown away; they've stopped breeding successfully. Since 2003 Atlantic Puffin colonies here have experienced what Erpur Snaer Hansen, director of ecological research for the Vestmannaeyjar-based South Iceland Nature Center, characterizes as "breeding failure, basically." For more than a decade, chick production in the Westmans has been virtually nil, with fewer adults breeding and only a scatter of chicks surviving to fledge (most of them dangerously thin). The result is a puffin population that's gradually aging away: Precious few puffins arriving in the Westmans each year are younger than 10 years old. While puffins can live (and breed) for more than 30 years, their average lifespan is about 16. Already the islands have seen breeding pairs drop by as much as 15 percent since the late 1990s.

I arrive at Hansen's home in Vestmannaeyjar the day before Thjodhatid, in late July. It's toward the end of Hansen's field season, a time when the 49-year-old biologist likes to blow off steam. His family hosts a tent at the festival each year (though they don't eat puffin), and in the Thjodhatid spirit of hospitality and excess, Hansen begins plying me with drink within minutes of welcoming me.

Over 20-year-old port, I hear about the "puffin rally," a cross-country road trip Hansen takes each summer, monitoring puffin burrows at 12 different colonies across Iceland. In June he and his colleagues inspect at least 40 burrows at each site, snaking a camera down the winding, four-to-six-foot tunnels to check whether each is occupied and, if so, whether its occupants have an egg. Hansen's team uses an infrared camera mounted to what's basically a drain snake—a custom-made device inspired by a plumber friend's invention.

In July Hansen and company return to each colony to see whether the eggs have hatched, to assess chicks' health, and to photograph adults carrying "food loads." Under normal circumstances, puffins with new chicks head to sea several times a day, returning to the burrow with cargoes of small fish. It's the classic postcard puffin shot: a close-up of that mime-white face, that melancholy eye, that splashy lobster-claw of a beak, with limp fish ends dangling out both sides like a silver mustache.

In southern and western Iceland, those dangling ends have historically belonged to sand eels, a cylindrical fish generally known to Americans as sand lances. In the Westmans, Hansen says, their relationship to puffins is "like the hare and the lynx"—a primary prey to the near-exclusion of any other species. And for 12 years, on the heels of gradually climbing sea surface temperatures, sand eels have gone missing from surrounding waters.

Well, not missing exactly, Hansen says, now pouring us tumblers of a peaty Scotch. Sand eel numbers have surged in Iceland's northern waters, where puffin populations once similarly relied on cold-loving capelin. The capelin, too, have shifted northward—but puffin populations in northern Iceland are stable, feeding on the sand eels that have flourished in the capelin's wake.

Around the Westmans, however, no suitable prey has thrived in the sand eels' place. And while adolescent puffins might shop around for an alternate breeding ground, once adults have chosen a colony, they're hardwired to return to it. In other words, the Westmans' breeding-age puffins can't just up and move to better fishing grounds, and it's a rare day when the puffin-rally photographer captures a returning adult with much of anything in its beak.

Icelanders love festivals, and considering the country has just 329,000 residents (dramatically outnumbered by 7 million to 8 million Atlantic Puffins), they sure seem to throw a lot of them. A handful of high-profile music and art fairs go down the same weekend as Thjodhatid. In November, Reykjavik's famed Iceland Airwaves fest has long attracted music industry VIPs. Of late, the Icelandic version of the international All Tomorrow's Parties festival has been one of hipsterdom's hottest tickets.

Thjodhatid dwarfs them all. It dates to 1874, when storms kept Westman islanders from attending a mainland celebration of the millennial anniversary of Icelandic settlement. So the islanders threw their own party, which has since evolved into a gonzo celebration of Icelandic and Westmans culture, with three distinct phases.

During the day, Thjodhatid is a family funfair, with ziplines and puppet shows for kids. Come evening—which lasts from roughly 7 p.m. until midnight, since there are 18 hours of daylight here in midsummer—the adults join in, wining and dining in the white tents and gathering in the steep natural amphitheater for Icelandic pop bands and fervent sing-alongs to folk songs and patriotic anthems. Then, at midnight each night, comes a different grand spectacle: an enormous bonfire on Friday, four stories of wooden pallets throwing heat across the whole valley; fireworks on Saturday that thunder off the crater walls; and on Sunday, following a climactic sing-along, a ceremony with 141 flares arranged around the crater's rim and simultaneously lit, creating a gargantuan ring of fire. Midnight at Thjodhatid makes the Super Bowl halftime show look like a kiddie party with sparklers.

Overnight, the carousing intensifies, with more drinking and singing and feasting in the come-one-come-all tents. Many celebrants are costumed, so you might find yourself in the small hours toasting a caped superhero or being serenaded by men in bunny suits. Other revelers wear PVC fishing bibs—a salute to Vestmannaeyjar's maritime culture but also practical protective wear should you lose your footing on the steep, muddy slopes of the concert area.

Insofar as it celebrates the Westmans' culture, Thjodhatid also celebrates seabirds. At the festival's entrance hangs a huge banner with a giant puffin wearing a crown of fire. The opening ceremony involves an elegant demonstration of spranga, a locally beloved sport of rope-swinging and rappelling that's rooted in the practice of collecting seabirds' eggs from cliffside colonies. Each year's Thjodhatid gets its own theme song, several of which lyrically invoke puffins and other birds. One I hear emanating from several tents is "I Brekkunni" (or "In the Slopes"), which jauntily declares: "With romance and smoked puffins, I set off to meet my friends!"

And so back to those smoked puffins. Historically, puffin hunting in the Westmans has meant standing at the edge of a cliff, swinging a long-handled net called a hafur to catch birds as they flit about. This method overwhelmingly captures non-breeding adolescents, since breeding puffins tend not to flit, instead flying directly in and out of burrows as they deliver and seek food. With a hafur net, a single hunter could once easily bag several hundred puffins a day. Hunters kept a few dozen, then gave the rest to the local hunting club, which sold the birds—to tourist restaurants in Reykjavik, say, or to families for Thjodhatid—and used the proceeds to maintain stately hunting lodges on the Westmans' wild islands.

It was hunters who, in the early 2000s, first noticed a dramatic decline in young puffins and petitioned the local government to recruit a specialist. Hansen's position was funded in response in 2007. He started by photographing birds, aging them by their bills and realizing that several years' worth of adolescents were essentially missing from the population. Hansen earned the hunters' ire when he subsequently called for a puffin-hunting ban. "They were a little angry with me," he says. "Some didn't believe what we were saying. It was really tough."

But spooked by their empty nets, hunters soon came around. Today puffin hunting in the Westmans is allowed on just three days in August—and catches are so low that few hunters even bother.

For Hansen, one benefit of the Westmans' hunting legacy is the harvest record, which dates to 1880. Since the catch has always consisted chiefly of adolescents, harvest numbers are a reliable proxy for chick production. Plot them alongside sea surface temperature records and inferred trends in sand eel abundance, and a pattern emerges: Puffin chick production is strongest during cool phases of a natural oceanic temperature cycle called the Atlantic multidecadal oscillation (AMO). But during the AMO's warm phases, sand eel abundance withers and chick production suffers. Hansen suspects that warm winters speed up the sand eels' metabolisms, so that the weakened fish don't survive to become next summer's prey. Higher ocean temps might also disturb sand eels' planktonic food chain, and they face competition and predation from mackerel that frequent southern Iceland's waters during warm periods.

A full AMO cycle is roughly 20 to 40 years of cool followed by 20 to 40 years of warm. The current warm phase began in the mid-1990s, and some predict the AMO could shift back to cool as early as the mid-2020s—unless climate change intervenes.

Hansen is among many scientists concerned that a linear warming trend may be overtaking the cyclical AMO. "If you look at the temperature record for the North Atlantic," says Morten Frederiksen of Denmark's Aarhus University, who studies seabird adaptations to marine habitat changes, "at least for the last 30 or 40 years, you'll see an upward trend that is not explained by those cycles."

What's more, says Tycho Anker-Nilssen of the Norwegian Institute for Nature Research, substantial breeding failure is also occurring in the Faroe Islands and Norway's Rost archipelago, which together host another 15 percent or so of the Atlantic's puffins, and where populations rely on prey other than sand eels. Since warming sea surface temperatures are the common denominator, says Anker-Nilssen, "it is likely that larger-scale climate variability and change is the key driver."

So what if climate change warms the North Atlantic to the point where even cool AMO phases are still too warm for sand eels to thrive in the Westmans? "That's exactly what we're super worried about," Hansen says. "That it's going to level off, and that means we've seen a shift northwards. And this place is done."

Puffins are inescapable around downtown Vestmannaeyjar. Everywhere you look, the bird appears like a totem: on murals, on road signs, wearing a bamboo hat and advertising Chinese takeout. Puffin bric-a-brac shops abound, as do fliers for puffin tours.

Vestmannaeyjar even has its own puffin celebrity in Toti, a charismatic rescue bird who draws visitors to the island's natural history museum. Famous enough to warrant his own segment on Icelandair's in-flight tourism video, Toti was brought in four years ago after fledging too late to join the migration to open-sea wintering grounds. It's a late-summer tradition in Vestmannaeyjar for children to roam the streets, gathering fledglings that emerge disoriented from burrows and head for the lights of town. Toti's caretaker, Viktoria Pettypiece, is among those who measure and weigh the wayward chicks (collecting data for Hansen) before releasing them to the sea. Twenty years ago, she says, kids would bring in 1,200 to 2,000 puffins a year. In recent years it's often dipped below 100.

Pettypiece, who once ran a gallery selling puffin paraphernalia, wonders how the breeding collapse might affect the island's image. "I think it'd be really hard for tourism," she says. "Most people who come here come to see puffins—even if it's the wrong time of year."

"I believe it might affect the number of visitors a bit," agrees Indiana Audunsdottir, co-owner of a popular waterfront restaurant called Slippurinn, "especially if we keep pushing the idea about puffins as part of the islands' identity." Slippurinn has earned accolades for its commitment to local sourcing and traditional Icelandic fare—but the restaurant doesn't serve smoked puffin.

"It's sad, but traditions have to end when traditions have to end," says Audunsdottir. Of course, she adds, stocking a restaurant with puffins is different than simply hunting or buying a few to take home. She laughs sheepishly. "I tried some the other day, and I was like, mmm! So I am a complete hypocrite."

A few blocks away, in the chic dining room at the Hotel Vestmannaeyjar, the special Thjodhatid menu does indeed feature plates of smoked, thinly sliced puffin. "Like carpaccio," says hotel owner Magnus Bragason. "Just to give a taste."

Until he bought the hotel four years ago, Bragason was the Westmans' go-to puffin smoker, but he was proud when hunters effectively gave up their hafur nets, since the prospect of wholesale population collapse has him spooked. "I think it would be very bad for our culture," he says. "I'm very happy that we are not killing them, and I'm not sure if we'll start again."

Still, Bragason misses the tradition, and his family is among those who bought some imported puffins to eat at home during Thjodhatid. Last year, before his son went on a student exchange to Maine, his host family asked over Skype about his favorite food. "Smoked puffin!" declared Bragason's son, without hesitation.

"Oh, my god!" Bragason laughs, remembering the host family's chagrin. It was hard for them to understand, he says. "People here love puffins, even if we eat them."

A hazily remembered (thankfully recorded) 3 a.m. scene from Thjodhatid: I've just emerged from a particularly boisterous tent, decorated inside with homemade (ironic?) Donald Trump campaign signs. A "Trump 2016" button is pinned to my vest. Inside, I was fed beer and pastries and made to pose with a cardboard cutout of the Donald. I'm relieved to have escaped.

Outside, a retired fisherman named Grimur Juliusson is telling me in spotty English how, with the Westmans hunt curtailed, imported puffins are too expensive to serve in the tents. I ask him: Are islanders saddened by the puffins' breeding collapse?

"Ja," he nods, "because the puffins is part of the island. He is our . . ." Juliusson hunts for words, then says slowly, "The puffins is the same as you and me."

I am touched by this sentiment. Then an eavesdropping neighbor chimes in. This puffin situation has happened before, he insists—we'll all be eating smoked puffin again soon. "Nature," he admonishes, "is a cycle. Nature is not like a straight line."

It's a common view around the Westmans, but Hansen is less confident. The day after the festival, around dusk, he leads me to one of his monitoring sites, a busy puffin colony on a rounded, windswept peninsula. Westman islanders have a saying when they're feeling run-down—"I feel like it's the Monday after Thjodhatid"—and Hansen and I are prime specimens. Whether it's the hangover or the stirring sight of a thousand puffins dotting the cliffs, Hansen is reflective. I recount the exchange outside the Trump tent.

"They're saying this because they believe it's going to come back," he says, "but they have no clue if that's going to happen. Nobody does. It's wishful thinking."

We watch a pair of puffins "billing"—rubbing their absurd beaks together in courtship. Puffins are silent above ground, and the only sounds we hear are the crying of gulls and the crashing of waves.

The twilight of puffin hunting and eating in the Westmans is a small victory for conservation. Islanders are doing what they can in the face of a warming ocean: preserving potential breeders and hoping for the best. But what's poignant about a Thjodhatid without smoked puffin is the reminder it provides that climate change doesn't affect only the natural world—or, say, where we build our houses. It's going to mess with our identities. It's going to change the meals we share and the songs we sing.

The puffins of the Westmans won't disappear soon and may never vanish completely. Even in the worst-case climate scenario, today's mature birds will keep returning without much breeding success, and island visitors will see what Hansen calls "shadows of the past." But today's immense colonies may indeed dissolve, and if they do, they'll take some of the freewheeling, open-armed Thjodhatid spirit along with them.

When Hansen and I leave the colony, it is every bit as dusky as when we arrived. In Iceland, the sun sets very slowly.

Ya-Ka-Mein: Old Sober

By L. Kasimu Harris

From *Edible New Orleans*

New Orleans-based writer and photographer L. Kasimu Harris,
whose work was featured in the HBO series *Treme,* knows his
NOLA culture from the inside out. Truly, only an insider could
school us in the ways of Ya-Ka-Mein, a polyglot Sixth-Ward staple.

Each step I took into the Ogden Museum of Southern Art hurt
worse than the one before. I moved lethargically and my head-
ache had contractions. I plopped on a bench, away from the music and
people gathered there on a Thursday night, almost two years ago. Even
the lights hurt my eyes. But I knew something was truly amiss when I
declined a bourbon on the rocks—offered by the museum's director,
who knew my affinity for the drink. All day, not water, a nap or even aspirin had made me feel better. Then, I paid $5 for a savory elixir dipped
from a slow cooker and served in a Styrofoam cup: Miss Linda Green's
ya-ka-mein.

I wasn't drunk or hungover, but that day, it was my Old Sober. For
the past 19 years, Green has served her dish of spaghetti noodles, beef
and green onions in a spice-filled broth topped with half of a hard-
boiled egg. As I ate and sipped the goodness, I grew stronger by the
second; it was Popeye the Sailor's can of spinach. Shortly thereafter, the
dish proverbially transported me back to my youth.

I spent a lot of my childhood on North Broad and Saint Phillips
streets, the Sixth Ward, where my parents owned Le Earth Florist &
Balloons and second lines often passed on Sundays. A few doors down

was Manchu's, a carry-out-only Chinese food place where I feasted on egg foo young, Saint Paul sandwiches and ya-ka-mein. My folks introduced me to the dish; for them, it was a quick snack on long days. For Green and so many other residents of the city, the dish dates back to their youth, family and neighborhood barrooms. And at those lounges, deep in those black communities, where the sounds of rhythm and blues reverberated around the walls and soul food was served from the kitchen, the legend of Old Sober was born.

"It was a unique dish. It was always a poor man's dish," Green said. "It was leftovers."

Green, who's known as "The Ya-ka-mein Lady," is 57 and grew up in Central City. Her mother taught her to make Old Sober when she was about 10. In the early 1970s, they lived in the 2600 block of Danneel Street, next to the Bean Brothers Lounge, which was owned by close friends of Green's family. Her mother, Shirley Green, often held court on her porch and chatted with people headed into the bar. Though she also sold fried fish, potato salad and stewed hen, it was her ya-ka-mein that was revered.

"I told her she couldn't take it with her and she had to give me that recipe," Green said. "And I'm grateful that she did." She added that food writers have perpetually tried to trace the origins of the dish. One theory has it coming from the extinct Chinatown, in New Orleans, where Chinese immigrants from California resided while building the railroads to Houston. Conversely, others believe the meal was introduced by black troops who fought in the Korean War and returned home with a hankering for the soupy noodle dishes they ate while deployed.

Green thinks it's the black soldiers. "But we know it comes from New Orleans," she said.

Green asserts that ya-ka-mein has been one of New Orleans's best-kept secrets. She recalls meeting blacks and whites who still hadn't heard of it though they were born here. Her version of the dish converts even the most doubtful eaters.

"Once it hits the palate, it goes to that part of the brain," she said, "and once it hits the brain, it goes right back to the palate and it wants more."

Before Green started selling ya-ka-mein at second lines in 1996 from her gray and black Chevy Blazer, it was difficult to find.

She reminisced about the '70s, when Old Sober was sold at a bevy of Central City barrooms including Sam's, Byron's and Pete's; all are shuttered now and the building that housed Byron's is a church. Green says from 1940s, until the '80s, from Danneel and Jackson, it was a bar on every corner all the way to Louisiana Avenue, with names like Big Time Crip, Mrs. Breaux, Jim's and Henry Three Way. Some of the joints changed names and owners, but most of them went dark. She can't identify a singular reason for the closures, but said she thinks many were family owned and the later generations didn't want to take the business over.

"They did their own thing," Green said of some children who spurned the family bar business. "Those kids went to college and they made a career for themselves."

My family's business was flowers; I went from cleaning to blowing up balloons and then making deliveries. I attended college in hopes of taking over the enterprise—my father, LeRoy Harris, encouraged me to pursue other endeavors. He grew up in Scotlandville, outside of Baton Rouge, where there were few bars in the late 1950s and '60s and none of them served ya-ka-mein. However, he still managed to get a taste of New Orleans. My father, 72, frequented Marico's around 1964, a bar he described as middle class because it was frequented by a lot of professors from nearby Southern University.

"That place used to be popping. That's when AFO was at the top of their game," he said, referring to All For One, the New Orleans–based record label, founded by Harold Battiste Jr., and featuring top jazz musicians from the city. "I was too young to go into the club, so we used to watch them through the kitchen window."

He moved to New Orleans a few years later and got his ya-ka-mein from Charlie's Corner and Joy Tavern in Gert Town, among other places.

"Everybody did it differently, some was good and some was trash," he recalled. "Seriously."

My father says most of the bars downtown didn't offer ya-ka-mein and only sold smoked sausage with mustard and crackers. "Maybe they didn't have real cooks."

Now, across the city, with the proliferation of food trucks, "real cooks" have become mobile. The downtown food options at barrooms have burgeoned well beyond boiled sausage and crackers. In the seventh ward, you can dine on ya-ka-mein outside of Bullet's Sports Bar on a Tuesday and get fried fish at Seal's Class Act Bar during the weekend. On a surprisingly cool night in May, Patrice Gordon parked on the corner of North Johnson and Lapeyrouse, across the street from Josie's Playhouse "Home of Magic Monday" to serve patrons of the barroom and other nocturnal eaters.

She hauled a white trailer around with a navy Dodge truck. Her menu was scribbled on a small dry-erase board and included hot sausage, cheeseburgers, fries and pork chops and chicken plates; at the very bottom was "yaki-mein" for $8.

"Right after the storm, everyone was getting super drunk," she said referring to Hurricane Katrina in 2005. She saw an opportunity to provide comfort for the increased consumption and had her aunt teach her how to make Old Sober. Gordon grew up in Vascoville, one of the three villages in the Gentilly neighborhood of New Orleans, and celebrated the city's cultures and is now a big queen with the Golden Blades Mardi Gras Indians.

Like Green and others attest, Gordon said the dish is simple. "But the spiciness of it brings you down and stops you from vomiting all of yourself after you get hungry," she quipped.

Gordon walked across the street and delivered a plate of food.

Inside the barroom, colorful lights flashed against the red colored walls and mirrors, a few couples danced as others sipped drinks and watched the highlights of the NBA playoffs. In the back room, the game on the pool table was the main draw. A bartender explained that all drinks are $5 on Magic Monday and usually it's all bounce music. That night, it was a mature crowd and the DJ played oldies.

Johanna Valdery, 46, has owned the bar since November 2014. She worked the kitchen for three years when it was named Mickey's Playhouse. Valdery's parents owned bars and restaurants and she has been in the business for 16 years. She said the kitchen will reopen soon at her place, but most neighborhood spots are not equipped to have full kitchens.

"And they just don't want the hassle of getting the permits," she said of bar owners. She added that is one of the reasons Old Sober is sold from food trucks far more often than the actual bar.

Green said she doesn't mind that more food trucks are starting to sell ya-ka-mein at bars and second lines. The food scene in New Orleans continues to evolve—but people drinking will always be consistent. She explained that the city is about food and having a good time and has been for hundreds of years with different influences. In recent years, Vietnamese restaurants have boomed in the city.

"People have asked me if I noticed the number of new pho places popping up," she said referring to a type of Vietnamese soup made with beef stock, spices and noodles. "The more the merrier, but it don't taste like ya-ka-mein."

Hot Sauce in Her Bag

By Mikki Kendall

From Eater.com

Mikki Kendall burst onto the scene in 2013 with lightning-rod Twitter posts on issues of feminism, racism, and gender. Since then, she's been published in Time.com, the *Guardian*, the *Washington Post, Ebony, Essence*, Salon, and other sites. Here, she lays bare rich layers of meaning in a Beyoncé lyric.

Five days ago, Beyoncé stepped outside of the expected pop-idol box and introduced "Formation," a song rooted in her family's mingling of Alabama and Louisiana heritage to create her, a self-described "Texas bama." The track opens with Messy Mya's distinctive voice, incorporates the iconic Big Freedia, and segues immediately into addressing some of the myths about Beyoncé, her family, and her choices. It's a track where she flips off her critics, and centers herself firmly in her heritage, right down to one of the song's most instantly iconic lines: "I got hot sauce in my bag. Swag."

Cornbread, collard greens, and hot sauce figure prominently in my childhood memories. Chitlins, ham hocks, neck bones and hog maws do too. I'm a Southern Black girl by diet, if not by birth, because the grandparents who raised me were part of the Great Migration, the exodus of millions of Black Americans out of the Jim Crow South, and into the rest of the country where, even though Jim Crow reigned, life was not as restricted as it was in the South.

Like Beyoncé's "Creole mixed with Negro," my family is a product of a journey that started during slavery, and demanded a mixing of customs and cuisines. My grandfather's family is out of Arkansas, my grand-mother's roots are in Louisiana and Mississippi. They came to Chicago in search of better opportunities, and on some level they found it—but they never lost their connections to the South. And so, in the way of families passing down more than DNA, neither did I.

One of the essential things my grandparents taught me was to be polite, and politeness in Black Southern culture means that you eat whatever is served to you. You do not reject food. You absolutely do not waste food. And if you have to salt your food? Do so only after you have tasted it. Hot sauce, as essential a condiment to the Black South-ern table as salt, is treated in much the same way. If your host has it, great. But it's good practice to have some in your bag just in case. The greens at the church potluck taste like water because someone forgot to make sure the right person made them? Hot sauce could make them palatable. You're visiting a white friend from the Midwest who doesn't season chicken the right way? Hot sauce helps.

I don't keep hot sauce in my bag any more, but for years I always had a little bottle of Tabasco handy. It was part childhood habit— my grand-mother always kept a bottle in her cavernous bag—and part the defense against my discovery that even though hot peppers and hot sauce were regular condiments at home, not all of the people who invited me over for meals kept a bottle of hot sauce in their kitchen.

There may be white Beyoncé fans who also carry around their own personal bottles of hot sauce, but hearing her say she has hot sauce in her bag isn't a shout-out to them. She's talking to the Southern and Great Migration Black Americans listening—to them, to us, it hearkens to home. To childhoods spent at fish frys, church picnics, and visiting relatives. It's a reference to a cultural connection, one that spans the diaspora of Black American identity. You might prefer Crystal to Loui-siana, you might only use it on greens that your Grandma didn't cook, you might rely on someone else having it, but you definitely used hot sauce. You definitely grew up seeing it used by the people that raised you, the people who gave you a sense of your roots, no matter where you were in America.

It goes deeper than that, though. Before, during and after the Great Migration, it wasn't uncommon for Black families to be splintered by distance, by danger, by the sad reality that it often wasn't safe to travel. Families moving from the South throughout America might not be able to take everything with them, but they could take their culinary traditions. They could have a taste of home on their plates even if they could never go back again.

For many, something as mundane as the way a pot of greens was prepared would set the tone for connecting not only with relatives, but also with new neighbors. When my grandparents separately arrived in Chicago, they lived in the city's Black Belt. They met there, raised their children there, and even though they came from two different experiences of being Black in the South, they found a common ground through food. My grandfather's habit of biting into an onion while he ate his greens might have annoyed my grandmother, but they loved the same cornbread recipes. They never did agree on their respective favorite hot sauces, but some was better than none, and it wasn't difficult for them to share the same bottle when they traveled—the one that lived in my grandmother's bag. Swag.

But there's another, much uglier reason that carrying your own condiments became a major part of Black American culture. While Jim Crow laws, extensively documented in print and historical record, are fairly well known, less well known are the unspoken etiquette rules for Black people, largely forgotten by anyone who didn't have to live under them.

During Jim Crow, Black people could pick up food at establishments that served white people, but they often could not eat in them. When custom demanded that Black people be served separately from whites, they were often required to have their own utensils, serving dishes, and condiments. So it was customary for Black families who were traveling to carry everything they might possibly need so that (with the help of the Green Book, the guide that helped Black travelers eat, sleep, and move as safely as possible) they could navigate America in relative comfort.

It's easy to think that there's no longer a need to preserve these customs. In theory, American culture has progressed to a place of being, if not post-racial, then at least racially aware. But the impact of "Formation" proves otherwise. Consider the imagery that surrounds Beyoncé's words about her family and her origins. Intermingled with images of little girls playing, a church service, and the day-to-day fabric of Black life, there are homes sinking under the flood waters of Hurricane Katrina. There is a dancing child facing down a line of heavily armed police officers, the words Stop Killing Us spray-painted on a wall, and a police car sinking under the flood waters with Beyoncé on top of it.

Jim Crow is over, but in the aftermath of Hurricane Katrina, New Orleans was treated shamefully by the very government that was supposed to be there for the residents in case of a disaster. Jim Crow is over, but police negligence and brutality is killing Black children for playing in parks. Is the video overtly political? Absolutely. And Beyoncé is committed to keeping the song political even without the video: at the Super Bowl, her dancers dressed in attire reminiscent of the 1970s Black liberation movement, wearing natural hair and Black Panther berets. In a society where people vocally take offense to the statement that Black Lives Matter, Beyoncé telling us she has hot sauce in her bag isn't just a line about how she likes her food. It's a relic, and a reference, and a reminder. The Jim Crow mindset isn't wholly in the past.

Neither the song nor the video for "Formation" is anti-police or anti-American. They are instead a look at what life is like in this country when your culture—in this case, Black culture—isn't the one considered mainstream. The politics of race in American culture play out in every aspect of life, from bearing the risks of police misconduct and brutality, to the way people eat their dinner. Even in our food, much of America is still segregated, especially when it comes to seasoning and expectations. It's not uncommon for Black Americans to joke that white cuisines here are seasoned with water and not much else.

At a recent weekend-long event, I kicked myself for giving up the habit of carrying hot sauce in my bag. Every meal was provided to our group, but none had seen salt, pepper, or garlic in any meaningful way. The event's organizers had made noises about wanting to increase the diversity of its attendees, but apparently no one involved had considered the diversity of cultural expectations of how food should be treated. Food may just be fuel for some people, but for many marginalized communities, it represents community, connections, a way of expressing your culture in public without care or concern for how it might be received by those who do not share it. And for communities that have struggled to have the right to eat in peace in public or in private, it can mean even more.

Although Beyoncé and her family are far from any sort of economic place where access to food is a concern (and it would be a very foolish restaurant that would turn Mr. and Mrs. Carter away), she's still a product of her family and her history. The flavor profiles of her youth are likely very different from those she might encounter as she travels. Her cultural heritage as a Southern Black woman dictates both that she eat what she is served, and that she be prepared for anything.

Some of the less favorable reactions to her hot sauce lyric have hinged on the idea that she's playing to stereotypes, instead of presenting a nuanced reality. Because our food culture is frequently presented negatively, it's easy to think that a racist overlay has erased the very real joy we find in our cuisine, or to assume that we reject our roots because they have been rejected by outsiders. Hot sauce in your bag may not be part of a culinary history shared by all her fans, but it is absolutely woven into the fabric of America.

This country likes to paint itself as a melting pot, a nation of immigrants that have come together into a shared culture. In reality, we are more a flawed tapestry: a nation of indigenous, enslaved, and immigrant populations, intersecting and interweaving but still retaining the integrity of our origins. That is never clearer than in our culinary customs. Yes, derogatory stereotypes have been built around the traditional foods of Black American cultures, but that doesn't mean we should give them up. Our traditions may have been forged in the wake of crimes against humanity, may reflect norms developed when American culture was less racially aware, but that does not mean that they have no value, or that we should attempt to do away with them to fit into the narratives of the American dream.

We have crafted our own traditions on a bedrock that may not resemble the stories of other communities, but they are no less valuable, no less important to making up the identity of this society. Assimilation isn't necessarily something to aspire to in general, much less so when the price of it includes going without the comfort of well-seasoned food. There's nothing wrong with a diet that spans watermelon, cornbread, collards, or hot sauce—kept on the table, or carried in a bag.

So too can Beyoncé's fans find common ground in their love of her music, even though they may not share her experience or heritage. Her hot sauce might be your mustard, your salsa, your sofrito, your soy sauce, or something else entirely. Either way, hot sauce is as integral to her cultural heritage as your traditions are to yours, even if it isn't something that you've had to carry with you in the same way. Beyoncé celebrates a very specific aspect of Black American culture with her references to soul food, to hot sauce, to the idea that now, fifty years after Jim Crow, we still need Black liberation movements to save Black Lives.

Glori-fried and Glori-fied

By Alice Randall

From *Gravy*

Novelist Alice Randall (*The Wind Done Gone, Ada's Rules*) may be
the only food writer mentored by Julia Child who's also written
a country music hit ("Xxs and Ooos"). She's also a food activist
and cookbook author (*Soul Food Love*) with a keen eye for
cultural signifiers—even in a bucket of fast-food fried chicken.

I magine yourself for a moment in a pew in a South Side Chicago
church, in 1965, or 1966, or 1967, with Dr. Martin Luther King Jr.
at the lectern—serious, head down, staring at his notes. A choir sings,
one voice rising above the others. Dr. King turns away from the con-
gregation toward the voice and smiles, the sweetest smile, a smile of
true joy, as the voice sings a battle cry: "Joshua fit the Battle of Jericho,
Jericho, Jericho, Joshua fit the Battle of Jericho and the walls came tumbling down."

The men and women in the pews begin to clap and sing even louder
as they are gathered into an army, not by Dr. King in the pulpit, but by
the woman leading the choir, a beautiful woman, large and brown, in a
crisp silk suit with giant buttons. When the song comes to its end, when
the crowd finishes thundering its readiness to fight, led by this singer
and this preacher, Dr. King says, "I think I can say, concerning this great
gospel singer in our midst, our dear friend, my great friend Mahalia
Jackson, that a voice like this comes only once in a millennium."

Mahalia Jackson was an international star, a principled artist who refused to sing music that was not gospel. A passionately political woman,

she could wrestle attention from Dr. King, even while giving him pleasure and respite. Why would she choose to lend her name to a fried
chicken franchise?

I have given a lot of thought to this question in the last few years.

I knew that my first husband's godfather, a black man named De-
Berry McKissack, had designed the iconic buildings that housed
Mahalia Jackson's Fried Chicken. I knew that John Jay Hooker, a prominent white lawyer, entrepreneur, and friend of Muhammad Ali's, had
backed both Minnie Pearl's Fried Chicken and Mahalia Jackson's Fried
Chicken. I knew that both businesses had failed. I sensed that country
comedian Minnie Pearl's was fundamentally wrong and Mahalia Jackson's was somehow fundamentally right, even if they shared the same or
similar recipes for fried chicken. I couldn't tell you why.

Glori-fried or glorified? Is there more to the franchise than yard-
bird, salt, pepper, and grease? Does the business exploit the Queen of
Gospel's associations with the sacred, or is her involvement with the
chicken enterprise a kind of savory and secular beatification?

I was born in Detroit in 1959. I remember my family waiting and
wanting a Mahalia Jackson's to open in Motown. I had a vague impression that Mahalia Jackson's was important to black America in the
1960s. But I couldn't tease out just why.

I was overeager to find the original recipe for the chicken, hoping
there was some magic in the formula that would prove Mahalia's genius, hoping there was something in the taste of the chicken equal to
the sound of her voice. There wasn't.

I have spoken with many, many folks who ate the chicken, loved the
chicken, adored the chicken. None of them thought it tasted more than
good enough. What they loved was the idea of Mahalia and chicken.

Born Mahala Jackson on Water Street in uptown New Orleans in
1911, the future greatest gospel singer of all time began singing at Plym-
outh Rock Baptist Church and Mount Moriah Baptist Church. Since
the mid-1950s, the New Orleans neighborhood where she lived has
been called Black Pearl. Back when she was born, it was simply called
"Niggertown."

Mahala moved to Chicago in 1927, joining a church choir almost
immediately. She renamed herself Mahalia in honor of her beloved
aunt. Four years later, in 1931, she recorded her first song, "You Better

Run, Run, Run." It would be nearly 20 years before she had a smash hit. In 1947, Mahalia Jackson recorded "Move On Up a Little Higher." It sold over 8 million copies.

Those 8 million copies sold meant that Mahalia Jackson impacted the South's understanding of itself, and she helped frame the North's understanding of the South. Eight million copies sold meant that some 80 million people likely heard the song. Mahalia Jackson was the first, and arguably the most significant, black female superstar of the 20th century.

Harry Belafonte declared her the "single most powerful black woman in the United States." He believed there was not "a single field hand, a single black worker who did not respond to her civil rights message."

"Move On Up a Little Higher" is a song that seems a simple promise about going to heaven. It is so much more.

When Mahalia Jackson first stepped into the national spotlight, she made a prediction about food. "I'm going to feast with the Rose of Sharon," she sang, declaring herself a black woman fit to eat with whites. She claimed an integrated table. She raised her voice like a mighty sword, singing, "Monday morning, soon one morning, I'm going to lay down my cross, get me a crown. . . . Soon as my feet strike Zion, lay down my heavy burden."

What was the cross that millions of women, mainly black women, understood Mahalia to be putting down at the end of a long Monday? Could it have been a cast-iron frying pan? Could it have been a maid's apron? In young Mahala's experience, where did black women like her mother and aunt go on Monday morning? To work in a white woman's kitchen and house.

Mopping and washing and frying chicken. And that's where Jackson eventually went.

Before she moved to Chicago, Jackson worked as a domestic servant in New Orleans. To feel the weight of that statement, remember: she was only 15 or 16 years old when she left the South for the North. Her first appearance in the white world was in a maid's uniform. She left school in the eighth grade to work as a cook and washerwoman. When she arrived in Chicago, she took jobs as a hotel maid, a laundress, and a babysitter.

By lending her name and her image to the fried chicken enterprise, Jackson was trying to put a choir robe over a maid's uniform before stripping them both off in favor of a knit business suit. She entered into respectability through the shaming kitchen door, kicking the door down as she stepped.

Jackson ventured into the kitchen to be far more than respectable: She used respectability to introduce radicalism. And like Floyd McKissick's Soul City in North Carolina, Mahalia Jackson's Fried Chicken empire was a fabulous failure. But before it failed, it enjoyed some very significant successes. Mahalia Jackson sought to use franchise food as a kind of Trojan horse to introduce economic vitality into the belly of black communities.

There was a bit of Marxism in her recipe. A bit of black Muslim self-reliance. And a whiff of gasoline. Here's what Gulf Oil had to say about the audacious plan: "We are pleased to be associated with Miss Jackson, a respected and renowned personality, and her company. Since Mahalia Jackson's Chicken System is black-owned, managed and staffed and is hiring in the communities in which it operates, Gulf hopes it is helping to provide blacks business and employment opportunities."

Beyond jobs and wages, Mahalia Jackson's offered employees paid vacations, low-cost life insurance, and major medical benefits. The System grew to include a management school.

In the late 1960s and 1970s, Mahalia Jackson's Fried Chicken opened in cities across the country. In her adopted hometown of Chicago, there were, at one time, five Mahalia Jackson's.

Mahalia moved on up from poverty-stricken New Orleans to European and Asian concert halls. Her face on the chicken bucket said, *this chicken is fancy, this chicken is fine.* The chicken gave pride back to black folk, just the way her music gave pride back to black folk on the hardest days that came.

In the black world, Mahalia Jackson's chicken enterprise is a culinary Camelot. A shining, vanished moment. A place where black people did the cooking and the eating, the sowing and the reaping. A place where blacks were the owners, managers, workers, and patrons. Such a place existed for a moment.

And this is what it looked like; this is how my godfather DeBerry McKissack designed it, according to New York's illustrious black newspaper, the *Amsterdam News*, "The white brick, carry-out chicken stores look like highly styled, modern churches with their red roofs climbing to high pointed peaks. Flying buttress wings, carrying signs shaped in the elongated oval of cathedral windows flank the stores on either side."

Despite the fact that Mahalia Jackson's Fried Chicken System lost money, Mahalia Jackson died a rich woman, leaving an estate of approximately four million dollars to various relatives. She didn't go into the chicken business only to make money. She went into the chicken business to help others make money, and quite possibly to redeem kitchen work, to transform it from a private hell into a public and pride-filled business defined by stock and dividends rather than slaps, insults, toting privileges, and rape.

Mahalia Jackson understood the power of food. She claimed as her greatest pleasure and entertainment feeding people in her home. She knew food to be a personal pleasure, a spiritual necessity, and a political statement.

Mahalia Jackson's Fried Chicken restaurants were embedded in the black communities they served. Due to a perfect storm of white redlining, poverty, Negro removal-slash-urban renewal destruction, and rising rates of drug addiction and unemployment, some of these neighborhoods were areas of concentrated crime. Mahalia Jackson franchise locations were often the sites and victims of robberies.

The very first Mahalia Jackson Fried Chicken franchise opened in Memphis, Tennessee, in 1968, just months after the assassination of Martin Luther King Jr. My own godmother, Leatrice McKissack, wife of the architect, was robbed there the day it opened. She entered the restaurant looking sharp, a twin daughter holding each hand. A purse with credit cards and cash swinging from the crook of her arm. After the official opening, she reached into her purse and discovered her wallet was gone. Ben Hooks and A.W. Willis, lawyers and activists who founded the flagship, called and cancelled the credit cards for her.

Today her daughters, Cheryl McKissack and Deryl McKissack, the twins who toddled into the opening of the first Mahalia Jackson's in Memphis, are the owners of two of the oldest and largest black-owned architectural and engineering firms in the world. Between the two of them they have offices in Los Angeles, Philadelphia, Chicago, Nashville, New York, Miami, and Washington, D.C. I like to think they developed a taste for franchise standing in Mahalia Jackson's nibbling on a fried chicken wing, listening to all the talk about black nation-building through black wealth-building.

Psyche Williams-Forson has written ably of building houses out of chicken legs. My god-sisters have built skyscrapers, national monuments, movie studio buildings, and roads inspired by Mahalia Jackson's chicken.

Respect, economic self-reliance, risk-taking, mutual aid: These were the secret ingredients in Mahalia Jackson's recipe. At the end of the day, the day that ends in Zion, the chicken was glori-fried and glorified.

Everyday Sacred:
A Personal Path to Gumbo

By Pableaux Johnson

From SeriousEats.com

Author of *Eating New Orleans,* among other books, writer-
photographer Pableaux Johnson is famed in NOLA for his
weekly red-beans-and-rice dinners (a concept he's taken cross-
country as the pop-up Red Beans Road Show). His gumbo
recipe, though—that's the dish that really tells you who he is
and where he's been.

I t's a cold winter's morning in New Orleans—don't laugh, we have
them—and, in accordance with the Ways of My People, I'm tending
my stovetop. Outside, the sky glows a neutral gray, and steady winds
force frigid air through unseen cracks in my house's weathered floor-
boards. The shadow cousin of Arizona's "dry heat," a Louisiana "wet
cold" easily penetrates the wool and heavy denim clothing I'm wearing
with a distinctive chill that triggers a primordial call—to gumbo.

This particular batch I'm making demands three burners on my
standard-issue gas range-top: one for the tall stockpot that contains a
dismembered turkey carcass (bones, skin, sinewy necks), the other two
for an oversize Magnalite roaster that's gingerly straddling two pulsing
blue gas jets. A soothing heat radiates from the stove, and a complex but
familiar aroma—smoke, sausage, and spice—floats through the house
and chases the cool air away.

Over the course of the afternoon, the roux-thickened elixir will bur-
ble away as flavors deepen and solid chunks of turkey meat dissolve

into individual shreds. Coins of smoked sausage, browned, crispy, and bacon-like, will soften and render, giving up their porky essence to a thick, nutty broth that's damned close to brown gravy.

By evening, I'll have four gallons of smoked turkey and andouille gumbo (my own trademark variation on the Louisiana classic) ready for serving. Around dinnertime, I'll add the final herbal touches—a blast of minced Italian parsley, a scattering of thin-sliced green onion—and feed eight hungry guests. In the morning, I'll ladle into quart-sized soup containers and freeze the remaining three gallons, which I will eat and share with my friends for months to come.

Our Culinary Cornerstone

In south Louisiana, gumbo holds a place of honor that transcends the restaurant soup course. In many New Orleans homes, making it is part of a tradition that represents culinary bounty, prosperity, and the joy of homecoming. But in the smaller towns along Interstate 10, gumbos are also a way of marking the seasons: Cooks in Cajun country shift into serious gumbo mode when that "wet cold" I mentioned earlier arrives and cravings for warmth kick in. It's a time when we start duck hunting, a time when fat Gulf oysters reach their decadent peak and the sugarcane harvest clogs the back roads with slow-moving tractor traffic.

Due to its relatively time-intensive nature, a well-made gumbo is what I refer to as an "everyday sacred" dish, and a cornerstone of Louisiana's multilayered cuisine. Ranked by degree of culinary difficulty, gumbo sits squarely between rice and gravy (a quick and savory workaday staple of the south Louisiana canon) and crawfish bisque (a high-handwork labor of love reserved for the most special occasions). A proper gumbo takes time and effort. Making it can be a deeply personal expression, developed over years of practice and slow evolution.

A Louisiana cook's signature gumbo is as unique as a thumbprint. In a land where cooking is a near-universal survival skill, and men and women share the stove, strangers often discuss individual styles and roux techniques in initial tail-sniffing conversations. Sure, my own gumbo, made in multi-gallon batches whenever the north winds blow, can be described simply in ingredient-centric shorthand as "smoked turkey and sausage." But how I got to this particular version involves a decades-long journey marked by countless hours of pot-stirring, onion-chopping, and culinary lessons along the way. Any truly personal gumbo develops in phases, triggered by curiosity, constant study, and happenstance. This is how I learned to make mine.

1986: The Barnyard Baseline

For many young cooks, culinary journeys begin with a wee bit of desperation. After years of dormitory life, I started my senior year of college in San Antonio, Texas, with the first real-life apartment kitchen that I could call my own. Having been raised at my grandmother's stove, I was excited by the prospect of expanding my admittedly minimal cooking skills. I'd already learned a few useful dance steps from watching my grandmother during my mostly latchkey small-town childhood, but the resulting repertoire (hot-rodded jarred pasta sauce, grilled bologna, tortillas roasted over a gas burner) got pretty old pretty quickly.

Back home in Cajun country for Christmas break, I sought the counsel of Michael Vidallier—an older friend and coworker from a youth misspent at the local guitar shop. During five formative teenage years, I learned many of life's great lessons from Mike: how to decode the sonic genius of Jimi Hendrix, the value of gutbucket country tunes, the importance of energetic curiosity, and how to recognize the good in people while letting acerbic assholes float into space. ("Them? I got no time for that kind of people," he would say.)

When I went over to Mike's for a yuletide visit that year, the tree was twinkling and, in accordance with tradition, a pot of gumbo simmered away, filling the house with a comforting savory aroma. It was a winter's version of the ubiquitous pot of coffee that welcomes visitors in Cajun kitchens—where there's always time for a long talk, and company knows to knock on the kitchen door instead of the rarely used main entrance. If you've got a pot of gumbo on the stove, it's easy to accommodate the inevitable arrival of folks who pop in for a quick visit: a little bowl of comfort to pass the time and encourage conversation. Mike's gumbo was a simple affair that he learned from his grandmother: chicken and smoked sausage, dark roux, onions, bell pepper, and celery, an affordable version that seemed easy enough for me to re-create in landlocked San Antonio, where a proper seafood gumbo would cost a semester's tuition.

Unlike other chicken and sausage gumbos, Mike's was smooth and hearty, with chunks of sausage but no chicken bones to get in the way of my hungry-boy appetite. He told me about the process in the abstract, employing lots of grammaw-inspired descriptors like "about," "until it looks good," and "not too big, not too small." I returned to Mike's house a few days later for an official gumbo lesson, paying careful attention as he browned the chicken parts until the skin resembled crispy *graton* (pork rinds), made the stock, and dredged and separated the chicken meat from its connective tissue and bones once the bird was boiled down with bay leaf and peppercorns.

I also learned how to make a basic roux, which required some grueling patience, and the hallmark of the "Mike Vidallier Method"—*ending* with a roux rather than starting with one. Then there was the marvelous moment when the diced aromatics hit the super-heated oil and perfectly browned flour, resulting in a fragrant steam and a consistency like bayou mud. After stirring that into the stock, we were an hour away from dinner, though I could hardly wait that long.

I grew up feasting on a wide range of gumbos—thin chicken/sausage variants served in public school cafeterias, my grandmother's okra-based springtime shrimp recipe, the occasional multi-meat affair thickened with earthy filé powder (ground sassafras leaf). But I loved the versatility of Mike's approach. Done correctly, in its simplest form, his gumbo was a pot full of rich, gravy-like goodness that you could pull off with standard-issue grocery store ingredients (poultry, smoked sausage, flour, and common aromatics), and it didn't require thickeners such as filé powder or okra. (When you thicken your gumbo with okra, you're beholden to your grocer's freezer except during summer and fall. And, while filé powder is ever-present on south Louisiana spice racks, venture too far north, even to Shreveport, and you could be hard-pressed to find it.) Plus, if I felt the need, I could always gussy up Mike's gumbo with shrimp (if they looked good), shucked oysters (if they were cheap), or, well, okra (if I damn well felt like it).

Living outside the Franco-centric motherland, and aspiring to life on the road, I needed a flexible recipe like Mike's that would travel well and deftly adapt to the local larder without too much flavor-based compromise. I needed something that I could pull off in a cramped kitchen, whether it was in San Antonio or Brooklyn or Berlin—any place where gumbo is considered Exotic Foreign Cuisine.

First, though, I needed to practice by making a few dozen pots of my own, using Mike's gumbo as my north star. Weeks later, I took to my Texas kitchen and proceeded to make some admittedly terrible batches. They involved rushed roux the color of wallpaper paste, burnt chicken, and spoonfuls of spongy, not-quite-edible cartilage. But I knew that if I worked on the basics, I'd improve over time. You can't hurry a good gumbo.

1994: The Turkey Bone Two-Step

Fast-forward a few years (and many batches of gumbo). After a couple of extended travel binges and a hilariously short stint in graduate school, I ended up in Austin and settled into post-collegiate life in the Lone Star State. I was living in a house that allowed for large-scale parties without fear of downstairs neighbors alerting the local authorities. My roommate and I (a friend from my hometown) began a Sunday tradition known as the "Big Food FooYay" (Cajun slang for "foolishness"). In the early days, we'd cook up big batches of food and invite folks over for a Sunday afternoon hang-around. Gumbo was always on the menu, and as the event gained traction, we found ourselves feeding upwards of 20, 40—then 60 people. But no matter how big the crowds grew, it seemed that a gumbo could always feed everyone. All we had to do was add another chicken, or make some extra rice. That's the beauty of large-format Louisiana cooking.

In a hat-tip to our Texas locale (and, honestly, to save browning time), I started buying smoked chickens from the plentiful local barbecue joints and grilling hot links, instead of the traditional andouille sausage, for the porky portion of the program. Smoke-on-smoke made for a wonderfully local adaptation. And, as the thrice-yearly parties swelled in size (eventually about 150 to 200 friends and neighbors would show up on a given Sunday), I dreaded the intricate handwork of dredging eight or nine petite chicken carcasses, with their little nooks and meat-holding crannies. Like a frustrated infomercial housewife, I yearned for a solution to my tiny-bird busy work. And the solution, I discovered, was a turkey.

Actually, it was a turkey bone. Big Food FooYay practically begged for a version of Turkey Bone Gumbo, a magical south Louisiana post-Thanksgiving treat. This gumbo variation transforms the picked-over carcass from our annual Pilgrim-focused feast into the richest of all possible poultry stocks, with the tender meat that Uncle Calvin often missed during the ceremonial carving process. It's an exercise in thrift and decadence, and one of my favorite gumbos of all time.

During a large pre-FooYay dredging session, I realized that turkey crannies are a lot more accessible than the ones on teeny-tiny chickens, and subsequently called a few local smokehouses to inquire about bigger fowl. The result was a richer gumbo with less fuss, muss, and bother that could accommodate an ever-growing crowd. And so I'd learned another gumbo lesson: Bigger birds are always better.

2010: Gumbo Claus Is Born

By the time I left Austin for New Orleans in 2001, I'd honed my gumbo's flavor and consistency to a proverbial fare-thee-well. While I was no longer cooking it up with the frequency I did in Texas, several times each year I would purchase a smoked bird, drive out to the country meat market for the best andouille, and commit myself to a two-day gumbo-making ritual (stock, dredge, roux, sauté, simmer). I'd serve some of it on Mardi Gras parade nights, and always had a spare quart or so left over for my sister at Christmas.

But one November, a buddy who was leaving town offered me his Weber Bullet smoker for long-term storage. ("If you don't take it, I'm just puttin' it in my sister's garage. You interested?") Like that, I had my very own smoker, just as turkey prices hit their annual low in American supermarkets. (Loss leader economics FTW.) The result was that I could experiment with my big-bird smoking techniques at bargain-basement prices, and give frozen quarts of gumbo as holiday gifts. I figured I could log precious kitchen hours and (as a bonus) *never have to set foot in a mall again.*

This stage of my gumbo education kicked off a kitchen-related obsession that bordered on madness. The first year with the smoker, I bought four turkeys for gumbo purposes. The next, 11. By 2014, the total was capped at 23. As the bird count increased, I simultaneously entered the realm of small-industrial production and roux-fueled insanity. During the peak years, I annexed the freezer space of non-cooking friends in exchange for quarts of the good stuff. I kept track of frozen birds with an Evernote document and took to describing myself as "a hungry squirrel with a large-format poultry fetish."

And now, from November until mid-March—my gumbo season— the stovetop perpetually heats my Uptown shotgun house, and my fridge turns into a solid block of one-to four-gallon industrial Tupperware containers. Around 50 gallons of smoky gumbo feeds my friends in lieu of Christmas-y baubles. To those in my circle, I have become Gumbo Claus—the bringer of cold-weather cheer, the filler of friends' freezers.

2015: One Final Touch

As time goes by, my gumbo ritual focuses on the little things, the minute refinements of technique and flavor that can sometimes come like bolts from the blue. After 20 years and change, I know the drill, I know what people enjoy. But that never stops me from asking friends this all-important question: How do you make *your* gumbo? While engaged in just such an exploratory conversation recently, the phrase "I put fish sauce in mine" stopped me dead in my tracks. A fellow New Orleans food writer tossed it off on Twitter, and I was so intrigued by the idea that I added a few tablespoons of the Asian condiment to my next batch of gumbo. Sure enough, it gave my old barnyard classic a delicious layer of funky, salty flavor that made every spoonful even more satisfying and addictive than before.

If you ask me, my fish sauce epiphany illustrates the most important lesson about gumbo: No matter what you *think* you know, keep on asking questions. It's a big world out there, and there's always more to learn. And so I will leave you right now to tend to the pot of gumbo that sits simmering on my stove, the one it's taken so many years to perfect. The one that is truly my own. I've still got work to do.

Dedicated to my friend and teacher Mike Vidallier (1958–2016). Thanks for teaching me many of life's most important lessons and pointing out the stars to steer by.

Dining Around

The American Diner at Age 143

By Max Ufberg

From *Pacific Standard*

An associate editor at *Pacific Standard* magazine, Max Ufberg
writes about a lot of things—technology, business, sports,
music. A native Pennsylvanian, he's still adapting to his new
California home. That's where the familiar comfort of an old-
school diner comes in.

Judge for Yourself Café is called a café, but really it's a diner. Those two words can be sort of synonymous, anyhow, especially these days. A café sometimes means the smell of espresso beans and the sound of polished indie-pop, but, as is the case with Judge for Yourself, a café can also mean slightly stale coffee and old rock songs. It is, for all intents and purposes, a diner.

Judge for Yourself sits directly across from the Santa Barbara Courthouse (hence the name). Surrounded by palm trees, basking in California sunshine, it's a far cry from the Pennsylvania diners that I grew up with—places with names like "The Gourmet" and "Bluebird Diner." Yet Judge for Yourself isn't really unfamiliar at all; it looks and smells exactly like the places my father used to take me to for eggs and pie on Sunday afternoons.

Sun-bleached photos line the walls of Judge for Yourself, including a poster from the 1988 Santa Barbara Greek festival and a wood-framed sign that reads "Old Lawyers Never Die They Just Lose Their Appeal." Oldies blare from a stereo sitting on a shelf above the cash register. Higher on the wall, a plaque from a local newspaper reminds patrons that the diner's bleu cheese and bacon omelet won the 2010 "Kill Your Hangover" award. A stack of newspapers occupies a stool next to the plain white countertop. The single-room establishment smells like bacon and butter. The place feels resigned—resigned to its average coffee, its over-worked staff, its role as a last outpost of sorts. In 2015, I'll take "diners" wherever I can find them.

The diner has rightfully assumed a mythical place in the American landscape, no less so than baseball or Elvis or old Chevrolet pick-up trucks. It is at once a place where young boys and girls with their guts full of beer can go to idle, writers to think, gangsters to scheme. In a country that seems to become faster and louder with each successive version of the iPhone, diners remain havens of unruffled simplicity, where the only big question that needs answering is what song to play in the jukebox and whether you want hash browns or grits with that "Kill Your Hangover" omelet.

A real diner, according to the American Diner Museum, is a "prefabricated structure built at an assembly site and transported to a permanent location to serve prepared food." So, by technical standards, the hole-in-the-wall on the first floor of an old row house isn't really a diner; that shiny, silver curiosity on the New Jersey Turnpike is. In 2015, though, the distinction has sort of ceased to matter. If there's a counter with stools, if people are consuming sandwiches, coffee, and eggs over music that sounds like it belongs in your uncle's garage, and *especially* if the linoleum counters boast a layer of grease that will outlive us all, then it's probably a diner—even if it calls itself a café.

To paraphrase a waitress I once knew: A diner is a diner is a diner.

The New Englander Walter Scott (not to be confused with the British author) is credited with inventing the diner. A part-time pressman in Providence, Rhode Island, Scott spent several years selling coffee and sandwiches to reporters and editors on the night shift. Having enjoyed surprising success with his entirely mobile operation, he decided to create a slightly less mobile version. In 1872, Scott—then 31 years old—began selling food out of a horse-drawn wagon that he would keep parked all night outside of the *Providence Journal* office.

There were plenty of milestones that followed: Charles Palmer receiving the first patent for a diner in 1891; the early diners—which were more like wagons, really—being mass-produced and sold throughout the northeastern United States in the late 19th century; the creation of the iconic streamlined diner design in 1939; Edward Hopper's famous 1942 oil on canvas *Nighthawks*; a post–World War II boom; a decline, followed by a resurgence in the 1970s; the corporatization of the diner, with places like Denny's and Waffle House taking the place of neighborhood joints; and today, once again, an effort to bring the authentic diner back (including yes, a new reality series). It's all there: the optimism, the competition, the inevitable disappointment, and the doggedness that defines the American experience. As much as *Happy Days* or *On the Road*, the diner and its constant renewal are undeniably, quintessentially American.

Gunter Grass wrote in *The Tin Drum* that America is "the land where people find whatever they lost." I'm not sure I agree with that. America is a changing, evolving place, and the effects of that change are both positive (accepting racial and ethnic diversity) and negative (the decline of manufacturing). Our country's nostalgia seems to survive—at least for young people—in skewed bits of refraction, through Planet Hollywood and kitschy Coca-Cola posters. The diners (the real ones, at least) stand as a testament to a past that is in so many ways impossible to find. Go to rural America and you're more likely to spot a Target than a stationary train car serving eggs. You can't rediscover whatever's lost in America; that America, too, has been lost.

That's why the smell of apple pie and stale coffee is so much more significant than the bill declaring its value in money. These places are relics, humbling but comforting reminders of what we ate while we were tearing down an old America to build a new one.

Elena is 41 years old and has been working as a waitress at Judge for Yourself for 23 years. "Right out of high school," she tells me. The job's been good to her; the customers are appreciative, and once in a while, she tells me while lowering her voice, a Los Angeles offshoot, like Michael Douglas or the doctor from *Emergency*, wanders in. (This is still Southern California, after all.)

My request for an audience with the owner and cook (Mr. Judge for Yourself himself!) is quickly rebuffed. "The owner doesn't like to talk," Elena says, with a knowing glance at a big-bodied man standing over a grill in a red apron. That's fine, I assure her; the last thing I want to do is get Elena in trouble with the chief. As we chat, I hear Elton John's "Tiny Dancer" in the background, an accompaniment to the smell of crisp, scorched bacon.

Judge for Yourself opened 35 years ago. Business has stayed steady, Elena says, thanks largely to the shuttering of other diners in town, a result of the area's wealthy population (why eat at a diner when you can get a proper brunch?) as well as of corporatization (there's now a Denny's about three miles up the road). But, owing perhaps in part to its central location, Judge for Yourself has managed to weather the gastronomic storm. Twenty-three years later, Elena still begins each day at 6:00 a.m., brewing coffee and setting the tables.

I ask Elena why she thinks people choose to eat at Judge for Yourself. What, in other words, makes this restaurant special? As I'm asking, a few other customers walk through the door. Elena is the only waitress there; I can't take up any more of her time. Before she leaves, though, she answers my question: "A lot of people come in here and I already know their orders. They feel at home."

I finish my cup of coffee and pay. As I'm leaving, I hear a familiar hum buzzing from the radio, a song that transports me, briefly, back to those trips to the diner with my dad: "I Second That Emotion," by Smokey Robinson & The Miracles. A diner is a diner is a diner.

Penn Station's Underground Raw Bar

BY TOVE DANOVICH

From *Edible Manhattan*

Tove Danovich's journalistic focus is generally serious issues of food and agriculture. (She's the founding editor of *Food Politic: Journal of Food News and Culture*.) In this disarming profile of a seemingly ordinary New York City restaurant, however, she discovers all the ways in which it is anything but ordinary.

Fifteen minutes before 11 a.m., when the doors open, two men in suits hover outside Tracks Raw Bar & Grill in Penn Station. It's not clear at first whether they're bartenders who have been locked out, commuters who meandered away from the Long Island Rail Road for a private chat, or just eager customers. At 11:00 the door is unlocked; the men grab seats at the long mahogany bar (customers after all). Within 10 minutes, four more people walk in, sit down and order a beer. They seem to quickly forget that they're in Penn Station, arguably the city's most hated transportation hub. Whatever else Tracks is, it's an oasis from the brake dust and human herds moving through tunnels during rush hour.

In the early 1900s, it wasn't "Penn Station" but Pennsylvania Station—two full city blocks of pink granite, vaulted ceilings and Doric columns. The station's waiting room was inspired by Roman baths and, at the time, it was the largest indoor space in the world. Pennsylvania Station inspired. Then, in 1963, the train tracks were hidden underground and the grand structure was demolished to make way for Madison Square Garden.

Even if it could, the Penn Station of today doesn't try to compete with stately Grand Central. The low-ceilinged, fluorescent-lit concourse that gets commuters from the subways and streets onto the train tracks is lined with newsstands and fast-food joints and a tie store called Tiecoon. During rush hour the hallways are crowded and hot. Off-peak it feels like a place a person might have wandered into by accident. Tourists don't detour to see the subterranean station—there's nothing to see. Penn is referred to as an "ugly stepchild" of Grand Central and commonly gets compared to the pathways rats use to scurry underground. But when Tracks owner Bruce Caulfield started making plans to open a bar and grill next to the LIRR, he wanted to create more than a Penn Station restaurant. "People said it could be a burger joint," Caulfield says of the restaurant, which finally opened in 2003. "But I wanted to do something more upscale." He got a lease to the place, sold his primary business and prepared to dive in. The space had last been known as McCann's—a rowdy bar with "a rough trade," as Caulfield describes it. "A real shot-and-a-beer joint" that didn't even have bathrooms. The place had been vacant for a few years and was not in good shape, but Caulfield buckled down, cleaned it up and put in a mahogany bar.

Since Caulfield and his partners were Irish-American, Tracks has some attributes of an Irish bar: staff with accents, Guinness on draft, a place for the commuter community to gather. But the food is better. "People come in and don't expect our food to be good—or as good as it is." It helps that they make it all from scratch and have items like lobster ravioli alongside hamburgers, fish and chips and an appetizer of root-beer-battered chicken tenders.

To cement the bar's new identity, Caulfield decided to throw in some shellfish, too. He began visiting raw bars throughout New York City, taking notes and planning. Grand Central had a raw bar, of course, but this was Penn. Raw oysters didn't exactly spring to mind when anyone descended under 34th Street. Could he change that? Maybe. Hopefully. He didn't really know.

But he put the raw bar in anyway, sandwiched between the bar and the "dining car." The service areas on either side are topped by black and white checkered tiles. Customers walking by can't help but be entranced by the neon blue glow of the lights illuminating the shellfish nestled into a bed of crushed ice. Tracks has a few different suppliers, including the family-run East End Oysters, which has been in business just a year longer than the restaurant. "He only brings them into Balthazar oyster bar," Caulfield says, "and us." Just like the clientele, most of Tracks' seafood comes from Long Island.

Many of Caulfield's employees are full-time and he gives them paid vacation and sick days. In return, six of his eight bartenders have been there for eight years or more. They can greet a majority of customers by name, know their regulars' drinks and what their kids have been up to or where that person just vacationed. There are often hugs or cheek kisses, a lot of laughter. While there is a seating area at the back of Tracks, the soul of the place is at the bar. That's where the regulars go.

At 12:30 Tracks fills up with button-down shirts as the lunch crowd files in from One Penn Plaza upstairs. Construction crews get off of work around 2:30 p.m. and enter in T-shirts and caps. Then there are the 9-to-5ers who still get out of the office on time—a Midtown luxury. A late rush might come in after a show at Madison Square Garden. Otherwise, by 8 p.m. the crowd is mostly people who worked too-long days at the office, people who own their own businesses and keep odd hours, or day-trippers with shopping bags getting ready to go home.

These patterns happen all day long, five days a week. Unlike most restaurants, slow time for Tracks is on the weekends. That's when you might find yourself in the company of a suitcase-toting New Yorker on her way home to meet family for the holidays. Or someone waiting for a delayed train as snow and ice pelt the city above. Travel in Penn this time of the year is even worse than rush hour—nearly a third of all Americans find themselves on the roads, in the skies or on the tracks. It's a time for drinking and hoping the travel nightmares will be over soon.

Staff and customers have hunkered down together for long hours during blackouts or blizzards when the trains stopped running. Many bartenders have become friendly enough with frequent customers to see them outside of work. Nearly half the bartenders are married to regulars who slowly won their hearts. Theresa, a daytime bartender who has been there for 12 years, says that her husband came in every day with the "three o'clock crowd" and that it was a few years before anything happened between them. When asked for the full story she laughs and says only, "I can't make it publishable. We'd all get in trouble."

Caulfield and his partners originally figured they'd have a "transient trade," people stressed out from traveling and getting ready to go on vacation or visit their families. A lot of rolling suitcases. Instead, it was typically commuters who visited three or four or more times a week on their way home from work. They didn't just get a drink and go but actually lingered, made friends, ate oysters. "People really decompress here," Caulfield says.

The phrase "Penn Station regulars" might call to mind a host of deviants and troublemakers, something closer to the crowd of the bar Tracks replaced. But this is a warm, friendly spot. There aren't many places like this left in New York City. One regular, Brendan, works in television and has been coming to this spot after work since it was McCann's. "I bring everyone I know to this place—my dad, my mom, my wife, my grandma." He says that he comes in four times a week (though he hopes his wife doesn't hear about that) and usually talks to the same group of guys every time. They're his Tracks friends in the same way another person might have co-workers or neighbors—only Brendan seems to actually enjoy their company.

Of course there are also one-off customers. A guy at the bar who is about to leave for a flight orders an Irish Car Bomb to settle his nerves. Another patron watches an old episode of Friends on his cell phone. A former interior designer named Trish has a few too many drinks after missing her train and really opens up. "I believe there are alien life forms that came and died off before humans," she says. "How else do you explain the pyramids?" A friend of hers for the last 35 years died over the weekend. Trish starts crying. She misplaces her glasses in the bathroom. She misses the next train.

It's a few hours until closing time, 1 a.m., and Tracks is still full if not bustling. Up on the street, it's empty except for a few police officers, stragglers and food cart owners on their way home. The lights of Madison Square Garden are bright. While it's odd that a place like Tracks exists in Penn Station, perhaps it's the only place where Tracks could be what it is. Neighborhood bars aren't stately; they're small. They make you feel like part of the family. Tracks allows its customers to make time for themselves to do anything: talk to strangers, share their biggest regrets, relax after work. It's a spa that serves oysters and beer instead of facials. It's purgatory for the lucky.

"I think Grand Central could use something like Tracks," Caulfield says. Once his customers find their way through those metal doors, they realize this is the only place they can go. Just like the water that gives each oyster its distinct taste, Tracks is the flavor of Penn Station, through and through.

Table for One

By James Nolan

From *Gastronomica*

Poet, fiction writer, and translator James Nolan lived in many exotic places—Spain, India, China, South America—before moving back to his native New Orleans a decade ago. From that citizen-of-the-world perspective, he makes a pithy point about American dining-out habits.

L et me finally admit it: I hate eating alone in most American restaurants. This is particularly vexing because I live in the French Quarter, which visitors to my native New Orleans think of as a culinary paradise. And with reservations—in both senses of the word—it can be, if you're part of a well-heeled gang out for a jovial night-on-the-town of dining with jazz in the background. But I'm not talking about my cousin's birthday dinner bash next Saturday, but tonight, a harried, workaday evening when I should be busy correcting galley proofs well into the wee hours.

Sorry, but I don't want to have fun every night of the week. I'm a hungry bachelor, one who has never gotten used to the concept of food as show biz. As I say to the street musicians approaching my outdoor café table whenever I'm back visiting San Francisco, "I'm from New Orleans—please don't entertain me."

Just feed me.

Every evening, the choices facing the hungry single person aren't easy: either the often tiresome steps of shopping, prepping, cooking, and then cleaning up involved in making a nutritious meal for one, or the shameful practice of eating convenience food—whether take-out, order-in, or frozen-and-nuked—usually at a granite-topped kitchen island. I'm hardly ever in the mood for the pricey fussiness of solitary "fine dining," and even if I did drive, the gastric suicide of fast food has always been out of the question. Sadly, the drugstore lunch counters, automats, and late-night diners ubiquitous in the black-and-white movies of my parents' era are long gone, although you can still pick up a package of ramen noodles at Walgreens.

What's left for people like me, those who love to cook, do so almost every day, but eventually grow weary of putting together a decent solo meal night after night? Aren't we one-person households supposed to be a growing demographic?

Few American restaurants cater to the single diner unless they're run by recently arrived immigrants, many of whom are bachelors themselves starting new lives in the United States. Asia, Middle Eastern, and Latin American restaurant owners understand the concept of a table for one, at which you might eat unself-consciously next to other hardworking single diners like yourself: a Chinese tailor between shifts, a Pakistani taxi driver, or a Mexican roofer.

In an American-style restaurant, on the other hand, a single diner will be seated at a table for two that waiters call a "deuce," usually behind a potted palm, near the swinging kitchen door, or around the corner from the restrooms. It's either that, or you'll wind up next to a boisterous party of eight singing "Happy Birthday," alongside a married couple silently dueling, or sharing the awkward intimacy of two people on a first date as their knees inch toward each other's under the table. Of course, just because we're single doesn't mean we've taken monastic vows. Sometimes we're only too happy to be part of a jolly restaurant party or to stumble through our own clumsy first dates. But not every night, the meat-and-potatoes of our weekly eating habits. Which is why, rather than suffer these indignities in restaurants, we'd prefer to stand at the kitchen island scarfing take-out or microwaved grub.

For much of my life, I lived in Barcelona, Madrid, and San Francisco, and these days I sorely miss the neighborhood bachelor restaurants I frequented in these cities: clean, utilitarian eateries that functioned as extensions of my own apartment and were similar in some ways to boardinghouse dining rooms. These places were economical, served home-cooked food, were set up with rows of double tables meant for one, and staffed by unobtrusive waiters who were probably the chef's brothers-in-law. As a matter of fact, everyone working there often came to the big city from the same village, either in rural Spain or Asia, and so offered a degree of community to the similarly displaced. The efficient but distant servers understood exactly what you wanted: to order, eat, read the paper, drink a few glasses of house wine, pay, and leave, without having to put on a party hat, listen to them recite in tedious detail the evening's specials, or pretend you were having the time of your life.

This, of course, was when the working class still could afford to live in these cities, and for various reasons many of them ate at least one meal a day out alone. In Spain, their workplaces were often close by, and so the suited bureaucrat ate lunch at a table right next to the bricklayer in his blue jumpsuit. The office-worker scanned newspaper headlines, the bricklayer stared at the TV blaring in the corner, and nearby a lone shaggy student was bent over a book.

And then there was me, after teaching my university classes or rattling around inside my apartment all day. We diners nodded, made eye contact with each other, and at times exchanged pleasantries, but otherwise respected each other's privacy. If we lingered over a coffee or cognac with an after-dinner cigarette—back when you could still smoke in restaurants—we might chat with the waiter as he bused tables. After all, we saw the same server three or four times a week, although we never exchanged names. No, this was a business, and he wasn't exactly a friend. Rather, the waiter was more like your mailman, someone who knew more about your tastes and habits than even those closest to you. On Fridays, one dashing waiter in Madrid, black hair slicked back like Ramón Navarro's, always seemed to know I'd order the cod, salmon, or trout. He never asked my name, religion, or even my nationality, but perhaps he'd noticed the Sainte Vierge Miraculeuse medal dangling around my neck.

Good walls make good waiters, so please, I pray to la Miraculeuse every time I'm seated in an American restaurant, don't tell me your name, just take my order. And there's no need for you to hover over the table, asking every ten minutes "Is everything okay?" or threatening to whisk away my half-finished dinner unless I'm "still working on it" here in my mastication factory. And don't wave that wooden dildo packed with peppercorns in my face.

Of course, American servers must be obsequiously entertaining and intimate because of the feudal economics of tipping, those sham roles of lord and servant long since vanished from European restaurants. And this has occurred on a continent, ironically, where real lords and servants abound, and class distinctions are closely observed. Yet in the labor-union economics of restaurant dining, everything in Europe is more equitable and democratic. There the waiter receives an automatic fifteen percent of the take from all of the tables in his section, in addition to a base salary. This is why, except in small family-run restaurants, the waiters traditionally have been men. It's a respected profession in which the waiter can actually support a numerous family on the steady income he earns. Most diners leave behind on the table a few coins from their change, either as noblesse oblige, a reward for a special kindness, or simply to get rid of a few heavy metal euros. But nobody expects it, and if you don't leave any coins, no hard feelings.

Along with the automatic fifteen percent service fee, the tax is also included in the price of each menu item, whether it's an à la carte or a prix fixe meal. So diners, whether alone or in groups, don't have to ruin their digestions by sweating over arithmetic when the bill arrives. And unless somebody in a group springs for the check, it's considered boorish beyond belief not to simply divide the bill by the number in the party. If you decide to argue about who needs to fork over more or less dough because of a dessert or extra glass of wine, no European will ever dine out with you again. Even today, I avoid going to restaurants with Americans who spoil a lovely dinner by ending it with an animated conversation involving addition and subtraction, never my strong suit.

The single diner in a European restaurant will often flip through a newspaper or book, or if it's a working-class bistro, watch the news on a TV mounted in the corner. In Spain, news broadcasts are timed for the lunch and dinner hours—2:00 and 9:00 p.m., respectively—so there's always something happening on screen to elicit a collective groan, cheer, or complaint, especially during soccer matches or elections. This entices the lone diner out of his shell and conversations often flow between tables. Nowadays, of course, here as well as in Europe, once seated, many diners immediately take out their things and start playing with them. For better or worse, glowing iPhones, those bottomless wells of self-absorption in public, have usurped the cigarette pack as personal place markers on the restaurant table, always close at hand.

Unaccompanied women often dine alone in European restaurants, where they are treated with courtly respect and discretion. I've seldom observed women dining alone in American restaurants, and have never doubted why. In her "Paris Journal," M.F.K. Fisher nails it: "*I do not enjoy* eating alone in American restaurants. . . . I am suspect: all single women are either lushes or on the prowl, good waiters and restaurateurs have assured me. So I am put near the bar if I look like a quick pickup (which I don't), and behind an aspidistra or a service table if I look like a troublesome drinker. . . . In even 'good' places I am served in a cursory way, something to be got through." Fisher then goes on to detail the delightful meals she ate alone in Paris restaurants, and concludes, "I am glad I am here, and alone here."

Savoring her words makes me feel not so alone in my nostalgia for the civilized atmosphere of single dining. Short of boarding a plane, what wouldn't I do tonight for a table for one at la Sanabresa or el Bierzo in Madrid, Bilbao or L'Havana in Barcelona, or Henry's Hunan or Yuet Lee in San Francisco? This April I'd loved to have been dining at la Sanabresa on Calle Amor de Dios seated alone at my table facing the TV newscast when King Juan Carlos abdicated his throne. I can only imagine the hubbub of shocked commentary exploding around me as I dove into my favorite first course of *berenjenas rebozadas* (deep-fried slices of eggplant), continued through my second of *pata de cordero asado* (roast leg of lamb), and finished with the usual *crema catalane* (crème brûlée). Or I could have skipped the food and would have paid the twelve-euro prix fixe just to eavesdrop on the heated family conversation.

In these bachelor restaurants, the bond between single diners and owners runs deep. This spring, visiting my old North Beach neighborhood in San Francisco, I made a beeline for Henry's Hunan on Sansome Street, where I'd often eaten dinner alone before teaching evening classes at the Chinatown campus of City College. Now, at the most un-Chinese lunch hour of three in the afternoon—over the years, my appetite has stayed true to the Spanish schedule—I found myself seated next to only one other customer in the empty restaurant, and he and I nodded, acknowledging with a smile that we'd both ordered the same dish. An African-American, perhaps also with Southern roots, he was eating the spicy house-smoked ham, as close to soul food as you can get in a Chinese restaurant and always my own favorite. In the middle of his meal, he glanced at his watch, patted his pockets, and told the Chinese waitress that he'd forgotten his wallet in his cab. Then the taxi driver offered to leave his iPhone as security for the bill while he ran back to retrieve it. But since he was obviously a habitual customer, the waitress wouldn't hear of it. A few minutes later, he sprinted in to pay and then leave with a carton of leftovers, reminding me of how many nights I'd raced from a table here to my classroom.

Tonight, back in New Orleans, on the day Juan Carlos's son Felipe is crowned the new king of Spain, I trudge into my kitchen, swing open the fridge door, and try to imagine what ingredients I can possibly scrape together to make an interesting meal before I get back to work on the galley proofs. What about a shrimp couscous, I wonder, using homemade shrimp stock from the freezer, pre-peeled Gulf shrimp, plus some raisins, a handful of pitted olives, cilantro, Aleppo pepper, and canned garbanzos? That might last me for three days, and even though I'll probably tire of it after the second, I go through the halfhearted preparations. Yet how much more enjoyable it would be to tuck today's newspaper under my arm and take a brisk stroll, only to wind up sitting at a table for one among clattering dishes in front of a freshly prepared meal at an unpretentious restaurant like la Sanabresa or Henry's Hunan, places that have always been like my second homes.

Except that there I don't have to do the dishes.

Dinner and Deception

By Edward Frame

From the *New York Times*

When NYC grad student Edward Frame's essay about his haute
cuisine service stint appeared on the *Times'* op-ed page, Internet
comment sections lit up. Which snooty restaurant's secrets
was he spilling? The social media buzz missed Frame's point,
though—about the co-dependent dance between the waiter
and the waited-on.

I t's 4:25 p.m. I make my way through the kitchen, past the prep cooks,
up to the locker room on the second floor. Getting dressed takes 10
minutes. That leaves 20 to get "family meal" before the porters break
everything down. At 4:55, I'm ready. Lineup is in five minutes—"live at
five." I double-check my uniform, an expensive-looking suit issued by
the restaurant, before I join the rest of the waitstaff downstairs.

Lineup is our final meeting before service. The managers report
on menu changes and our ranking on the world's top restaurants list.
Sometimes they test us. "Where did Chef get his first Michelin star?"
"What kind of stone is the floor made of?" But tonight we just taste the
new wine. A classic Burgundy: red fruit, rose petal, underripe cherry;
med-high acid, soft tannins. It'll pair well with the pork.

The dining room has four "stations," each with six or seven tables
overseen by a four-person service team—captain, sommelier, server
and assistant server. As a captain, I'm in charge of my team. It took me
eight months to get promoted to this job; some captains waited for
years.

Six food runners also roam the floor, along with three managers. Two expediters—the "expos"—stay in the kitchen to decide when food leaves and where it goes. At most other three-Michelin-star restaurants in New York City, the system is much the same.

Doors open at 5:30. Tonight, the book says 152 covers. About 120 used to be normal, but the owners are opening a new place next month and need cash. So tonight it's 152. The service director calls this an "opportunity for more guests to experience the restaurant." But this is spin, and everyone knows it. Thirty-two more covers means we need to turn eight more tables, two more in my section, which means I'll be taking a cab home at 3 a.m., not 2.

My team is good. Not perfect, good. The sommelier knows his wine, but on busy nights gets buried fast. I can rely on my server. My assistant server is great. Every captain knows that an assistant server can make or break you. "Crumb, clear, water"—that's all an assistant server technically does, but a good one keeps things moving in your section.

First table gets seated at 5:31. I print and scan the chit, a digital dossier we keep on every guest, new or old. *Who are these people?* V.I.P.? ("Soigné" is the preferred term.) It's the first seating, so I know they're not, but I check anyway. Have they been here before? Do they have a water preference? Food allergies? Likes? Dislikes? Spend big on wine?

I announce my presence on the greet: a flourish, a hand gesture, a pressing of the palms, anything to signal that everyone at the table needs to pay attention, that I'll be dictating the pace of the experience tonight, not the other way around. "Good evening." Big smile. "Do you still prefer sparkling water? Or would you like something else this time?" The assistant server stands by the credenza next to the Champagne bucket, waiting. A slight wiggle of my fingers behind my back means bubbles; a slashing motion, still; a twist of the fist, ice water. Like magic, he appears with the correct selection. "May I take a moment to explain the menu?"

Captains compete for the briefest menu spiel possible. The key is to eliminate unnecessary choices; most people just want to be told what to do. At 5:35 I'm back at the table for the order. I memorize every guest's selection; writing things down would suggest a "transactional" relationship, something I want to avoid. Each guest should feel special. A minute later I dictate the orders to the server, who transcribes and then places them while I stay on the floor.

In an ideal service, the captain never leaves the floor. After that, it's all about table maintenance until I drop the check with some complimentary cognac in three or five hours, depending on whether they go four-course or tasting. I'll do this 13 more times tonight.

Marx might have called this kind of work "estranged labor," but the phrase isn't quite right. My experience working in fine dining was marked by hard, repetitive and often meaningless work. But it wasn't completely "estranging," not at first. To the contrary, I found that hard, repetitive work, however "estranged" in some abstract or theoretical sense, could be incredibly affirming. Executing the same tasks with machine-like precision over and over and over again, like one of Adam Smith's nail-cutters, offered a special kind of enjoyment. There was no reflection, no question about what my job required of me, and I could indulge, for hours, in the straightforward immediacy of action.

Next to a doorway leading into the dining room, a sign in the kitchen summed up the job in the form of a commandment: "Make it nice." Make it nice means you hold yourself accountable to every detail. It means everything in the restaurant must appear perfect—the position of the candle votives, the part in your hair. Everything matters.

Most of us internalized this mantra quickly. One of my first assignments as a food-runner was to polish glassware. I worked in a small alcove, connected to the dishwasher. Glass racks came out, I wiped away any watermarks or smudges, and then, just as I finished one rack, another appeared. This went on for hours, like some kind of Sisyphean fable revised for the hospitality industry. By hour two my fingers hurt and my back ached. But I couldn't stop. The racks kept coming. Slowing down never occurred to me. There wasn't time. I needed to make it nice. I *wanted* to make it nice.

I moved up the ranks quicker than most. Each promotion required a new but reassuringly mechanical set of skills. When setting food on a table, I learned to obey the maxim "raise right, lower left." My movements had to be perfectly synchronized with the other food-runners, our arms dropping together like weighted levers. To replace a tablecloth, I would smooth it out with an antique iron, reset the table with glassware, silver and charger plates, making sure the labels on each were squared-off and facing the guest, all in under three minutes. Another server suggested that I hum the theme to "The Bourne Identity" under my breath to stay motivated. I did, and he was right. It worked.

Duck came out on a special cart called a guéridon. Captains did the carving tableside. Slicing off the left breast was easy, but to get the right side required a little finesse. You couldn't turn the bird around, which felt natural to do, because the cavity could never face the guest. Chef decided this would be "unappealing." So you had to switch hands, carving ambidextrously. Regardless of your abilities wielding a knife with either hand, both breasts needed to be on the plate in less than a minute, before the kitchen sent out the sides. If you took longer you'd be caught finishing the job while some runner hovered awkwardly next to you with a tray full of saucepans and tweezers.

Not everyone can do this kind of work well. Captains joked that it wasn't worth learning a person's name until he got promoted at least once. But get promoted and suddenly you were admitted into an inner circle of people who excelled at this sort of thing. Most members of the service staff shared one thing in common—a quiet alliance against our betters: the guests, and our managers. When someone spoke about the "swan" in lineup, a metaphor for the ideal server, churning tirelessly beneath the surface while maintaining the impression of absolute poise to the casual observer, there was never a hint from management that, like us, they understood the psychological dividedness their favorite symbol suggested. But as captains or servers or sommeliers, our job wasn't just serving food, it was playing a part, and we did it with a degree of self-conscious irony that our bosses seemed incapable of.

Acting out your role during service could be fun. You could play guessing games like "hooker or daughter." Or the "adjective game," where you competed to successfully sell a wine with the least helpful descriptors possible. "Haunted" was a good one. You learned to read people. I still remember the Chinese businessman at Table 43. He had two companions that night: a pair of young women whose skin looked oddly synthetic. Right away he ordered a bottle of 1990 Krug—a thousand dollars, like that.

"May I take a moment to explain the menu?"

"We want the tasting menu," he said.

The two women stared at their phones, indifferent to our exchange. They clearly weren't planning to eat anything.

"Sir, the tasting menu is a five-hour experience." I looked at him, then at the two women. "Are you sure you wouldn't rather spend some of your evening elsewhere?"

He opted for four courses.

You experience a special rush when your job is to project an aura of warmth and hospitality while maintaining an almost clinical emotional distance. It's the thrill of the con. This pleasure in deception was suggested by another metaphor popular with upper management: lipstick on a pig. The key to fine dining, I was told by one manager, was to ensure that the guest never noticed the pig, only the lipstick. Guests wanted to believe the make-believe; they wanted to believe everything was perfect. But the moment someone noticed a minor imperfection—a smudge on the butter, a fingerprint on the fork—other imperfections would suddenly become noticeable, threatening the illusion we all worked to maintain.

In a playground for the superrich, I was an overpaid chaperone wearing a bespoke suit. Gluttony was common. So was sex; more than once we had to interrupt coitus in the restroom. Once a woman asked to leave her baby at the coat check. When the maître d' explained that dinner lasted at least three hours, she stared back at him, unfazed. "Yes, I know." Grown men wearing Zegna and Ferragamo would sit at the bar chanting, "We are the 1 percent!"

The nightly grotesquerie was almost exciting. But something happened after spending too many nights delivering four- or five-figure checks on silver trays. Estrangement *did* set in. I imagine pick-up artists experience something similar. You learn what people want from you, and, for a while, you get a high making all the right gestures: the perfectly timed joke, the wry smile. But, deep down, you feel nothing. Until something forces you back to reality again.

When the guest falls, I'm standing at a credenza near the bar. It's lunch. The dining room is full. I don't see him go down, but he makes a loud, gasping sound before he hits the floor. We all know him. He's a regular. He's been to the restaurant maybe 150 times and always orders the same thing: double vodka on the rocks to start; first course lobster; second course duck; no dessert. Usually he comes with his wife, who freely complains about his diet. He tips well, and, like most regulars, he is generally considered to be a jerk. But now, as he's lying there, his skin turning a kind of grayish-white, it is impossible to feel anything for the man who has just had a stroke in the middle of our dining room except pity.

He is lying on the polished terrazzo floor, flat on his back. People are staring, not quite sure what to do, their thoughts clearly teetering between concern and that other more ugly thought—*I waited three weeks for this reservation and this is ruining my experience.* Everything leading up to this moment has been so carefully orchestrated: the timing of the courses, the neat folds of each napkin, the levels of every water glass. But not this. The normally composed servers are visibly shaken. How can anyone sanely elaborate on the virtues of left-bank Bordeaux next to a body?

Impossible, I think, so I turn to my manager and ask: "What should I do?" I assume somebody has called an ambulance. The manager has just finished hurrying to push a Champagne cart in front of the possibly dead man on the floor, a lame attempt to hide him from nearby diners. Nothing in the service manual can tell him how to answer my question. This isn't planned; the moment demands real empathy, real human understanding, and not the counterfeit variety he and I earn our living with.

"I'm going to go turn the music up," he says. "Just keep going."

So I do. I keep going, pouring wine, giving spiels on food and dropping handwritten checks until the paramedics arrive 10 minutes later. The manager comps the bill for those people seated near "the accident." No one else seems to mind.

The guest, I learned a few days later, survived. But he never returned to the restaurant. Neither did I, after I left a few months later to go to graduate school. In the end, "making it nice" for 80 hours a week left me feeling empty and tired. As the regular's wife used to say when he ordered his usual lunch, "eating like that is bad for you."

The Hunger Games

By Howie Kahn

From *Travel & Leisure*

Veteran travel and culture writer Howie Kahn is a contributing
editor to the *Wall Street Journal,* though his work has also been
published everywhere from *Details* to *The Oprah Magazine.* He's
traveled to a lot of places—but something about Singapore
clearly revs up his taste buds.

W e were four courses into dinner in the private room of Shinji
by Kanesaka, an *omakase* restaurant in the arcade behind the
stately hotel Raffles Singapore. Already we'd been served biolumines-
cent squid; *hirame,* conjugally wrapped around morsels of *uni*; and glass
fish, tiny and transparent except for the blacks of their eyes. Now it was
time for the abalone, which had been soaking up mirin, soy, and bonito
broth vapors for the past five hours. As our host, Chris Lee, a 45-year-
old local designer wearing a Kanye West–style man-skirt, lifted the first
mollusk to his mouth, he asked the table, "Is it male or female?" He
chewed ruminatively, then answered his own question. "Male. Textur-
ally, it's more dense, more like the sea. It's more comprehensive."

"You have to chew it twice as long as other foods," chimed in Henry
Hariyono, 43, the general manager of Artisan Cellars, a dealer of rare
wines. "But it's twice as rewarding."

As the meal progressed, Lee, Hariyono, and Teng Wen Wee, a
33-year-old restaurateur, competed to drop the most food knowledge.
They debated the merits of *bafun uni* (richer) versus *murasaki uni*
(sweeter). They informed me that our squid, flown in from the Toyama

prefecture of Japan, is in season for only three weeks. When the sushi courses began coming over the counter, the chef—Shunsuke Kikuchi, one of founder Shinji Kanesaka's protégés—sent out multiple cuts of *otoro*, or tuna belly, each sliced through with a $3,000 knife. "The middle cut," Hariyono said, "should look like the first day of snow."

Though this epic feast (stats: 17 courses, eight bottles of wine) was especially decadent, it was also characteristic of the way devotion and scholarship amplify the pleasures of food in this cuisine-obsessed 5.5 million-person city-state. Eating here also means constantly talking about eating—passionately, proudly, and knowledgeably. Ask any Singaporean stranger—cabdriver, store clerk, bank teller—about where and what they most like to eat, and you are likely to end up with a friend for life. Foodie-ism is a national religion, and the melting-pot dining culture, with its innovative, critically hailed restaurants and habit-forming street food, undercuts the notion that Singapore is, as some call it, "Singa-bore"—a hypersanitized snooze fest long on global financial services and short on fun. For a culinary adventurer like me, the place is irresistible.

I started eating before I'd even left Singapore Changi Airport. Minutes after deplaning, just past midnight on a balmy, tropical evening, I headed to the Killiney Kopitiam kiosk to marvel at the simple, craveable wonder of *kaya* toast. Killiney, which opened in 1919 and became a chain in 1993, browns its toast evenly on a grill, then slathers it in butter and *kaya*, a sticky-sweet coconut jam. The bread is then assembled like a sandwich and served alongside soft-boiled eggs in a small ceramic bowl, the yolks serving as a dip. I was jet-lagged and needed a shower, but couldn't help downing a second order while catching up on Hariyono's Instagram feed, which featured glossy, alluring, Helmut Newton–style close-ups of local dishes. At home in New York, these images had only provoked wistful fantasy. But now I was back for my third visit in a year (that's about 144 hours of transit time and more than 60,000 air miles, all told) for around-the-table camaraderie and around-the-clock caloric indulgence with my newfound comrades in food.

The next day didn't really get going until I was served a fish head. Specifically, a kingfish head, prepared by David Pynt at his restaurant, Burnt Ends. After a restorative morning round of more *kaya* toast at my hotel, I found myself sitting at a long, boomerang-shaped bar watching Pynt cook on the other side. Sporting a dark, burly beard and a leather apron that resembled body armor, the 31-year-old Australian worked the three elevation grills and the four-ton brick, steel, and concrete oven he built himself, which stands over six feet tall and reaches a temperature of more than 1700 degrees. "I just call it my baby," Pynt said.

For the next several hours he worked his creation with paternal tenderness, manipulating fire to get all the delicate bits of meat cooked and smoked just right for me and my dining companion—Loh Lik Peng, the co-owner and one of Singapore's most prominent restaurateurs. Lee had told me that Loh possessed a tremendous appetite, something Loh immediately confirmed: "I ordered half a baby goat last time I was here," he said. This time we started with smaller cuts of meat and seafood—quail with *salsa verde* and aioli; marron, a freshwater Australian crayfish, sprinkled with capers and parsley; lamb loin with carrots. Then came the fish head. Enormous, spade-shaped, and thatched with swaths of lemongrass and a mortar of miso, the dish was the embodiment of the country's eclectic taste in food. Cooked by a progressive Aussie, it combined Chinese, Malaysian, and South Indian culinary techniques that were in play here long before Singapore became a sovereign nation half a century ago. We ate with our hands. Eventually, Loh brought part of the skeleton to his lips, corn-on-the-cob-style. "I'm eating the brain and the eye," he said with a grin. "Who says Singapore is so clean?" Pynt laughed, plating a series of smoked ice creams and pastries. "It's all pleasure here," he said as Bob Dylan crooned over the restaurant speakers: *your next meallllll.*

A few hours later, Hariyono texted to tell me it was dinnertime. We met at Izy, a bustling *izakaya* in Chinatown that his company has a minority stake in. An IT professional turned wine savant, he was wearing hip, frameless glasses and a woven porkpie hat. Understanding I had come from a big lunch, he recommended a bottle of champagne as a digestive aid. "Champagne really works well with everything," he said, "including a full stomach." The bartender filled our glasses with a 2008 Chartogne-Taillet and set them on colorful coasters printed with a kaleidoscopic blossom of samurais, *luchadores,* cigarettes, soda bottles, and tattooed arms holding swords. A mural in the same maximalist, pop-iconographic style was on the back wall. The dishes, from a menu that executive chef Kazumasa Yazawa devised in consultation with Japanese star Yoshihiro Narisawa, were more restrained. "This is Narisawa's influence right here," Hariyano said as he plucked a lobster claw from beneath a small mound of wasabi sprouts, okra, and *kai-lan* flower, one of our 12 courses. "You can taste the green, still alive. But what's more amazing is that Yazawa used local vegetables, which is unheard of here."

Farm-to-table eating isn't yet a driving force in Singapore the way it is in the West, but its slow emergence shows a desire to stretch the boundaries of menu-making and cooking. It also underscores Singapore's growing pride in both its homegrown products and its local kitchen talent. At the just-opened Sorrel, for example, instead of importing a foreign chef, as is the common practice, Loh Lik Peng turned over the reins to a pair of talented young Singaporeans: Johnston Teo, 24, and Alex Phan, 27.

For the first time, Singaporean-style sensibilities are being exported, too: Loh has opened hotels and restaurants in London, Shanghai, and Hong Kong; this month he opens his latest property, the Old Clare Hotel, in Sydney. Lee has commissions throughout Asia, Europe, the Middle East, and North America. All of this industry was sensationalized by Kevin Kwan in his international best seller, *Crazy Rich Asians*, which is being turned into a movie by a producer of *The Hunger Games*.

"People follow passion here and the rest of the world is responding," Hariyono said before suggesting an excessive (but not unexpected) nightcap. We walked around the corner to Luke's Oyster Bar & Chop House, an elegant, low-lit, New England–style place whose chef Travis Masiero hails from Boston. Singapore may be finding its own voice, but it's also still a place where tried-and-true dining concepts from around the world are executed to perfection. "When people like food this much," Masiero told me, "it makes cooking classics from anywhere a lot of fun."

Teng Wen Wee's new restaurant, the Black Swan, is another irresistible foreign import. It serves timeless bistro fare, from beef tartare to oysters, in a beautifully renovated three-story Deco building, formerly a bank, tucked among the skyscrapers of the Central Business District. "Burnt Ends is also like that," Masiero said. "It's an Australian concept made better here. And Shinji by Kanesaka. Every time I go in there, I think, *Man, this is the best* omakase *in the world.*" He set a tin of caviar and a couple of mother-of-pearl spoons on the bar. "Just go for it," he said, looking in my direction. "Finish it."

By the time I met Cynthia Chua, the following morning, time as I knew it had collapsed, the hours, minutes, and seconds replaced by a looping circuit of big meals, small meals, and snacks. In other words, "you feel like a local," suggested the diminutive 42-year-old restaurateur. She piloted me through the village-like enclave of Tiong Bahru in her chocolate-colored Porsche convertible. "Everybody wants to live in this neighborhood," she said. In part, that's because of its distinctly desirable 80-year-old Deco housing blocks, which look like they could have been airlifted in from Miami. But it's also because this is the area where Singapore's diverse traditions mix so thrillingly with a sense of cutting-edge entrepreneurship. Four of the nearly 20 restaurants and coffee shops Chua owns in Singapore are here.

As the afternoon passed, she shared her future ambitions: an artisanal butcher shop, a charcuterie, a rooftop farm. (She has since opened two urban farms.) At Tiong Bahru Bakery, one of her first investments, we sampled salted-caramel pastries known as *kouign amann* and smoked-salmon sandwiches on supple squid-ink buns. "I want to curate entire streets," Chua said. This is a long-standing impulse in Singapore, epitomized by the centralized hawker centers that were set up for street vendors in 1971. At their best, these clean, orderly rows of stalls feel like personal invitations into the homes of aunties and uncles who want to serve you delicious family recipes. There's concern about the long-term survival of these businesses, since young Singaporean culinary entrepreneurs seem inclined to aim for higher profit margins than two-dollar chicken dishes—no matter how sublime—can provide.

As we sat in Tiong Bahru's own hawker center eating *jian bo shui kueh*—tiny steamed rice cakes with radish chili and shallots, sold four for a dollar—Chua explained how she matches buildings with big ideas. Recently, in a duplex on nearby Martin Road, she launched Common Man Coffee Roasters, a third-wave espresso joint with a stellar menu of comfort foods, and Bochinche, a clubby meat-and-cocktail-driven Argentinean-inspired establishment. "Every time I stand in front of a vacant shop here," she said, "people think I'm taking it."

On my last day, Hariyono and I visited a food stall on a working-class street in the area of Jalan Besar to load up on *laksa,* a silky, briny noodle soup beloved by locals. Then, already full, I met Chua at Tippling Club, another of her restaurants, for a 22-course send-off dinner prepared by the 36-year-old British chef, Ryan Clift. Chua lured Clift to Singapore in 2008, promising him his dream kitchen. "Once I get somebody here," she said, "they stay." When I had last visited, the restaurant was operating in a former army barracks, but it was now located in an elegant, central, two-story shop-house.

Working fast in the bright, open kitchen, the chef sent out courses in sealed jars, test tubes, and pill bottles, but they were anything but clinical. Clift lives to misdirect and surprise. Traditional chicken curry came in a combination of white crisps—like small packing peanuts—and flavored foam. Sweet bell peppers had become carbonized lumps. Clift had tenderized the Wagyu beef by placing slices between kombu leaves and zapping them with sound waves. Small bites carried huge flavors. Large ones were unexpectedly subtle. All was engineered to provoke excitement through complexities that weren't obvious to the eye. The meal represented the ambitions of Clift's adopted country well, and he knew it. "Things have been bubbling up around here for a long time," he told me. "But now Singapore is finally hot. Singapore is boiling."

As I headed back to the airport for my 4 a.m. flight, I began scrolling hungrily through Hariyono's Instagram again. There were cuts of fish I hadn't tasted; chili-spiked breakfast noodles I hadn't slurped; plate-crowded tables my friends had not yet suggested we visit. There would be a last snack of sweet *kaya* toast in the airport followed by a long flight home, and eventually, a return ticket to book.

Eating and Drinking in Mexico City: A Diary

By Todd Kliman

From the *Washingtonian*

A master of long-form food writing, Todd Kliman—who
contributes to many publications alongside his regular gig as food
critic for the *Washingtonian*—goes well beyond what's on the
plate to draw readers into the essence of wherever he's dining out.
A trip to Mexico to sample tacos? Hold onto your sombrero.

W hen the magazine with the buff dude showing off his six-pack
on the cover every month called up and said, *We want to fly
you down to Mexico City to eat tacos,* I didn't envision having a Benito, or
all that having a Benito entailed.

Benito was my butler for the week. When I met him at the airport,
he had not only a sign with my name on it, but also lemon-scented towels and a bottle of mineral water.

"Welcome to Mexico City," he said in stilted, heavily accented English. He wore a starched black jacket with gold buttons down the front
and a solicitous smile that seemed only to emphasize a certain sadness.

I'd arrived more than two hours late because of a delayed connecting flight, and then it was another hour through traffic-clogged streets
to my hotel. By the time I dropped my bags in my room, it had been
nine hours since I'd downed a quick sandwich at the Houston airport.
I was ravenous and light-headed, and all I could think about as I hus-
tled down the winding staircase that smelled of club-goers' cologne was
running to the nearest taco stand.

But apparently, I would not be running alone. I wouldn't even be running.

Standing at the door of the lobby, barring my exit, was Benito. And there was my driver, too, waiting at the curb, his car door open.

I said I thought this was maybe just the tiniest bit unnecessary, given that I was only going out to a taco stand.

No no, Benito said, with the gravest of expressions.

Benito had a nervous, deferential manner that made me nervous and deferential toward him, which in turn made him more nervous and more deferential. I could already see what kind of week it was going to be.

A week before I left, my editor had overruled my first choice of hotel as not expensive enough, and upgraded me to a new boutique property in a trendy neighborhood with 24-hour concierge, car service and, as it turned out, a Benito on call.

"We want you back in one piece," he said, reminding me that I would be journeying to a land of carjackings, robberies, and kidnappings. *Bon voyage and bon appetit!*

I had never been to Mexico City, but I had read about it, and in the two weeks before I left I read more and more about it. If you're looking to be scared about something, the internet is great for confirming your worst fears, as anyone who has ever searched for information on an ailment knows—everything from that little bump on your leg to that indigestion that won't go away is potentially cancer.

I read about buses that had been stopped at gunpoint on the way to the Aztecan pyramids in Teotihuacan and robbed. I read about express kidnapping, in which victims are taken around to one ATM after another, forced to withdraw small amounts of cash at each to avoid systemic detection, until the account is drained, at which point they either are thrown from the car or killed. I read about the okay taxis and the not-to-be trusted taxis. I read the solemn and exhaustive report from the State Department to Americans traveling to the city, a document that kept me up late one night, imagining all the terrible, horrible things that might befall me.

The good thing about imagining the worst, of course, is that the worst never comes to pass. I was fine, as it turned out. The city worked on me in other ways. Got in my head, got in my bloodstream, altered my system, made me feverish, made me agitated, made me sick, made me walk around in a haze.

Every major city is a little like other major cities, and Mexico City is a little like New York in its frenetic pace, and a little like Los Angeles in its sprawl and traffic, and a little like Tel Aviv in its faded '60s architecture, and a little like Miami in its color and pulse.

At the same time, it is nothing like those cities. And the ways in which it is not the same are a lot more interesting than the ways in which it is.

Picture it from the vantage point of an airplane window: a city perched 10,000 feet above sea level, situated on what was, long ago, a lake, belted in on all sides by mountains and volcanoes. The effect is of a cavernous bowl sunk down into the earth, atop which a thick perma-cloud of smog rests like the top layer of cheese on a French onion soup. Beneath it, the city boils away: 21 million people living, working, play-ing, coupling, killing, creating, oppressing, thriving, eating, sleeping, starving. Pujol chef Enrique Olvera, who also commands the kitchen at the modern Mexican restaurant Cosme in New York, told the *New York Times* last month, "Mexico City is like a wave; you need to surf it. You don't make plans, you just move."

I longed to surf it. I longed to be able to walk out into the city, alone, and just move. That meant wandering the streets and getting myself lost. That meant ditching Benito.

I called Martin. If I was going to risk venturing into the city without my buffer who had vowed to do anything for me, I should at least have a warm body by my side.

Until the day he picked me up in his 4×4 to take me out to the pyra-mids at Teotihuacan, forty-five minutes northeast of downtown, Mar-tin and I had never met. A friend of a friend of a friend had introduced me by email, and Martin, understanding that I had traveled to a city of 21 million where I knew not a single person, took it upon himself to look after me—to be part tour guide, part culinary explainer, and part (the part he loved) demonic Virgil.

Hurtling toward Teotihuacan, we discovered that we had been born within a month of one another, that our fathers were both brilliant, difficult men, that we shared a mutual love of Negronis, and that we both subscribed to the principle that if the night was good, then you stayed out late and made it great (and if the night was bad, then you stayed out late to make it good). The bond had been established, and with it the conditions for exactly the night of excess that came to pass.

We began our tour of Teotihuacan in the museum, taking in the burial plots of the ancients, the skeletons lit with an eerie light, glowing like coals, then began the ascent toward the Pyramid of the Sun, a perilous trek up 248 narrow, often uneven steps. Halfway there, my heart began to pound. I could feel it in my chest, and by the time we reached the top I was wheezing.

The view was majestic, and it was humbling to think of the civilization that was, of the city below that had once thrived. At the time of the arrival of Cortes and his men, the conquest that would lay waste to a people and culture and transform the place from a Nahuatl culture to a Spanish culture, the city was one of the largest in the world, larger than Paris and London. Down below us, I could hear the hawkers sounding the jaguar whistles they sold as souvenirs—a strange and primal sound, like that of wind whipping through a tunnel, only with more hint of animal danger, a sound that emphasized the feeling of being on the very edge of a society.

Which was so very apt, given that I was at that very moment struggling to breathe. It was as if some unseen hand were goring me between my eyes, not unlike the feeling you get when you guzzle a Slurpee too fast, only fifty times more intense.

If Benito were here, I thought, he would revive me, with a bottle of water and a cold cloth.

Or catch me if I fell.

But Benito was not here because I sneaked out of the hotel without Benito's even knowing, a schoolboy cutting class.

Desperate to be out and about on my own, desperate to experience the city without a buffer. And now I was desperate.

The lonely, piercing sound of the whistle, the fact that I was gasping for air, the memory of all those stark and eerily lit skulls . . . for a moment, I had a vision of myself tumbling down from this perilous height, and I thought of Juan Escutia, the 19th-century warrior who wrapped the Mexican flag around his body and leapt from the top of Chapultepec

Castle—one of the six *niños* heroes who died defending the city from invading U.S. forces in the Mexican-American War, and the most resonant, perhaps because his death recalls that of another momentous descent from the sky—the great Aztec eagle, who, according to legend, swooped down from the sky to devour a snake on the swampy island of Texcoco and convinced the Aztecs to build their metropolis.

Falling, tumbling, descending . . .

It was not a religious experience I was having—there was no epiphany, no vision of the future, no moment, even, of clarity—but it was an experience all the same. Something was happening to me, in me. For a moment, I was not all there, or maybe I was all there, maybe I was more there than I ordinarily was, maybe I perceived and felt with a greater intensity, being so high, so woozy, so far from what I knew, so far from home.

And all this without even a drop of alcohol. I had yet to take my first sip of mezcal. I was under another influence as I stood there at the top of the Pyramid of the Sun. I had Roberto Bolano's *Savage Detectives* on my brain, which was one reason I was thinking in long, shifting sentences like those above.

I had begun reading the novel, set partly in 1970s Mexico City, on the plane and by the time I met Martin it had taken hold of me like a narcotic.

"I'll be Arturo, you can be Ulises," he said when he saw me that morning, speaking of the Quixote and Sancho Panza of Bolano's mock epic.

I felt pretty sure that whatever I saw, I was seeing through a Bolano filter, I was seeing the city through his depiction—a city of irrepressible vitality, of endless incident and color, of danger and violence lurking around every corner. *The Savage Detectives* doesn't touch on the pre-Hispanic age of Mexico City, and yet it was hard not to think that Bolano's ragged energies and panoramic vision were in some way informed by this history, by all that the city had suffered and assimilated.

"You okay?" Martin asked, searching my eyes.

I had gone somewhere, clearly.

As we descended, my breathing returned to normal, and with it the feeling that I had come out on the other side of something difficult.

Martin, looking to capitalize on my euphoria, suggested that it was time for drinks.

I consulted my phone; it was a little after 2.

"And tacos, of course," he said.

Our destination was Taqueria Gonzalez, back in the city, not far from the San Juan market. The market has many adherents, among them chef Rick Bayless, for whom the sight of young rabbits shorn of their fur except for a tufted patch approaching the feet must be roughly equivalent to that of a penitent Catholic gazing upon the vault of a cathedral.

I knew the taqueria was going to be great when we walked up to it to discover both men in suits and men in sweaty T-shirts, both tourists and locals.

This was not a sit-and-eat operation, it was a stand-and-gorge operation. The focus of everyone's attention was the great concave griddle, or *comal*, in the corner, a teeming mess of *rajas*, cubed potatoes, *longaniza*, and chopped pork of uncertain and possibly dubious provenance. A squat man working with the speed and efficiency of a short-order cook heaped massive quantities of meat and potatoes on my palm-sized tortilla, which I doused with guacamole. It was gloriously sloppy. We returned for seconds.

Martin thought it was good more than great, which is the sort of discernment you're lucky to be able to indulge in when you live in a culture with tacos at every turn.

No, they were not at the level of the tacos I had had the night before, at a wonderful Oaxacan restaurant called Yuban. And the tacos at Yuban were not at the level of the tacos I would have later that night at Quintonil, honored by San Pellegrino as one of the 50 best restaurants in the world, where, at my waiter's prompting, I converted a gorgeous hunk of wagyu chuck draped with a chili demiglace into three small tacos, embellishing them with an ink-black swipe of sauce made of *huitlacoche*.

But I came from the land of store-bought, mass-produced tortillas with crummy fillings and weak salsas, which was why I was so sorely tempted to wrap the squat man at the comal in a great big bear hug.

"I don't want to pull you off assignment," Martin said (meaning he did), "but you can't come to Mexico City without visiting at least one *pulqueria*."

I'd done my homework. I knew what *pulque* was, the fermented sap of the agave plant, a drink the Aztecs deemed the "drink of the gods." But knowing something on paper is not the same as knowing something tangibly—the difference, the crucial difference, between book learning and experience. Las Duelistas was like nothing my reading had prepared me for, hot and moist like a sauna, crammed tight with sweating patrons of varying ages, intricate colorful art covering nearly every inch of the space, including the ceiling, which bore, like a Renaissance cathedral, an image of a God.

Martin had been here before, and suggested going with the *degustacion*, a tasting flight consisting of five samples of pulque of varying colors, red, green, orange, light yellow, and pearlescent. The least appealing was the pearlescent, which Martin informed me was pulque in its natural state, unadorned, without flavoring.

"This is the one we start with," he said, "and work our way up."

I peered into the glass. It didn't look promising.

"A little salty, a little bitter, a little viscous," Martin offered.

I reached for the glass.

As I took my first taste, he said, "I've been told it tastes like semen."

"Thanks," I said, setting the glass down.

"No problem."

The *pulque* got better, much better. But of course it had only up to go. From there we moved to beer, and then from beer to mezcal. By dinner time, I had slipped into a haze and was grateful that Benito had appeared by my side, to guide me to dinner.

In *The Savage Detectives*, the aging poet Amadeo Salvatierra, one of the novel's 52 narrators, keeps reaching for his bottle of mezcal as he recounts his memories of the bohemian poets Arturo and Ulises. The brand, Los Suicidas, is no longer in existence, he notes, and in lamenting its passage he laments the passage of time.

At dinner I ordered a glass of Alipus, whose bottle features a stark, black-and-white woodcut of a warrior on a horse, looking down at a poor, harrowed soul on the ground. The poor, harrowed soul has his hand up, begging surrender. In my reading of the image, the warrior is mezcal, the poor, harrowed soul the unsuspecting drinker: *No more mezcal! No more assault!*

My rationalization for more mezcal was that its smoky bite made for an ideal pairing with the food, and that I was here, after all, to learn about the culture, which only goes to show that when you want to you can rationalize anything.

Meeting up with Martin later (he had had the good bourgeois sense to return home to his wife and four children for dinner before giving in to his bohemian impulses), I had no more excuses. I was simply indulging.

Our first stop of the night—at the time, I had thought it was to be both our first and also our last stop—was a "mixological speakeasy" hidden beneath an unassuming cantina in his neighborhood, the trendy, restaurant-laden Polanco. I was interested, was I not, in knowing what a mezcal Negroni was like?

The unsmiling linebacker barring our entrance didn't care about my research needs as decided by my new best friend Martin. We were not dressed all in black. We were not in our 20s. But Martin strode right up to him and, in the manner I imagined he had perfected years earlier in the courtroom, addressed the stern judge with all the charm, confidence, and certitude he could muster.

The judge listened without appearing to and relented, waving us in without so much as looking at us.

"What'd you say?" I asked Martin, as we descended into mezcal hell.

"That you were a figure *muy importante en los Estados Unidos.*"

The mezcal Negroni went down like punch, as did the mezcal cocktail in the place we went after, a small bar several blocks away, where my research needs took us.

Liquid fire, dressed up to look like innocent refreshments.

I woke up in the middle of the night, heart racing, mouth parched. When I went to get a drink of water, I was so light-headed that I had to brace myself against the furniture in the room.

The next morning did not exist. I did not wake up for it. I wanted to not wake up for the afternoon, too, but I was not so lucky.

Martin texted to inquire how I was doing "the day after."

I was not doing. I did not want to do.

I ticked off my symptoms.

Sounds like altitude sickness, he wrote back, and advised me to go to a pharmacy and buy a box of Dorixina Relax, a muscle relaxer. The otherwise simple act of walking to the store sounded, now, like a massive effort of will, and I knew that I could not just slip off to the pharmacy, that Benito would be shadowing me. Maybe a nap would help. Maybe I would wake up and all of this would just go away.

But when I woke up two hours later, it had not gone away, it was just as bad as before.

No, I thought, getting out of bed, it was not just as bad, it was worse. I put pressure on my foot, and the throb went zoom!—all the way to my head. Yes, I thought, it was unequivocally worse. I was torn between wanting to go back to bed and vomit.

The last thing I wanted to do, the very last thing, was go to lunch, but being a professional means playing hurt, playing through pain. I got dressed and went downstairs, clutching for the railing that wasn't there as I descended the narrow, winding steps.

Waiting for me in the lobby was Benito. I nodded. He bowed.

Whether we had now passed to the phase of making awkward conversation in our broken versions of each other's language, or whether he had simply taken my measure and decided to be upbeat, I wasn't sure, but as we walked outside to the waiting car Benito said, "How are you in love with Mexico City?"

I lay limp against the backseat, feeling as lively as those mounds of bones we had seen at Teotihuacan. They, at least, glowed like coals. No amount of production value, I knew, was going to revive me. My skin was flushed. No, it was cool. No, it definitely was flushed. I reached for the cool, lemon-scented towel, hoping for refreshment. Uh uh: too cold. I rolled up the window. I began to sweat.

Hurtling toward the restaurant, I wondered if Los Suicidas had been rebranded as Alipus.

Midway through lunch, Benito came in to check on me. I asked for an aspirin, desperate to ease the pounding. The pill arrived in ten minutes on a small saucer, like a mid-meal palate cleanser.

Benito, from the Latin: *blessed.*

After the meal, he smiled and bowed when I slipped him 100 pesos and asked where I would like to go next, prepared, no doubt, for another multi-stop adventure: a trip to a taqueria, followed by a pit stop at a taco stand, followed by a coffee refueling, and then maybe a trip to another taqueria.

"Farmacia," I said weakly.

In the States, you need a doctor's prescription for a muscle relaxer. In Mexico City, only a valid form of ID, and some reassuring words from a Benito.

Take one and call me in the morning, Martin texted.

Host, chaperone, culinary advisor, tour guide, and now doctor, too.

I had plans to meet my friend Ines, the editor of the magazine *El Gourmet,* for dinner later that night at a restaurant she was high on ("they have very good insects," she wrote via email the week before). I set my alarm for three hours and popped the pill.

I had also picked up altitude pills at the farmacia. I popped those, too.

It was six o'clock. I never did hear the alarm. I woke up the next day at 8, 14 hours later. The last time I had slept 14 consecutive hours was— no; there was no last time; I had never slept 14 consecutive hours.

What the hell was in this stuff?

Martin drugged me, was all I could think.

First he drugged me with mezcal. Now he has drugged me with strange pills.

This was what I needed Benito for; not to save me from kidnappers. To save me from Martin.

I texted Inés my apologies, citing the mezcal hangover and my altitude sickness.

Is this your first time drinking a lot of mezcal? she wrote back. *Welcome to Mexico City.*

A walk in the park—the Parque de Mexico was cattycorner from my hotel—was still not a walk in the park: I could manage only a few hundred yards at a brisk pace the next morning before becoming winded. But the hangover had lifted. The nausea was no longer a constant but came and went in waves. Improvement: I would take it.

The lingering effect of the Dorixina, however, was to make me feel as if I had been wakened prematurely from an anesthesic slumber, while the pitiless city whipped by me in a blur.

Martin picked me up and we drove down to the village of Coyoacan, south of downtown, to meet with Alejandro Escalante, a taco scholar who owns a restaurant, La Casa de Los Tacos, not far from the electrically colorful house where Diego Rivera and Frida Kahlo lived.

Before I arrived in Mexico City, I had thought that the taco was roughly equivalent there to the burger in a city like New York. Both street foods, both highly democratic in their appeal.

But the taco penetrates life in Mexico City in a way the burger, for all its popularity, never has or will. I saw tacos at the large, centralized markets and tacos at the temporary markets, called tiangis, tacos at street stands, tacos at corner stands, and tacos on bikes—sold by kids pedaling through neighborhoods. I saw tacos at every rung of the gastronomic ladder, with chefs taking the humble snack to new levels of refinement. I ate tacos for breakfast and lunch and dinner. I ate tacos between meals, on the way to more tacos. I ate rolled tacos and fried tacos. I ate flat tacos, called *tlacoyos*, and folded tacos. I ate tacos *sudados*, sweaty tacos, tacos stored in covered woven baskets and allowed to steam.

It hardly seemed possible, but every taco I had tasted so far had been better than the last, and at each stop I had been forced to recant my prior declaration that I had found the best taco in the city of tacos. But now, at Escalante's, I came to tacos *pechito*, beef breast tacos, the rich, tallegio-soft meat slipped inside corn tortillas pulled hot off the comal behind us. These were tacos so vivid and intense that it was as if I were eating something other than tacos.

Was this the effect of the Dorixina? To simultaneously slow me down and heighten my senses? Or was this simply what Mexico City did to people, seeped into their system and made them vulnerable to stimuli, overpowered them with sensation?

My appetite was coming back, though how cruel that my nausea should be at high tide when I sat down to lunch at a pillar of contemporary Mexican gastronomy but ebb just in time for me to sample the wide world of insects.

I had eaten grasshoppers before, more than once, but grasshoppers are generally regarded as the gateway critter in the world of pre-Hispanic cuisine, as easy and accessible.

With Escalante looking on, a waitress brought us what her boss described as one of the great delicacies of "pre-Hispanic cuisine"—an oblong dish containing hundreds of tiny corn kernels, called *escamoles*, which had been tossed with onion, garlic, cilantro, and *epazote*, a minty herb used in stews, soups and beans.

Just how pre- were we talking about? I wondered silently.

Plucking one of the mystery kernels between his thumb and forefinger, Escalante said, "These are not just any ant eggs."

"No?"

"No no," he said, and locked eyes with me, making certain I understood the seriousness of what he was saying. These were carefully sourced eggs, he said, the eggs of soldier ants.

I was still in the zone of slowness and heightened clarity.

Ant eggs.

Would-be ants.

Ant babies.

They looked like little pills.

I took them into my mouth. Tender, delicate. Rich. A little nutty.

I made a taco. I took a bite. Another taco that didn't taste like a taco, with flavors for which I had no point of comparison, for which there was no personal precedent.

Of all the insect-eating countries in the world, I learned from Inés when we finally connected, Mexico is at the top, with 504 of what she called "known edible species."

She was proud of this standing, lamenting that food globalization has made beef and chicken king and "displaced" the "wide spectrum of possibilities that insects have to offer."

Possibilities. Inés had come prepared; she was determined to plead her case for their worth and importance and open my mind.

Was I aware that a hundred grams of crickets have more protein than a hundred grams of beef?

My eyes widened.

Did I know that insects are organic? That they are good for the environment? That they are both seasonal and local?

We could have been talking about four-dollar tomatoes at the farmers market.

Her great hope, she said, is that as a new crop of Mexican chefs revives interest in insects as it seeks to reclaim its terroir, in much the same way Southern chefs like Sean Brock and others have with benne seeds and heirloom varieties of pork, it will "bring in others to look into the variety of products in the markets and restore the traditional Mexican diet, which is by far more diverse, healthy, nutritious, and tasty than what supermarkets offer. Just like Louis XVI did with potatoes in France."

She had one last thought for me, one last attempt to sway me and bring me into the fold.

"Just the thought of entomophagy repels some," she said, "but we define what we eat by what we've learned to think about it."

Nick Gilman, who writes the blog Good Food in Mexico City, had urged me to speak with a man named Juan Pablo Ballesteros, owner of a restaurant called Limosneros. On my last night in the city, I went to meet him.

It was raining, a hard drizzle that glazed the streets and rendered the old, colonial-era buildings heavy and forlorn. Benito and my driver waited for me in the car, like movie mobsters.

A tall, strapping guy with tight, curly hair and the impish expression of Georges Perec, Ballesteros is descended from taco-making royalty. More than a hundred years ago, his grandfather opened a restaurant called Cafe Tacuba, in the city's historic center. The place is still standing, a beloved relic of the scene. Limosneros, with its chandeliers, handsome wood tables, and dark mood lighting, doesn't just extend the family line; it attempts to extend the possibilities for the contemporary taqueria.

Ballesteros let me order a few dishes on my own, then began sending out treats. The first dish was tuna tacos garnished with citrus foam. Light, trendy, the sort of thing you can find in the States at most upscale Mexican restaurants and, as it turned out, a sly bit of misdirection, because this was not what Pablo was here to show me. Out came a superior mezcal, served in a thin, carved cup that nestled perfectly in my palms, along with a bowl of ant eggs and a basket of fresh tortillas.

"You eat insects, right?" Ballesteros asked, with only the faintest trace of a question in his voice.

Because he was not asking—he was confirming. Of course I ate insects, right? As a food writer, a professional eater of food, I of course did not presume that I could hope to understand the culinary culture of Mexico City and not eat insects, did I?

He smiled as he watched me spoon the ant caviar onto the tortillas.

The next plate was among the most gorgeous of my trip, vibrantly colored, harmoniously arranged, the sort of intricate culinary artwork that tasting menus exist to display. Even in the low-lit room it was impossible to miss how dazzling an arrangement this was, but I sat forward, now, to get a better look it: four squash-blossom canapes set off dramatically by thick dabs of orange and green sauces and garnished with what appeared to be pieces of fried meat.

"Beetles," said Ballesteros.

He eyed me carefully, gauging my reaction. It was no doubt the readiness with which I had taken to the tiny white eggs that had persuaded him that I was prepared to graduate to the next level.

Ant eggs, at least, resembled tiny corn kernels. There was no mistaking what this was. My first thought was that my beautiful plate of food had been infested by a small army of bugs. My second thought was: *I can't.* Followed immediately by my complicating third thought: *I can't not.* With him standing right there, eager and proud? And call myself a food writer? And not feel like a hypocrite for espousing adventurousness and open-mindedness?

I lifted the nigiri-like pad and tilted it slightly toward a dab of sauce, as if I were about to eat a bite of yellowtail. The bug fell off, and I jumped.

Enough dallying.

I picked up another pad, exhaled a deep breath, and ingested the thing all in one bite.

I immediately sought precedent in my data bank of food memories. None came.

Well, wait, no. A sort of meaty toastiness, like a pecan that had been roasted for forty minutes.

Literally, though, this was a taste of the earth, much more than any plant that has been lifted up through the soil. I was sitting in a trendy restaurant that plates its dishes to resemble works of art, and I was eating a bug that took me back to the roots of the city, before it was a city, before the Spanish arrived to lay waste to it and construct a new culture in its place. The place now was not the place then. Its grid was that of a European city. Its people were of mixed identity, and spoke Spanish. A new culture had evolved. The bugs, though, remained. They hadn't been snuffed out. To eat them was to reach back at least 500 years and taste the earthy essence of that vanished time.

Limosneros had done what most museum curators aimed to do with their exhibits: to present the past in a way that was accessible, modern, and above all interactive. My meal was nothing if not interactive. I did not learn about that past. I ingested that past.

I got up from the table, feeling woozy. No, it wasn't wooziness. I was definitely ill again.

This, too, felt right, even if it felt wrong. I would struggle to digest what I thought I had learned. The hard, intense place was showing me once more that it was harder and more intense than I had reckoned with.

I walked outside. The rain had dissipated to a drizzle. Benito regarded me with a smile I didn't understand, a quizzical smile that mingled deep concern and amusement. Or maybe he was just trying to understand me, something that even after a week in my company had eluded him.

"Come," he said.

Blessed Benito.

He took me by the shoulder with the tender guidance of a nurse and led me toward the waiting car.

"I will take you back," he said.

The other book I brought with me to Mexico City was *Down and Delirious in Mexico City*, by Daniel Hernandez, an exhilarating, sometimes frightening chronicle of a modern metropolis that feels at once familiar and strange.

At his best, Hernandez is as exuberant as Dickens writing about London and as observant as Balzac writing about Paris. His relentless drive, however, owes a debt to Hunter S. Thompson, with whom he also shares a fondness for visceral detail. In the very first paragraph, he takes the car from zero to sixty, and doesn't ease up on the gas for the next 288 pages.

"Life in Mexico City," Hernandez writes, "is a contact sport. It might be scary at first, unforgiving, violent, but to really grasp it, you gotta get in, release all inhibitions, all cultural blinders. You have to get down and play."

I reached out to him when I returned home, and he confessed to worrying that the city's "intensity maybe sometimes ventures toward becoming second-nature. I bet it is for a lot of people who were born and raised and continue living here."

And as for Hernandez?

"I just usually need a little visit to the serenity of the strip malls and highway interchanges of the United States," he wrote, "to remind me that where I live is a beautiful lake of fire and I should be thankful every day that it doesn't eat me up. . . . The daily barrage of wonders and averted disasters transforms you."

Someone's in
the Kitchen

Bo Bech Discovers the Bounty of Virginia

By Jason Tesauro

From *Travel & Leisure*

It's a perfect pairing: Jason Tesauro's day job as sommelier for Virginia's Barboursville Vineyards and his writing gigs as co-author of *The Modern Gentleman* books and website. Given his twin commitments to Virginia *terroir* and the good life, who else could best profile Danish chef Bo Bech's American odyssey?

I t was less than two hours until the premiere dinner of Bo Bech's New York City pop-up series. The Danish chef stood in the kitchen of Cosme, the Flatiron District restaurant helmed by chef Enrique Olvera, who had lent Bo kitchen space in which to prep and serve his eight-course menu. Bo's feet were firmly on the ground, shoulder-width apart. Both his palms were flat on the table and his eyes were closed like a yogi's. He was rolling the movie of the menu, setting the tempo and the physicality of each act, previewing the playlist's texture and flavor so that courses progressed in power throughout the meal.

Earlier that day, six strangers had received a text message—their golden Wonka ticket—inviting them to the first iteration of the guerrilla-style dinners. No one knew until 90 minutes out exactly where, when, or how they would gather. The Virginia-inspired menu was still in flux even as attendees arrived, but the foundation of flavor, sourcing, and soul had been marinating for weeks.

This is the story of how that dinner came to be. It's the story of how a force of nature named Bo Bech whipped through Virginia in the hopes of flooring an often-jaded New York City food scene. It's the story of how a road trip inspired an extraordinary meal, and of how an extraordinary meal marked the New York arrival of one of Denmark's most fascinating chefs.

Before the Trip:

"I kept sensing this itch that I wanted to do something risky," Bo told the *New York Times* in October. The Danish chef, who gained international renown at his Copenhagen restaurant, Geist, had just announced his plan to launch a pop-up dinner project, which he was calling "Bride of the Fox," as a first step toward opening a more permanent NYC outpost. Each meal would be a stand-alone event in a different space with a distinct theme. The locations—and, more notably, the invitees—would remain secret until just 90 minutes before the meal.

This wasn't just marketing. Bo's motivated by what interests him, and what interests him is pushing his own boundaries. His somewhat unique career trajectory is a living graph of this pattern: total immersion followed by success followed by a sharp turn toward something new. He started cooking in his early twenties, after a brief career as a General Motors salesman and a tour with the Danish Royal Guard in the former Yugoslavia. After deciding to try his hand at cooking, Bo's first job in the kitchen was at Krog's Fiskerestaurant in Copenhagen, his hometown, where he worked under culinary wunderkind Frank Lantz. Bo headed abroad next, to train at Le Gavroche and Marco Pierre White's the Restaurant in London, followed by Lucas Carton and l'Arpège in Paris. After returning to Denmark and working under several of the country's top chefs, Bo opened his own place, Restaurant Paustian, for which he obtained a loan by cooking leeks over a camp stove for bank employees. Within four years, he had earned the restaurant a Michelin star.

Rather than use this acclaim to propel himself into bigger culinary waters, Bo's next project was Bo Bech Bageri, a bakery that made just one bread, a naturally leavened organic sourdough. This type of obsessiveness is part of what makes Bo the kind of chef other chefs have a crush on. "He's the opposite of full of shit," said Thomas Carter, restaurateur of Estela in NYC's Nolita, where Bo is a regular when he's in town. "Bo's provocative, but always looking for truth. He's super respectful of the ceremony of food and company and he wants to strip the pretense away very quickly."

I read the *New York Times* piece on October 12. I wanted to be a part of what Bo was doing. By noon on the 13th, I'd hatched a plan and made contact. "I'd love to take you on a road trip to explore Virginia bounty," I wrote. I told him the tour through my home state would include visits with the best chefs, bakers, millers, and winemakers in the area, and that I was sure he'd discover more than just brilliant ingredients for his pop-ups. Four emails and six texts later, he was booked for Richmond.

Day 1: Richmond, Virginia, 6 p.m.

The first time I actually spoke to Bo was when we greeted at the Richmond airport: "Bo f——g Bech!" I said as we embraced outside baggage claim. We hopped in the car, which is where we'd spend much of our time together over the next week, and I began a fast-track immersion course in Bo-speak.

Bo's words, like his flavors, are deliberate and measured, if occasionally mysterious. "I'm rediscovering my language. Challenging my alphabet," he said, explaining the reasoning behind his decision to open a restaurant in New York. The pop-ups would help him get a feel for the city, its geography, rhythm, and diners. Also, it would give him a head start in establishing relationships with the chefs and restaurateurs who could help him source ingredients, talent, and equipment.

Day 2: Sub Rosa Woodfired Bakery, Richmond, 9:30 a.m.

Our first morning together began with coffee and fire. I took Bo to Evrim Dogu, the Turkish baker who founded Sub Rosa Woodfired Bakery in Richmond. Dogu and Bo got granular. They talked about the ritual of bread, the progression of heat, the role of nigella seeds, and the baker's brain. "Equanimous," said Dogu. "To do this work, your mind must be even." We pulled loaves from the oven, thumped on crusts, tore open the gluten matrix, and thrust our noses into warm crumb. Behind the bakery, we fired up the wood and stone mill and ground an heirloom red corn called Bloody Butcher. Radiant morning light washed through the tiny mill room illuminating fine polenta dust like incense smoke in a holy chapel.

Before we left Richmond to explore the countryside, I introduced Bo to artist Ed Trask, Richmond's most important muralist, painter, and street art curator. We toured a formerly blighted power plant that's become a hub for visual art and revitalization. Bo paused over a graffiti collage by pop artist Pose and the piece "Bullseye" by Mark Jenkins, its squash-yellow disk lodging in our minds like the scent of jasmine. Bo is another kind of street artist—see his cooking-outside-the-bank-to-secure-a-loan performance piece—and the pop-up restaurant project he has embarked on has the drive-by feel of improv.

Behind the concrete walls, Trask took us along a semi-secret pipeline that runs over the James River. Swollen and turbulent that day, white water rendered the walkway treacherous. Bo was nervous—it was the most spooked I saw him the entire time we were together. But he pushed onward. "The sound of the water flipping—I kept telling myself, you have two hands, you can hold onto the sides," he said after crossing the slippery pipeline. "If you put one foot in front of the other, it's impossible to get hurt."

Day 3: Barboursville Vineyards, Barboursville, 4 p.m.

We set out for the mountains. At Barboursville Vineyards, a Piedmont-area winery on a historic estate, winemaker Luca Paschina cleaned the deer he'd shot a few days before. Bo and I foraged for oyster mushrooms on fallen logs and picked greens from Paschina's garden in the fading Blue Ridge dusk before sitting down to a dinner of Italian-inspired rabbit and coarse polenta. To venison-leg carpaccio, Bo added walnuts, nasturtium flowers, and more salt than seemed advisable. He used nasturtium leaves like a torn piece of injera to scoop up the meat, nuts, and flowers. Bottles of unctuous Viognier, elegant Nebbiolo, and a long-lived red blend called Octagon were passed around the table.

Day 4: Caromont Farm, Esmont, 12 p.m.

Vegetables have seasons and so does milk. Autumn is a great kidding season, but when a buck is around, the goats go into heat and the milk gets gamier. To adjust, Gail Hobbs-Page of Caromont Farm in Esmont, a tiny town southwest of Charlottesville, makes her fresh chèvre in the early spring. While showing us around her farm, the cheesemaker talked of teat placement and worm resistance the way some parents brag about report cards and piano lessons. "This one," Hobbs-Page said, "is the daughter of my very first goat." We followed a herd into the woods, their hooves schussing through fresh-fallen leaves.

Bo leaned in to marvel: "Eighty-one goats and she knows each one's name." He inhaled and sighed. "This smells like home." Over a bottle of rosé in Hobbs-Page's kitchen, chef and cheesemaker bonded. "Food does something," Bo said. "It triggers you, it's not just a tomato. We do agree on that, don't we?"

Day 4: Autumn Olive Farms, Shenandoah Valley, 3 p.m.

Dragging ourselves from the goats, we realized we were two hours late for lunch with pigs. After arriving at Autumn Olive Farms, we filled our plates in the kitchen and stepped through a door off the dining room. A makeshift plywood ramp carried us into the back of the farm's food truck, which was set with a table fit for Thanksgiving. Clay Trainum, the deacon-like farmer, served his beloved Berkabaw pork chops cut thick as a family Bible. He beamed with adoration at a playful litter of heritage piglets and their 400-pound mother: "We ate her sister for lunch."

Bo followed Trainum into his cellar, where the pork is dry-aged. The chef caressed a side of hog meat ripening to a beefy red, layered and marbled with white fat. "Most people can't afford to eat this way," said Trainum. "We couldn't, so we had to grow it."

Day 4: Foggy Ridge and the Shack, Staunton, 8 p.m.

Further west, near Shenandoah National Park, we ran into Foggy Ridge cider maven Diane Flynt and her husband while checking into Stonewall Jackson Hotel in Staunton, a mountain town of 25,000 with hills like San Francisco. It's far enough inland to be equidistant from the Atlantic coastline and the easternmost edge of Ohio.

We were all four headed to the best restaurant in town, the Shack. The Flynts, who make the finest handcrafted ciders in the U.S., had a reservation and cozied into a table for two the size of a TV tray; we waited an hour, but there was no bar or lounge or extra chairs. Instead, we put ourselves against the back door of the tiny kitchen. I fetched a bottle of Foggy Ridge and some flutes. Bo scoffed. "In the kitchen, we drink from quart containers," he said. The Shack's chef and owner, Ian Boden, grabbed a stack and tossed them over. Bo poured the bottle into the plastic tubs and we toasted.

Bo and I drank cider and admired Boden's tidy mise en place of crosnes, romanesco, and boiled peanuts. At last two seats freed up. Bo told the server: "Feed us as you like."

Day 5: Casselmonte Farm, Powhatan, 1 p.m.

On our last full day in Virginia, we visited a farm with an unusual metric for success. Bill and India Cox don't use yield or shelf life to evaluate their Bradford watermelons or pasilla peppers. They've spent years finessing their soil and plants.

Bo, who was known for the avant-garde vegetarian tasting menu he offered at Restaurant Paustian, was impressed. After a blind flight of Southern sorghums, cane syrup, and three varieties of farm-raised ginger, India served us a lunch of her wild shiitake hot-and-sour soup. Bo said it was the most delicious thing he had eaten all week.

Later, we wound up in the basement gawking at a record-setting stuffed bison that Cox took down with a bow and arrow. At the feet of the bison, Cox and Bo rummaged through a box of Hayman sweet potatoes, an heirloom variety grown on only one other farm in the state. Bo took his time to select two to salt-roast at the pop-up. "I'm very passionate about trying to slow down. There's something sexy about being slow when there's chaos," he said. On the way out, we ogled a massive moose mounted over the hearth. Another bow-and-arrow kill.

Day 6: RIC > LGA, 12 p.m.

Our plan was to road-trip to New York City the next morning, but once word of Bo's presence spread throughout Richmond, our final evening on the town became a Bo Bech bacchanal. Chefs in the city wanted to cook for Bo. By night's end, we'd had three dinners, four group photos, and five rounds of drinks that might as well have been called Why-Not-Skip-the-Drive-and-Just-Fly. Twenty-four hours later, that's just what we did, deplaning at LaGuardia with a suitcase of Virginia bounty that didn't fit in the overhead bin. On that flight, Bo had begun to sketch out a menu and prep list for the first pop-up, which was taking place the next night. Fifteen hundred people had registered for the Bride of the Fox, but Bo's plan was to invite six guests and use the groceries we'd collected. One rule: he couldn't serve any dish he'd ever cooked before.

I get it. Bo hates status quo. "It's about getting ideas out of my head. I don't like having prisoners in my mind. I think wherever you are in the world, pick your disease, but also choose your sun." For Bo, his source of warmth and light is cooking and breaking bread. The diseases are those ills that come with the craft: brutal hours, no free weekends, the physical toll and pressure of launching pop-ups and opening new restaurants.

"How can I find a beautiful spot that I can afford? How can I do a build-out that doesn't sink me so I become Titanic before I even get out onto the ocean? How can I get a crew assembled that's willing to go through the same journey?" He paused. "But it's the right challenge. It's a proper challenge."

Day 7: Cosme, NYC, 3 p.m.

The curtain was set to go up at Cosme in the Flatiron District at 6 p.m. on Monday, November 16. "He called me three days before," said Enrique Olvera, the restaurant's chef and owner, of Bo's request to host the dinner there. "Bo-style, everything at last minute. I like his way of thinking and doing things. His cooking looks like it's simple but it's not, and I feel pretty identified with that."

Yana Volfson, Cosme's beverage director, shed a little more light. "Bo and Enrique are on the same frequency," she said. "They change dishes on the fly and they always look like they're dancing. They lead with the confidence of experience versus the confidence of knowledge."

Of course, Bo's not fearless. He had blanched above the swirling white waters of the James River before stepping onto the thin metal walkway. But he didn't turn away: he gripped the railing, put one foot in front of the other, and walked. "Entering the arena," he calls it.

He enters the arena.

4:25 p.m.: Bo hands me his phone. "It's time to tell the guests."

4:52 p.m.: Bo slices walnuts and plans seating. He decides to put us on the pass—the table in the middle of the kitchen where the finished plates are set out. We'd be sitting a foot away from the dishwashing station.

5:16 p.m.: Wines are on the ice, sauces on the stove.

5:19 p.m.: Bo selects the plates and flatware. "No tablecloth," he says. He's in the same uniform of black pants and two-tone Nike Zoom Elite B sneakers he'd worn all week.

5:21 p.m.: "When you have time," he says, holding out his knife to Cosme sous chef Sarah Thompson, "can you please sharpen?"

5:27 p.m.: Menu is typed up.

5:31 p.m.: Bo pulls out the raw fish, makes three precise cuts, rinses his knife, and puts the fish away.

5:33 p.m.: He responds to some text messages and fills a pot with water.

5:39 p.m.: "Go upstairs," he tells me. "Walk out of the restaurant and then walk back in anew. From now on, you are my guest."

6:00 p.m.: The Bride of the Fox begins. Bo Bech is ready for the dance.

The kitchen hummed with action, a wild cadre of stainless steel and white jackets. Cosme chefs Mariana Villegas, Daniela Soto-Innes, and Sarah Thompson were all on the line, and the restaurant's 140 seats turned over and over while we six sat on the pass in the middle of the kitchen. Printers whirred around us, spitting out orders until tickets filled the window.

Within each course, I glimpsed a moment of genesis. The sea bass with barbecue sauce would have seemed a preposterous combination had Bo and I not sucked down smoky-sweet chipotle oysters at Merroir on the banks of the Rappahannock River. The pumpkin, a bright Pantone 138-C cut in perfect circles, hit the bull's-eye and harkened to the vivid street art we saw in Richmond. The second course took me back to Bo nosing through Caromont's woods, and how he thought mushrooms would pair splendidly with the fecund chèvre. The grains we milled with a Turkish comrade; the wines were bottled on land where we had foraged, cooked, and communed with the winemaker. Even the very idea of eating on the pass recalled our time at the Shack with the chefs, when we drank cider close enough to the fryer to speckle our sleeves with hot oil.

Afterward, over mezcal in Cosme's dining room, Bo reflected. "For a whole week, I listened and tasted. Tonight, I'm an immigrant interpreting what he saw in America, in a state, in a small town, on a farm. No artsy-fartsiness, nothing weird, nothing technical. A nice piece of pork with a kiwi and a coffee sauce. Simple. Complicated simple."

Bo held a second pop-up a week later at Harry & Ida's Meat Supply Co., an East Village provisions store and Jewish-style delicatessen that is at once nostalgic and innovative. The theme of the night was "Fire and Smoke." Bo cooked the entire meal using only the grill, serving grilled smoked eel and grilled pigeon that had been aged for 30 days and glazed with carrot juice, mustard seeds, and smoked maple syrup. The next dinner is scheduled for December 11—Bo has hinted that it might take place in a private apartment. Meanwhile, the success of the first two pop-up dinners has cemented Bo's commitment to putting down roots in NYC: he has moved out of a hotel and into his own place, and is scouting spaces for his new restaurant.

Back at Cosme that night after the first dinner, I looked around the dining room. It was getting late, but all but one of the pop-up guests were still in the restaurant. No one could bear to break the spell.

Two pop-uppers sidled up to Bo's table as he offered a toast. "If we're not afraid, not so blocked, six people who don't know one another, they can have a night where a server is fooled into thinking we are old friends," Bo said, looking everyone in the eye. "How beautiful is that?"

Smoke Signals

By Julia Kramer

From *Bon Appétit*

Bon Appétit senior editor Julia Kramer may be a city girl who grew up in Chicago and now lives in New York City, but she can spot an authentic food artisan when she sees one. Hence her journey to the North Carolina countryside, where baker/pizzamaker Tara Jensen is the real deal.

Tara Jensen hosts a monthly pizza night, and every time she's sure that no one will come, and every time, nearly 100 people show up, finding their way to the town of Marshall, North Carolina, then heading six miles northwest on Route 70 along the French Broad River, winding around the knoll called Walnut, and stopping at the dirt driveway leading to her compound, which consists of an algae-covered pond, a shack in the woods, a brick oven, and two pitched-roof houses, one of which is a bakery that goes by the name of Smoke Signals. People out here are getting by on their passions—but just barely. There are still women in this area who make lace and sing ballads. Fiddle players, weavers, herbalists.

Some of the people who arrive for pizza night live nearby and just walk over the hill to Jensen's house. Many come from Asheville, 16 miles south. Others drive three or four hours from Georgia or Tennessee. They're here for the pizza, blackened from the wood-fired oven, misshapen from the slow fermentation of the dough. They're also here for the sense of community: people sprawled on picnic blankets around an outdoor hearth, drinking six-packs and watching the sun go down. But mostly they're here for Jensen, a 33-year-old guru for an era in which naturally leavened bread has become something of a religion. To aspiring bakers and established chefs and food geeks and fawning journalists, she represents an elusive ideal: the young breadmaker who structures her life around the rhythms of a wood-burning oven, not the demands of a high-volume production facility. At a moment when "artisanal" has gone the way of cliché, Jensen actually embodies it. Her dedication shows in each bread and pie, which she patterns with intricate handmade stencils and cutout shapes.

Unlike at most other bakeries, gallery-worthy sweets are not Jensen's goal; they're the medium. Her aspirations are deeper and, well, a little more abstract. The bakery is a way for her to grow as a person. To share stories. To connect. Through breadmaking, she believes, people can learn to trust their intuition, to accept themselves for who they are. Baking is not the essential truth about Jensen. She's just here, having an experience.

Jensen wakes up at 5:30 a.m., when the November sky is still black. She makes her way to the kitchen, puts on a kettle for coffee, and reads her horoscopes for the day. Then she replies to the e-mails that have come in during the night. These are her office hours, her primary way of talking with people. Strangers seeking her advice. Amateur bakers who want to make pies with her. Fans who think that Smoke Signals is a regular bakery, with regular hours, where you can drop by and pick up a loaf of sourdough to take home for dinner. Being present in your life is the topic of most of her replies. People build up this mystique around making bread at home, and Jensen gives them a starting point. People are scared to make pie crust, and Jensen tells them to just do it. Don't be stuck in your mind. She needs to hear that too.

Jensen finishes her e-mails and posts a photo, as she does every morning, to the 90,000 people who follow her Instagram account, @bakerhands. This one is of a table of pies from a recent baking workshop that she led. She knows that a lot of what's on Instagram is painstakingly curated, but it's her nature to use it with sincerity—to use it to connect. Some people show a product removed from its context; she wants to show the handprint of the person who made it. On the Internet, she tries to be exactly who she is, and who she is is vulnerable. Several months ago she went through a bad breakup, and since then, there's been a lot about heartbreak on her feed. A tree changing color: What is love if not a beautiful waste of time well spent? A buttermilk dessert: To make this cake. Fall in love. Let it destroy you. Go in to find your strength. Surrender. Prepare to love again.

But sometimes she has to wonder at the phenomenon of Instagram. Really, what is this? She can post about an upcoming bread workshop and it will sell out that day. She's part of this world, even though she's out here in the mountains. It's how the producer of a documentary called The Grain Divide found her, and then he brought bread god Chad Robertson from San Francisco's Tartine Bakery out to visit. Holy s**t!

As Jensen gained a following, there have been people who have tried to capitalize on her visibility. She's received offers to write a cookbook, but none of them felt right. She wants her book to contain stuff about, like, the moon. About astrology and poetry. And people said, Okay, that's great, but do you have any recipes?

Earlier this week, a restaurateur invited Jensen to see a space in Asheville. That's not the kind of growth she's interested in. She doesn't want to have a retail bakery, with a German-made steam-injection deck oven and perfect white subway tile. She loves her oven—even though it doesn't lock in as much steam, and so her loaves come out looking all matte and rustic. She wants to have a small farm, where she can grow the vegetables for her pizza nights. She wants to have a school, where bakers of all levels can come together.

That's why she's focusing on her workshops, all-day sessions that she holds every other weekend. Each has four to six slots, and they always sell out. The workshops are modeled on her daily practice, which means they include baking and art. Pies in the morning, stamping gift wrap in the afternoon. Forming bread dough, then carving stencils and making patterns with flour. She shares her principles: Observe the process closely. Walk away when something isn't working. Don't become attached to the outcome. This weekend, there are people coming from Alabama, Colorado, South Carolina, and New York. A typical mix.

She started Smoke Signals nearly four years ago with $500. She pays all her bills, but she also runs everything on a shoestring and lives humbly. She doesn't want a closet full of shoes. She's willing to make sacrifices so that the business can live.

Today is Tuesday: the start of the baking cycle. Jensen walks down the cobblestone path from the side door of her house to the building next door, which is her bakery. It's a single, plain room—low ceilings, fluorescent lighting—most of which is taken up by two stainless-steel workstations. Before the owner of the property, Jennifer Lapidus, turned this space into a bakery, it used to be a living room. A temperamental walk-in refrigerator divides the kitchen workspace from the front nook that Jensen calls her studio, where she keeps her journals, her art supplies, and her radio.

She turns on NPR; it makes her feel more connected to the outside world. She dips her fingertips into a bowl of water, gauging its temperature, then combines it with flour—a mix from two local mills—and the starter. She squishes it all together until it forms a wet, lumpy blob of bread dough, then divides it among three bins: one for her base sourdough, one for sunflower loaves, and a third for pepper-and-herb. Over that final bin, she pours a stream of olive oil, then dusts the surface with black pepper and the leaves of oregano, thyme, and sage from her garden. She folds the dough into and over itself, incorporating the herbs until they're just faint specks. The dough is stiff and dense and gets stuck under her fingernails. Jensen measured the flour, water, and starter on a scale, but everything else, she eyeballs. She can only follow the rules to a certain extent.

Jensen has been baking since she was a kid, spending her days with her mom in the kitchen of a house at the end of a dirt road in rural Maine. As a teen, she dreamed of going to art school in New York. She ended up taking classes in feminist theory closer to home at the College of the Atlantic instead, where she developed as an artist, exhibiting Yoko Ono–inspired installations. One day during college, she walked into a bakery in Bar Harbor called Morning Glory, and there were all these punk-rock women wearing black, listening to Patti Smith and mixing dough for scones—whatever she had to do to get into that, she would do it.

She fell into a group of anarchists and moved with them to Montpelier, Vermont, to open a bookstore, where she gave lectures on gender and capitalism. To pay her bills, she started working at Red Hen Baking Co. in nearby Middlesex. That was back in 2003, when people would still bring their CD binders into work. They would bake to dance music on Friday nights. She liked making baguettes, but mostly she was drawn to the sense of family among the bakers. She could connect with people by talking about food.

At some point Jensen started to grow apart from the anarcho-feminist cohort, and she became disillusioned with the art world. At her shows, the conversations weren't really about what was on the walls. But in baking, there was something real. When you put a piece of bread in someone's mouth, they have this visceral reaction beyond their control.

She bounced around for a couple years before moving to Asheville and landing her next baking job, at Farm and Sparrow, which occupied the space that is now Smoke Signals. She worked there for three and a half years, learning how to laminate croissant dough, use buckwheat flour in cookies, roll tart crusts. In 2009, Farm and Sparrow moved out; three years later, Jensen decided to lease the space. She moved into the little house and turned the bakery into Smoke Signals. Whenever she enters a new stage of her life, she starts a blank journal. Writing down her goals makes her accountable to them. On one page of the journal that she started in the early days of Smoke Signals, she wrote: Long-term goal: Use my business for social justice, community organizing, and individual empowerment.

Jensen began baking bread and pies in the property's wood-fired oven and selling them at the Asheville City Market every week. She became known for her bread: the intensely nutty flavor from the fresh Carolina Ground flour; the sticky-moist yet featherlight interior; the thick, substantial crust that shatters as you bite into it. But after a year and a half, she knew in her gut that she didn't want to dedicate her life to increasing production. She had more to offer than commodified products. She wanted to teach. She wanted to host pizza nights. She wanted to use bread as a vehicle—not an end in itself.

Back in the kitchen, Jensen prepares her baskets, lining each with a pale gray cloth to keep the wet dough from seeping out. The three mounds of dough are no longer so tense and firm. After sitting in the cool room for four hours, they've slowly inflated with air bubbles, creeping up the sides of the bins and doming at the top. Jensen dusts the cloths with cornmeal and flour. She divides each blob of dough into smaller blobs, folds and pats and rolls and squeezes each one until it looks like a giant empanada, then sets it in a basket, where it will rest overnight. She reaches for the next blob, folds in one side, then the next, pats it into a cylinder, rolls it up, pinches the edges, transfers it to a basket. Then the next. Over and over. Forty-eight times more. Every week the bread will be different, because the weather's different, or her mood is different. When people come to bake with Jensen for the day, they glimpse her lifestyle. But to really learn? That's in their hands. It's about repetition.

By the time the loaves bake the next day, the oven will be on a slow descent from its peak temperature of 800 degrees, and the heat trapped inside the bricks will shape the shaggy lumps into crackly, crusted loaves. Fifty total. This will be her production for the week. She'll tuck each still-warm loaf into a hand-stamped bag, pack them into the back of her Subaru, and drive around Madison County, delivering them to an outdoor-gear outfitter in Hot Springs and two stores in Marshall. When she arrives at each stop, there won't be Cronut-esque lines awaiting her loaves. There will just be a couple feet of empty shelf space among dream catchers or Clif Bars or packs of gum, where she'll set down a dozen or so of the brown-paper bags. She's not interested in selling her bread anywhere else. She lives here. She's part of a history of people who have made bread in this oven, on this knoll, in this town.

Around midday, Jensen covers the bread dough, puts on another kettle, and starts the fire. First with shards of slab wood—by-products from a local sawmill—which she busts up into kindling, snapping the six-foot lengths across her knee. She arranges the wood in the center of the oven, which was built in 1998 by Alan Scott, the Australian blacksmith who became a legend in the world of wood-fired bread and pizza. Scott saw brick ovens as a way of bringing neighbors in rural areas together—building the ovens was like a barn-raising. He constructed this one for Lapidus, the owner of the Smoke Signals property, who had the idea to convert one of the houses into a bakery. Jensen thinks of herself more as a steward of the oven than the controller of it.

She lights a crumpled piece of newsprint tucked among the wood, and the kindling takes hold. She listens to the sticks pop as the flame catches. The fire should roll from the floor of the oven, along the walls, then back in on itself. The clean walls should turn black, and then burn themselves clean again. The oven is very much a living thing. The flames wrap under and around the logs as the wood breaks down into glowing orange-red embers. The chimney sputters until the oven reaches 250 degrees, and then there is no more smoke, just a different texture in the air above the oven: wavy and pulsating. By the time Jensen wakes up, the oven will be nearly 800 degrees and just a bed of coals will be left. She likes these evenings, when the fire burns and the dough rests. She sleeps differently then.

With the oven temperature climbing, Jensen goes back inside the bakery to make pie. In a small tabletop mill, two granite stones crush a few handfuls of soft winter wheat berries. She runs her fingers through the golden flour. Its flavor is just different. More present. The body recognizes this as food. Jensen separates out some of the larger pieces through a tiny sifter, tap-tap-tapping it against her palm like a tambourine as the fine powder drifts into the bowl below. She cubes the butter and smears each tiny square between her fingers as she adds it to the flour. It's her way of keeping it alive.

Jensen has no interest in the myth of the tortured creative person. The lone genius. The baker who's going mad. That does a disservice to the hard work that creativity requires. In a craft as ancient and elemental as breadmaking, there are only going to be so many innovations. The stencils that she uses to decorate her breads and pies? They've been around for ages; you had to be able to identify your bread in a communal oven. Freshly milled grains? Not a new idea. When people make pie designs that look like hers? Oh, she thinks that's nice. That just means they're interested in being creative too. They'll find their own voices one day.

After the pie dough has rested, Jensen cuts it in half, revealing a million tiny sheets of butter layered into the amber mass. With a thin rolling pin, she coaxes it into a smooth, sprawling circle, pressing down on it with the full weight of her body—yellow tank and Levi's, brown bangs that graze her eyelids, arms tattooed in graphic symbols, each of which marks some kind of overcoming.

She cores and slices Granny Smiths and Jonagolds and Pink Ladies from a nearby farm, squeezes the juice of a few lemons over the apples, and shakes in some ground ginger, cinnamon, nutmeg, sugar, and vanilla extract—none of which she measures. She inverts pie tins onto the thin sheet of dough and traces imperfect circles around them. The dough lifts easily off the surface, and Jensen tucks it into each dish, trimming the edges with kitchen shears. With both hands, she scoops up the apples, piling them high in the dough-lined tins. She tops each mound of apples with another round of dough, crimps and folds and pinches it into place, and brushes it with a wash of beaten eggs and cream.

She gathers up the scraps of pie dough, scrunches them together, and then rolls them out into a level canvas on the steel work surface. Without pausing to plan or sketch, she begins rolling a pizza cutter through the dough, drawing lines and arcs that soon become shapes: simple and elliptic like bay leaves, another that looks like feathers, or maybe a sea creature. With a fork, she gives each shape its own texture: pressing the tines one way and then the next to crosshatch, using the base of the fork to create indentations, drawing the prongs along the dough in a swirl, making dots with the tips. One after the next. Each one the same, each one totally different. Tomorrow she'll sell the three pies to the Laurel River Store in Marshall for $15 each. It's not a profit-making venture; it's part of her practice. She's bringing something to an area that doesn't have it. She's the town baker.

When the pies are baked, she posts again to Instagram. Then, as she does most nights, she walks across the street to her neighbor's, a woman in her 50s who fosters dogs, and they watch the sun go down from the porch. Before Jensen goes to sleep, she sets her alarm to check on the fire—once at midnight, then 2 a.m.—even though she knows she'll wake up a few minutes before it buzzes each time. She'll walk out to the oven in the moonlight in her pajamas, add a log or two to the fire, and make her way back to bed.

That's it for today. Tomorrow Jensen will wake up at 5:30 a.m., put on a kettle, return her e-mails, and walk over to the bakery. She'll check on the baskets of dough in the walk-in, then step outside to look at the fire. The oven will read 782 degrees, as it should. She'll rake out the coals, mop the inside clean, and replace the oven door. Then she'll wait.

Why Serious Bakers Have Mother Issues

BY ANDREA STRONG

From SeriousEats.com

Writer/blogger Andrea Strong (*The Strong Buzz*) found her vivid voice as a food writer after careers in law and restaurant management. In her refreshingly colloquial style, she gets top bread bakers across the country to answer the yeasty question: Who's your mother?

They came from all over Europe—a village in Poland, a farm in Tuscany, a town in Bordeaux. They were carried across the continent, and trekked from the Old Country to the New World. There were arrests and clashes with the police. But through a combination of luck and love, they arrived in New York City where they now work quietly, often in the small hours of the morning. Not many people have even seen them; just a modest, elite group of artisans truly know them intimately. The bakers know their mothers, and these are their stories.

But, wait, perhaps I should clarify. These aren't their actual mothers, as in the women who gave birth to them, who raised them, who are now, undoubtedly, the subject of therapy for one 45-minute hour per week. No, no. These are their "mothers"—also known as *madre*, seed, chef, and *levain*. Natural yeasts starters destined for some of the world's best sourdough breads, typically born of a combination of apples, grapes, and honey, left to ferment on a warm windowsill and grow a frosting of wild yeast and *Lactobacillus* bacteria. Yup, *those* mothers.

Mind you, starters do share qualities often associated with matri-archs (. . . and pets)—they often inspire love-hate relationships marked by serious dependency. Unlike commercial yeast, which requires little more than sugar and warm water to activate, mothers are needy. They demand regular feedings of flour and water in order to produce the or-ganic acids, alcohols, and carbon dioxide necessary to make bread do that cool thing it does: rise. Bread made from wild ferments don't just give them that characteristic tangy sourdough flavor—they also im-prove the bread's texture, nutritional value, and shelf life.

This rigorous regimen of constant attention can become difficult for anyone who might want to have a life outside the confines of the bakery. (*You don't call! You don't visit!*) Chad Robertson, the breadmaker at Tar-tine Bakery in San Francisco and a leader of the wild-fermentation movement, used to bring his starter to the movies with him so that he could feed it on time. And who can forget the monolithic mother from Anthony Bourdain's memoir *Kitchen Confidential*, which Adam the baker was tasked with feeding. "The bitch," described Bourdain, was "a massive, foaming, barely contained heap of fermenting grapes, flour, water, sugar and yeast." A mommy monster!

To be sure, there are easier, less taxing ways to get a rise out of flour and water than coaxing mold out of rotting fruit. There's that convenient little envelope filled with commercial yeast. But given the Brooklyn-to-Portland rise in artisanal, DIY everything, the wildly-fermented mother has become the darling of the craft bread movement. Indie bak-ers would rather starve than bake predictable, personality-less loaves made from commercial yeast. Instead, they're playing wet-nurse to wild yeasts, obsessively feeding their goopy, gloppy slurries with their eye on the prize: Heartbreakingly beautiful breads with unparalleled flavor, shattering crusts, and a cavernous crumb.

The other rather priceless quality mothers share is that, like wine, natural yeast starters also have terroir—while all mothers include the same strain of bacteria, they pick up their personalities from a region's yeast, flour, air, and water. All of those magical microbes get infused into the starter, like a strand of DNA that gives every mother a unique fingerprint—hence why you'll find sourdoughs labeled by provenance, from the iconic San Francisco starter to their East Coast and European brethren.

In fact, if you stick your nose inside a jar filled with starter, it's like you're inside a wine cave. Your head is dizzy with the musty, sour sweetness of fermenting grapes. "It's those acids and alcohols that contribute to the bread's flavor, texture, and keeping quality," explained Scott Kendall, head baker at Le Pain Quotidien's Fashion Island Bakery in Newport Beach, CA. "Even if the recipe is the same, regional changes will affect the yeast and beneficial bacteria strains grown in the levain. A sourdough made in Southern California will have subtle variations in texture and flavor to those made in New York, London, Paris, and around the world."

With proper love and attention, mothers can live a long, long time, and they often have mythic, legendary histories. The story goes that when a woman was getting married, her mother would send her off with a piece of her dough. This way, her daughter would not have to wait two weeks to create a new starter of her own, she'd be able to bake the next morning (right to work, missy!). The other advantage, of course, is that the mother becomes a kind of family heirloom, passed from generation to generation, a lifeline in every loaf. All of which goes a long way to explaining why some of the best bread you're eating right now was born from a mother with a history all her own.

Kamel Saci, the head baker at New York City's il Buco Alimentari, made his mother nearly twenty years ago when he was a teenager living at home in Bordeaux. A Mixed Martial Arts fighter, Saci was injured in a judo match at the age of 19 and tore his ACL. While recovering from surgery, he took a job at a bakery. "I walked in with no experience and they taught me how to bake, and how to start a mother, and I fell in love."

Saci made his mother from a combination of honey, apples, and grapes left out in the warm kitchen until a bloom of mold developed. He and his mother have been together ever since, traveling the world. From its birth in Bordeaux, his mother accompanied him to Paris, where he worked with master baker Eric Kayser, to London, where he was head baker at Aubaine and worked for Joel Robuchon and Pierre Gagnaire. Then it was on to Barcelona where he opened Baluard's, then to Miami at Le Rendez-Vous, and finally in 2011, to New York City, to open Alimentari where he bakes 500 loaves a day—Ciabatta, Filone, Focaccia, Figs and hazelnuts, Country, and Buckwheat sourdough— and many more.

Not that these journeys have always been seamless. Saci has been detained twice by airport police—once in New York and once in Mexico City—and questioned about the mysterious liquid he had frozen in a container in his carry on. But he and his mother were freed without incident. "I said, I am a baker, this is my mother, and it was okay. They let me keep it. I was glad because I would have been very sad to lose my mother," he said.

Not surprisingly, Saci takes very good care of his mother. On Mondays, he feeds her a mixture of flour and room temperature filtered water. 12 to 16 hours later, often sometime between midnight and 2 a.m., he returns. The question of sleep is a good one; Saci says he usually catches a few winks around 9pm, before waking to make the dough: mixing the mother with additional flour and water, which activates for one hour. Then comes the salt, and more resting, this time for about two to three hours. Then an hour in a proofing bowl, after which it's shaped and left in the cooler for 24 to 48 hours before it's baked and makes it onto your plate, where chances are it will disappear within a minute or two.

Though Saci has cared for his mother since he was a teen, he isn't stingy with it. He shares it freely. "It's something I made, it comes from my experience, and I like to share a part of me," he said. When Justin Smilie, the acclaimed former chef of Alimentari, left to open his own restaurant, Upland, Saci handed him a jar; a piece of his mother tucked inside. "I gave it to Justin to make pizza," he said. "I taught him how to take care of it. And when I was there and I had his pizza, and it was so good, I thought, they are taking good care of my mother."

Other bakers also share their mothers. In the late 1980s, Eli Zabar, the owner of Upper East Side institutions such as Eli's, EAT, and The Vinegar Factory, was on a quest to find a good Jewish cornbread: a super dense grainy rye, which actually has no corn flour in it, but has cornmeal dusted on its bottom to prevent it from sticking to the bread peel. "I was looking for a cornbread roughly the weight of a bowling ball," Zabar said, in all seriousness. "I dreamed of slicing it thin and eating with the fresh unsalted butter." (Are you getting a Larry David visual here, because I am.)

Anyway, through word of mouth, Zabar learned of a bakery in Tarrytown making Jewish cornbread and decided to pay a visit. There he met a Mr. Schwartz. "He was in his 80s, working with his son, and he was in fact making the most delicious cornbread I've ever had in these big wood-fired ovens," recalled Zabar, who continued to travel up to the bakery to get to know Schwartz and, obviously, to buy more bread. One day, Schwartz handed him a bucket. It was filled with a shimmering blob: a piece of his mother, the one his family originally brought over from Poland before World War II. Nearly every slice of bread you eat at Eli's today is made from Schwartz's starter, still going, still giving life to bread. "Ten years ago, I was in one of my stores and Schwartz's son came in to say hello," said Zabar. "His father had passed, but I thought, in some ways, he lives on in our bread."

Jim Lahey, the award-winning baker behind Sullivan Street Bakery, says he'll give a piece of his mother to anyone who asks. "I probably shouldn't say that, because I'll have a line at the bakery for mothers to-morrow," he added, with a laugh, "but I'm happy to share it."

Lahey made his mother at a turning point in his life, while travel-ing through Europe in the early '90s. "I was a young kid, I had been kicked out of art school, and I was trying to learn to bake," he recalled. "I wanted to find something that spoke to me, something that I felt comfortable doing, something that gave me a form of pleasure. That, I found, is the making of the bread."

Living on a farm in Tuscany, he lifted the bloom off a black kale leaf and made his mother. "I knew you could lift a must from grapes and fruit, and I thought I'll try to lift it from the leaves of some black kale, and feed it flour and water." And so his unique mother was born. He brought it back to New York City and started baking with it, using it to launch his now renowned Sullivan Street Bakery.

Nearly 30 years later, Lahey's mother is still working, being fed a very strict diet of flour and water, with trace quantities of salt. "My mother lives in a retirement home for old sourdoughs in Pensacola," said Lahey, chuckling to himself. (Baker humor, gotta love it.) In reality, his mother is not playing Mahjong, but is living in a production kitchen on West 47th Street, where it's fed at 4 a.m. daily and left out to ripen and make bread. "We rot it, portion it, form it, design it, mold it, proof it, and then bake it," said Lahey by way of explanation. "It's not easy. Fermentation is a moving target. It's like life. You have to know when to fold it, know when to hold it, know when to walk away. (Yes, you can sing that last sentence.) That's the practice of bread."

Jean Paul Bourgeois, the chef at Blue Smoke in New York City, uses a mother that was a gift, but whose origins he cannot divulge. "My mother was given to me by a chef friend," he said. "But he asked that I never tell anyone where he got it from. All I can say is that it comes from one of the best bread bakers in the world," he told me, in a hushed, James Bond, "if I tell you I will have to kill you" tone.

Whatever its origin, Bourgeois is very fond of his mother. "The mother does two essential things to my waffles—its sour fermentation gives the waffles a unique savory tang, and the natural rise makes the waffles fluffy and delicate, airy and crispy." But Bourgeois says his mother gives the waffle something more. "When you use a mother, you are telling that story of something handed down from generation to generation," he said. "I feed my mother White Lilly flour, so I have changed it, and made it my own. As your mother is passed down, the story may change depending on the baker. But it's that story we continue to tell in every waffle we make." Which brings us back to the true nature of the mother: she doesn't make you who you are, but she sure helps you find your way.

Cooks Are Different

By Michael Ruhlman

From *Tin House*

The line between writer and chef is porous with Michael
Ruhlman, whose culinary school days led to his 1997 book *The
Making of a Chef.* Gastronomic stars such as Thomas Keller, Eric
Ripert, and Michael Symon have since enlisted his wordsmith
gifts. For the literary journal *Tin House*, he spills the truth about
his adopted tribe.

Not to brag, but I think I may have written one of the most stolen cookbooks in America. The first hint came a few years ago,
when I read the following on Twitter: "My copy of @ruhlman's #salumi
was stolen. #heartbroken."

The writer attached a photograph of the passenger side of his car,
shattered glass covering the seat.

Someone had not simply stolen my book, but had caused consider-
ably more damage than the book was worth in doing so. What would
have been petty theft became a second-degree burglary. For a book?
I found this curious enough that I asked chefs if they had ever lost a
copy of *Salumi*, or of its precursor, *Charcuterie*, to theft. Every one I approached said yes. Four of the chefs I asked have had thirteen copies
stolen between them. (Another responds to the unspoken rules of the
kitchen by taking her book to and from work with her.) All of which
would explain why a ten-year-old book containing recipes that take
days and even months to follow—some of which can kill you if you do

them wrong—remains such a steady seller. The same people have to keep buying them.

Salumi's theft from restaurants rather than home kitchens makes some sense. Professionals love its unabashed embrace of fat and salt and complicated preservation methods, plus the perfect recipes of my collaborator, chef Brian Polcyn. But it's a $35 hardcover, and young cooks, who earn a subsistence wage, are at once the people who would benefit most from it and who are least able to afford it. So it gets stolen. A lot.

I grew so proud of this dubious distinction that I bragged about it to *New York Times* reporter Alex Witchel, who regarded my claim skeptically. Later, however, she told me that she asked a chef if he owned *Charcuterie* or *Salumi* and had either ever been stolen?

Yes it had, he told her. Twice.

That a single book in our ocean of cookbooks may be more pilfered than any other makes it unique, but its theft from restaurant kitchens does not. There may be more general thievery in the restaurant industry than in any other.

The restaurant is more vulnerable to theft than most other retail businesses. It requires a large number of low-wage workers to make it run profitably, and all manner of food, alcohol, silverware, and tools must be accessible to these employees, not to mention to diners. But I think, also, that there might be something in the nature of restaurant kitchens and the people who work in them that encourages theft. While I'm sure servers steal, the stories I hear are almost always of cooks stealing, which leads me to consider a most intriguing possibility: that there is something built into the job of professional cooking itself that generates the desire to steal.

This idea occurred to me after rereading a book called *But Beautiful: A Book About Jazz*, by Geoff Dyer. In it Dyer notes the high incidence of drug abuse by and early deaths of great jazz artists—Chet Baker, Charlie Parker, Billie Holiday, Lester Young, Coleman Hawkins, a list that goes on and on. Even some of those jazzmen who made it into their sixties and seventies (Ray Charles, for example) ultimately succumbed to alcohol-related organ failure. Dyer suggests not that high-risk personalities are drawn to jazz, but rather that there is something dangerous inherent in the form itself, some unseeable power that wreaks havoc on those who play it. The same might be said of early rock and roll, even beyond the "27 club" (Hendrix, Morrison, Joplin), or, more specifically, of rock-and-roll drumming, which is satirized by the exploding drummers in *This Is Spinal Tap*.

It was M. F. K. Fisher who made a similar observation about cooks, noting "the grim picture drawn by statistics which show that in many great prisons there are more cooks than there are representatives of any other one profession.

"Most cooks, it would seem," she goes on, "are misunderstood wretches, ill-housed, dyspeptic, with aching broken arches. They turn more eagerly to the bottle, the needle, and more vicious pleasures; they grow irritable; finally they seize upon the nearest weapon, which if they are worth their salt is a long knife kept sharp as lightning . . . and they are in San Quentin."

Cooks certainly are a singular breed. Most would have you believe they are artists, not criminals. Passion, heart, love. Chefs will say these are what they cook with and the qualities they want in a cook. "Show me a young cook with passion and I can teach him the rest," most chefs will tell you. They will fall over themselves explaining how they *cook from the heart*, how they *cook with love*.

This, of course, is bullshit. Professional cooking is a kind of addiction available only to a select kind of human, typically a manic youth with ADD who is willing to follow eight hours of monotonous, stand-in-one-place prep work with six hours of action that's not unlike playing a soccer match while juggling knives, hot steel, and scalding oil.

I learned to cook at the Culinary Institute of America in Hyde Park, New York, and it wasn't out of love; it was out of anger. I'd talked my way into the CIA to write a book about learning to become a chef. The process of persuasion had taken more than six months (eating up half the book advance) before the administration agreed to let me in. I had to rent our house in Cleveland and move my family to New York's Hudson Valley before the CIA acknowledged I wasn't going away. Still, it took months of daily phone calls before I got into my first kitchen.

But I did.

Once, on the day of an important test, a blizzard hit the Hudson Valley. I called my chef, Chef Pardus, and told him I couldn't make it out of the driveway, let alone twenty-five miles south to the school. He said, "Fine." I said, "I'd get there if I could but I can't."

He said, "Fine."

Frustrated, I said, "You've got to believe me, Chef, if I could get there I would."

He said, "That's fine, Michael. You have your work, we have ours. We're chefs. We get there. We like it like that."

The motherfucker.

I drove twenty-five miles through a blizzard to make a béchamel sauce. I was a writer, but goddamn him, I would be a cook. And a cook I became.

I discovered that anger is valuable. It's what gets you through a service—the work is just too hard, the pace too fast, to rely on anything so squishy and elusive as *love* or *heart*. And once you are through it, if you didn't get your ass handed to you but rather sent out plate after plate of perfect food until that ticket machine's incessant chatter ceased, the adrenaline and testosterone will make you want to head-butt your fellow cooks in jubilation.

Anger is dependable, as is its twin: fear. Fear motivates. The second reason I (like so many others in the industry) took up cooking was fear of poverty. I was an unemployed, unknown writer living in Cleveland with a wife and baby daughter to support. Cooking was the only job I could get. The restaurant that hired me, a fancy French Mediterranean place called Sans Souci, was owned by Marriott, and the chef to whom I'd applied for a job looked at me (I had no resume; I had just told him I could cook) and said, "You have to take a drug test, you know." He held my gaze, eyebrows raised. I said not a problem, and he hired me on the spot. Ah, the irony! How we've glorified the chef, made The Chef a celebrity and media star, when, really, the only qualification for the job is to be able to pass a drug test.

The last quality defining the true cook is itinerancy. The profession is the closest thing we have these days to medieval journeymen traveling from town to town. Cooks are vagabonds. Until they are ambitious and lucky enough to own a successful restaurant that keeps them grounded in one place, they travel from restaurant to restaurant, city to city, practicing their craft. There are exceptions, of course. But I've written about a lot of restaurants and cooks and chefs, and I have often returned to a restaurant I've covered to discover I don't recognize a single cook beyond the chef owner.

So. Compile a fleet of men and women who are motivated by a volatile mixture of anger, fear, and adrenaline addiction, people who are perpetually broke or on the edge, and who are spiritually homeless, and you have a workplace primed for small crime.

"I had a cook walk out on his last day with a New York strip between his butt cheeks," a cook in Seattle told me. While taking a smoke break, he watched the departing cook reach his car, unbuckle, and pull out the beef before driving off.

I asked chefs on Twitter for stories of cooks stealing. Matthew Grover wrote back: "Tenderloin down the pants—he had to saran it in place. (And unfortunately my kitchen copy of *Charcuterie* is gone. Will get one again.)"

Some thieves are more clever and ambitious than knucklehead cooks pinching protein. The guy who entered a restaurant wearing a gray Hobart work shirt and pushing a dolly, for instance. Hobart is one of the leading suppliers of appliances to restaurants. The man in the shirt hefted a Hobart meat slicer onto the dolly. When the kitchen steward, in charge of keeping track of what's in the kitchen and in the coolers, halted the man and said he didn't have a work order for this slicer to be taken, his sous chef stepped in, screamed at the steward, and told the workman to take the slicer. An hour later when the chef arrived, he asked, "Where the hell is the slicer?"

Cooks don't just steal from the restaurant; they steal from each other, such as a guy in San Francisco who stole shoes and clothes from the lockers and sold them to his roommates.

Jason Royal, a cook at a restaurant in New Hampshire, remembers a cocky young cook just out of culinary school, nicknamed Skittles, who brought in a set of handmade knives forged in Japan. His father had paid $8,000 for them. They were dark, dull steel, not shiny like factory-made knives. The blades were etched with exotic Japanese insignia. To cooks, knives can become intensely fetishized; and the rest of the kitchen marveled. The executive chef, concerned for the young cook's valuable set, told him to keep the knives in his office, which would be locked. After a hard night's service, Skittles left, forgetting the Japanese knife set in the office. When he returned the next day, the knives were gone. Infuriated, the executive chef made the kitchen stay late after service to hunt for the knives. They were never found. (Skittles, too, was gone three weeks later.)

Of course, everybody believed the thief was the executive chef, who was the only one with a key to the office.

This kind of theft does not happen in finer restaurants, one would think. The most common stories are of dishwashers in lower-tier restaurants finding hiding places for booze to consume after work and of cooks stealing food and expensive tools and books.

Actually, theft does happen in finer places. The finer the place, the bigger the heist. This past winter, seventy-six bottles of wine with a total value of more than $300,000 were stolen from the French Laundry. A month later, the wine was discovered clear across the country in Greensboro, North Carolina.

Chef/owner Thomas Keller, one of the most respected men in the industry, told the *Los Angeles Times*: "We have 130 employees, we have dozens of delivery people every day, we have hundreds of guests. Someone close to the restaurant? Yes. Somebody who knew where the wine cellar was? Certainly.

"But that could have been the linen delivery guys, the wine delivery guys and any of the people who service the restaurant, as well as everybody who ever worked at one of our restaurants over the years. That's a lot of people."

Keller invoked the crux of a restaurant's vulnerability. All those people required to make it run, all that expensive equipment, food, and wine. That and the fact that most of those employees are people for whom minimum-wage work is the only option.

Except for the cooks. Cooks are different. They could easily trade their apron for a bow tie and earn a living wage as a server. But they don't, because they're cooks, and cooks are different.

The restaurant kitchen is a world dominated by high heat and speed and knives, which often come in handy. Among my favorite theft stories is the following, which comes from one of my culinary instructors, certified master chef James Hanyzeski. At the restaurant he ran prior to joining the CIA, he learned that not one but two of his cooks were stealing from the restaurant. The next day he fired them on arrival. At the end of the night, he found that his car had four flat tires.

Hanyzeski shook his head. I could see he was still kicking himself all these years later. "I knew I was going to fire those guys," he said. He kept shaking his head. "Why didn't I bring four spare tires to work with me?

That was *stupid*." Hanyzeski knew the nature of kitchens and who you become when you work in one.

Only when you enter the rabbit hole of the professional kitchen, where theft is built into the culture, do you recognize the peculiar laws of the cook's universe, where wine and knives and books go missing and one must plan accordingly. You don't leave copies of a book your cooks want on the passenger seat of your car. Or if you do, you don't *lock* the car.

Midway through my reporting at the CIA to write about becoming a cook, one of my classmates asked if I paid tuition. I explained that I was writing a book and therefore wasn't paying tuition. He narrowed his eyes at me and, in a heavy Boston accent, said, "Man, I shoulda thought a dat scam."

This was the main reason no one had wanted to let me in, the president of the school told me: too many chefs thought I was trying to get a free education. All I'd wanted was to get in and get out with a story so I could write the book I'd taken an advance on. Instead, Chef Pardus infuriated me into becoming a cook.

It wasn't until many months later, having returned to Cleveland, having finished the manuscript for the book, having eaten through its advance, having tried and failed to sell another book, going quickly broke and nearing the end of my rope, that it dawned on me: *I've scammed a free education! I can get a job as a cook!*

I did. And that cook's job led to another book, and to another book after that, and, eventually, to a book that would be among the most stolen in the country, thanks to my fellow cooks.

And I could do all this only because I'd stolen the most valuable thing of all: an education. I was a cook, it seems, from the beginning.

Rites of the Caquelon

By Tim Nevile

From *Ski Magazine*

Tim Neville's freelance journalism slants toward adventure travel, in his pieces for *Outside*, the *New York Times*, and *Skiing*, among other publications. A two-year stint with the Swiss Broadcasting Corps in Bern afforded him plenty of time on Swiss slopes— and plenty of time to indulge in his *après-ski* food passion.

Before he was the King of Cheese he was just Fred Fischer, a dairyman, a ladies' man, a man with hands well accustomed to curds and teats. As cheese kings often do, Fischer lorded over a cheese shop. His was called, simply enough, the Cheese Shop, and it sat in the Swiss village of Grenchen near a lake not too far from Bern.

The Chäsi, which is how the Swiss say "cheese shop" in their funny German dialect, was not your average cheese shop, for Fischer was no average monger. Just as his father, his father's father, and his father's father's father had done, and just as his own sons were doing now, Fischer had dedicated his life to the stuff. Cheese was a business, yes, but it was also a torch he carried down from his Alemannic forebears and a passion for all the delightful things that one can do with milk.

On weekends and mornings, especially before the holidays or when the forecast called for snow, the townsfolk would bury chins into scarves and amble down Schild-Rust-Strasse to the Chäsi, inside a building the Grenchen Dairy Cooperative had owned for 90 years. They'd lean into the glass doors and feel their nostrils flare. Inside, the cool showcases glimmered with colorful trophies of Alpchäs and round, spruce-wood containers of vacherin mont d'or. Fischer had hard, lumpy chunks of Sbrinz, one of Switzerland's oldest cheeses, and creamy cylinders of tête de moine. He had wedges of raw-milk Erguël and wheels of l'Etivaz, a semihard wood-fired cheese made from the milk of cows that graze on wildflowers that grow at 6,500 feet. He had cheeses that no other monger had.

A fine cheese shop in Switzerland is hardly rare, but Fischer wasn't through. On days when he wasn't skiing at nearby Adelboden in his bright red jacket, he'd pull out his kitchen scales and a sheet of paper and measure and blend his ingredients into strange and wonderful fondues. These were not the sad, sallow versions your mother made in the '70s. No, Fischer's fondues were sensational brews that could transport a dinner party back to a favorite time in the Alps or deep into the recesses of a childhood Christmas memory. "I want people to take a bite of my fondue, close their eyes, and feel something," Fischer would say.

Back in the day, if foreigners wanted to become Swiss, agents of the Einwohnerdienst might knock on their doors and ask for a fondue. Did the applicants rub the pot with garlic? Did they use the right cheeses— always a base of vacherin and Gruyère? Did they get the right wine and just enough kirsch? The agents weren't hungry. It was a test to see how well immigrants had integrated themselves into Swiss society.

Fischer's fondues would have resulted in instant deportation. Instead of just cheese and booze, Fischer made "Al Capone" fondues with pesto and mascarpone. He made "English" fondues with mustard and whiskey. His "James Bond" fondue called for the cheese to be melted in champagne and a martini, shaken, not stirred. In all, Fischer penned 50 recipes for fondues that the Swiss had never seen.

From there his popularity soared. Real estate companies hired him to organize team-building parties that focused on fondue. Bankers brought him in for lavish soirées in Zermatt. He invented special forks and special belts with detachable breadbaskets so his friends could eat fondues while standing in a forest. The local newspaper hailed him king.

Slowly, though, the kingdom began to crumble. After 20 years, the Chäsi needed costly repairs, but Fischer and the cooperative disagreed over who should pay for them. A full-blown supermarket with mass-packaged fondues moved in 1,000 feet away, and sales began to slide. "Fondue King Retiring," blared the Grenchner Tagblatt in 2011, when Fischer announced that he was calling it quits. "Future of Chäsi Uncertain."

In a way, though, Fischer's legacy had never been more sure. For unbeknownst to him, 5,399 miles away in a snowy Oregon ski town, a man he'd never met was laboring over his own scales and working out his own formulas on his own sheets of paper. He'd been working for years to cement his own fondue fame among a precious group of friends.

And while this man, much to his wife's consternation, once bought most of a wheel of rotting vacherin that had miraculously appeared in a local delicatessen one day, and while his blends were good and his love for the ritual great, the man needed more. He needed an Old Country master to lead him deep into the ways of the cheese, to show him the quiet corners of the country where the ingredients are born, and to reveal the techniques that could transform his own fondues into memories.

That man was me.

I was meant to be him. It all began one frigid winter day in 1991, when I was 18, heartbroken, and living for a year outside Geneva with a Swiss family I'd never met before. That night my host-father, a powder skier and a wealth manager for a rich Saudi minister, made a fondue at the family home on Old Willows Way just as snow fogged the panes in frosty spandrels. The miasma could have made Dr. Scholl question his vocation, but one dip and swirl of a bread cube later, my little mind popped.

Maybe it was the alcohol that hollowed out my head or the interactive, merry nature of the meal, but henceforth I had cheese on the brain. I logged 33 days at ski resorts in the Alps that winter, and fondue factored into many of them. I ate it in Zermatt, Verbier, and Champéry. I ate it in Meiringen after my first real powder day. Each fondue made me feel so worldly. There I'd be with legs glowing from a ski day's burn, babbling in French with mes amis, stirring the schmaltz of adolescence. From then on nothing could complete a day in the mountains like a steaming pot of cheese. A sausage? No, thanks.

I cried uncontrollable tears when I had to come home, and over the next decade or so I put my love for fondue on simmer. It was impossible to find the right cheeses in Western mountain towns in the '90s.

I couldn't have afforded them anyway. But 16 years later, in 2008, my wife, Heidi, and I returned to Switzerland, where I'd been offered a job. At last I could become a fondue fiend.

It took me all of a month to buy our first fondue pot, a red caquelon adorned with a white Swiss cross, which I got before securing our newborn daughter a crib. Fondue was not something "a divorced dad makes for his kids," as a Planet Money reporter once cracked, but an art that I mucked up aplenty. I made it too runny or too thick; I burned it and drowned it in booze. It didn't matter. You could find the critical cheeses—real vacherin and Gruyère—easier than you could find tortillas. Soon fondue became our frozen pizza, the thing to cook when no one felt like cooking.

But it's a myth that the Swiss eat fondue all the time. Six times a year seems about right. And even Swiss cheeseologists, bless their moldy souls, say there are as many origin stories about fondue as there are ways to make it. Homer mentions a similar dish in *The Iliad*. A Zurich woman penned a recipe called "To Cook Cheese with Wine" in 1699. Ultimately the French name for the dish stuck after master chef Vincent La Chapelle included "Fonduë," meaning "melted," in *The Modern Cook*, published in 1735.

Today the French, Italians, Germans, Austrians, and even the Portuguese and Chinese have their own ways of making fondue. But no one has folded the dish into their national identity like the ski-loving Swiss. Iron Age farmers in Switzerland were making cheese in alpine huts 3,000 years ago. Surely they melted it. Or if not, then the blending of cheeses to make one unique dish serves as a tidy metaphor for a tiny country with four languages and cultures—e cheesius unum, if you will.

Whatever fondue's provenance, when we went back to our cozy home in Bend, Oregon, in 2011, I was determined to keep the spirit alive. I returned to Switzerland often to ski and work, and each time I came home with cheeses to last the winter. It became a thing. After skiing at Bachelor we'd tap "Schweizer Volksmusik" into Spotify and invite friends over for a hot night of fondue. Eventually I developed equations for perfect proportions every time. To make my fondues required algebra.

Indeed, I had become my own Stephen Hawking of cheese, yet I yearned for more. Had I truly rubbed the edges of this universe like so much garlic in the pot? One day last fall I wrote an e-mail to the most proudly Swiss guy I knew, a colleague back in Bern, wondering whether he knew of a fondue expert who might be willing to take me under his wing.

As a matter of fact he did.

Ah, Fischer! I'm eating a Chäschüechli, a little cheese pie, outside the train station in Spiez, a 13th-century town near Interlaken, when the king himself drives up. It's February, and a light snow is falling.

I guess I was expecting a portly dweeb with Roquefort slicks across his chins, but Fischer is athletic and handsome. He's 54 years old with a black soul patch. I toss my skis into his Nissan Qashqai and we zoom off toward a ski area called Engstligenalp, near Adelboden.

"You said it right when you e-mailed me," Fischer says in his sing-song German as the countryside squeezes in around us. "Fondue does foster friendship and Gemütlichkeit. I think you're going to have some 'emotions' over these next few days."

A T-bar whisks us high onto the broad face of the Dossen, a 7,500-foot pyramid of limestone looming over a massive hanging valley. The sharp roofs of alpine huts struggle to peek out of the four feet of snow that have fallen over the past three days. For safety's sake we stick to the runs. It's midweek and no one is here. Fischer loves places like these.

"In the summertime this is all green," he booms, sweeping his poles across the vista. He explains how the cows that graze up here produce rich, aromatic milk thanks to the 50 types of grasses, herbs, and flowers they find in every square meter of pasture. Fischer, who grew up over his father's dairy near Solothurn, used to spend 100 days a summer living in a hut high in the Alps not far from here, tending cows and making cheese. He loved the ancestral ritual and how simple variables (like cooking times) and simple tools (like rocks) could transform basic milk into complex cheese. People now pay him upwards of $100 a person to attend his fondue parties. Otherwise he's buying cheese for a dairy distribution company called Baumann. "It's a nice way of living, up there on the alp," he says, somewhat wistfully. "It can be lonely, but cows don't care if you're late or sick or hungover."

The light turns flat, so we ski down for lunch inside a spectacular multichambered igloo perched at midmountain. Edelweiss entombed in airless ice and backlit with soft LEDs glow from inside the frozen walls. Candles flicker from tables with wooden benches softened by thick sheepskin covers. The air smells of hot wine and cheese.

The fondue is excellent but not light-years better than mine, which makes me kind of proud. Fischer didn't make it, but he clarifies the rules for eating it. Always drink wine, black tea, or kirsch—never beer or cold water—to avoid a "cheese baby" forming in your belly. Save the crusty burned bit on the bottom—called the "nun" in French, the "grandmother" in German—to eat at the very end. Lose your bread in the pot and you must kiss the chef. "For some reason the ladies always throw their bread into the pot when they're with me," says the king with a smirk. "It's a real problem."

Fischer takes me deep into his world over the next couple of days. We visit dairies in the rolling pre-Alp region of Fribourg, where I procure large wedges of Gruyère and vacherin from the Bongard family, one of the most decorated cheese families in Switzerland. He shows me how curds should feel in your hand when they're ready to be pressed. We drink warm whey straight out of the tank.

There is no doubt this man is worthy of his crown when I witness him at his best one night. A hardware company hired him to throw a fondue party, then canceled, but word got out and 30 mostly random people have shown up on a moment's notice. We all huddle in a cozy cabin in Biel, divide into groups, and make "Fireman," "Pyrenean," "flambé," and "English" fondues at our tables using his extraordinary blends of cheeses, creams, spices, wines, and champagne.

Fischer tells jokes as he marches around the room in a traditional Swiss wrestling shirt, barking instructions on when to add more wine and how to properly stir (in a figure eight with a wooden spoon that has a hole in it). "I love fondue, but I've never made it like this before," says a giggling nurse at my table. Fischer rings a bell and we pass the pots around so we each can sample them all. The laughter peals for hours.

But the real "emotion" comes unexpectedly another evening when Fischer leads me to the edge of a hillside forest called the Freiholz, north of Bern. Dozens of strangers have gathered here in the icy dark for a fondue al fresco. We strap on belts with metal breadbaskets attached, fill them up with cubes, and stir large witches' cauldrons of burbling cheese with these extra-long forks that Fischer invented.

Tiny Swiss villages flicker below. Cross-country skiers slip by on a cushion of moonlit snow. The kirsch flows as freely as my poorly conjugated verbs. So warm. So beautiful. By the end I'm hugging strangers and tears threaten my eyes.

Such is the power of the cheese.

A few days before I meet the King I linger around the French-speaking regions of western Switzerland to make the most of an epic snowstorm. I log face shots in Villars and Gstaad, recharge over wedges of tomme de Vaud in the Hôtel de Rougemont, and track down slabs of l'Etivaz from the country's only l'Etivaz cellar (in the hamlet of l'Etivaz, of course). One night I slip through the snow-wrapped hemlocks to a fairy-tale hut called Solalex and gorge on warm, gooey bins of pungent vacherin mont d'or while a cat snoozes by the fire.

My plan to ski while gathering ingredients for a spectacular fondue party is well on track. By now Fischer has helped me net enough stinky cheese to make any contraband-sniffing canines at customs keel over from the fumes. I just need the wine—a chasselas or a fendant—and a bottle of kirsch. As with the cheese, I want them from the source.

The kirsch proves tough to find, but after asking around I luck out and score a precious bottle from a quiet man named Oliver Matter. Matter, 45, once made news for making absinthe with Marilyn Manson. His kirsch is no less eye-popping than the shock rocker.

The fourth-generation distiller combs the countryside for the scattered remains of Switzerland's old-growth cherry trees, harvesting fruit from one tree here, another tree there, until he's gathered enough to distill a small batch of the clear brandy. "Switzerland is kirschland," he tells me, "but, yes, I like to think this bottle is unique."

A former ski-school director and restaurateur named Raoul Colliard helps me with the wine. In winter, Colliard will burn through 12 tons of cheese serving fondues at one of Switzerland's most authentic cheese chalets, a historic place called Le Tsale in the small ski town of Les Paccots, above Châtel-Saint-Denis.

If Fischer is the Jerry Lee Lewis of fondue, Colliard is its Chopin. At 74 years old, ruddy-cheeked, with thumbs calloused from decades of milking cows, Colliard is a purist who lets his cheese stand alone. One of his most remarkable fondues uses a vertical flight of a single-source vacherin with a mix of ages from about three to seven months. No thickeners. No wine. No kirsch. He's used the same fork to stir so many of these fondues that the tines are nothing but nubs.

"I'm supposed to make a fondue for the Prime Minister of Canada in Montreal next month, and they can only get me one vacherin," he sighs when we meet over a pot of his vacherin at Le Tsale. It's stunning—far cooler than most burbling mixes but rich and delicate, with the consistency of latex paint. "You need at least four vacherins to give it this character, so I don't know what I'm going to do," he frets. "C'est terrible!"

The next few days are magnificent, however. I ride the surface lifts at Les Paccots, finding stashes of soft powder on the edges of the pistes, and sled down from a mountaintop chalet in the dark, loopy on wine. All in all I eat six fondues in five days—an entire year's worth in less than a week. The Swiss are mortified. My cheese baby is full-term.

Sadly, in the spectacularly terraced Lavaux wine-making region on the shores of Lake Geneva, my mission comes to a close. There Colliard's friend Jean-François Cassy and his family have made chasselas for generations. We sit around Cassy's table eating charcuterie and sampling smoky garanoirs as wind whips great banners of snow off the Alps across the lake. By the time I fly home I have four liters of his best whites in a duffle. The customs agents never blink. All of my loot is legal.

ACTUALLY, there's one more thing to do. The ski season is winding down when I throw my grand fondue fête. My wife and I cover our table in fake gems, put on the Volksmusik, and prepare to get rowdy with cheese.

Friends invite friends who invite more friends, and I worry I won't have enough cheese for all 14 of us, until I remember, oh yeah, I have 15 pounds of it.

I do as Fischer told me to do and get my proportions dialed. I let the cheeses soak in wine for at least an hour before firing up the warmers. I explain the rules—the stirring, the kissing, the nun and the grandmother. We crack open the wines and do shots of kirsch while the anticipation builds.

Soon the house smells like Old Willows Way. We have pots bubbling with Gruyère and vacherin, and another with Appenzeller and raclette on top. My pure vacherin fondue turns out a separated mess, the result of getting impatient and heating it too quickly, but the James Bond fondue is a resounding hit. That caquelon will be licked clean when the night is through.

I duck out of the room for a minute to eavesdrop and savor the moment.

"Oh my God!" says Erin. "This is amazing!"

"Wonderful!" says Chris.

"This one is spectacular," says Mark.

And then Siobhan delivers the money: "This reminds me of being a kid."

The king is gone.

Here lives the king.

The Chef Who Saved My Life

By Brett Martin

From GQ

GQ correspondent Brett Martin writes a lot about food, culture, and food culture for publications ranging from *Vanity Fair* to the *New York Times*. But this time it's personal: how a routine encounter with the great chef Jacques Pépin retooled his life. *Twice.*

Here is the story of The Day Jacques Pépin Saved My Life. That's how I tell it, anyway—at parties, over dinner, on those occasions when a friend finds himself drowning in his own life and I'm cast as an unlikely dispenser of wisdom. That's when I try to assure him that salvation can come in the most unlikely of guises: in the guise, say, of Jacques Pépin, who, when I, too, was lost and deep in dark waters, came along and showed me the way back to the light.

It had been a bad breakup. We had lived together for three years, a first for both of us, which may have fueled our fever to stick to it long after it was clear we had probably been a mistake from the beginning. By then, our needs and dependencies had locked as neatly as pieces of a jigsaw puzzle, a perverse compatibility that eventually turned to reinforcing and confirming the worst suspicions of each about the other. There followed, finally, a kind of plummeting death-lock in which she and I could do nothing but cleave together and grimly wait for the ground to arrive. When it did come, it was complete with screaming, sobbing, drinking, all the flourishes that make you think, even in the midst of it, not without a certain amount of grim pride, "Good god. So, this is what *this* looks like."

It had left me, when I had finally wrested myself away from the apartment we shared in Brooklyn, living in the windowless, though carpeted, basement of an old friend's house in Cobble Hill. Mornings, I lay in the complete darkness, listening to the shuffling and creaking of him and his wife and his two children preparing for the day. There had been a time when I'd still felt close to that domestic future, but now the truth of my life had been revealed, like the corners of a nightclub when the lights snap on: I was no man. I wasn't moving toward anything. I was a troll in the cellar.

Of all the fallout, physical, psychological, and emotional, that my spasmodic lurch out of the house and into the world had engendered, one effect was most worrisome: I had lost my appetite. Believe me when I tell you that this never happens—not when I'm sick, not when I'm sad, not when I'm busy. I do not understand when people "forget to eat." As a friend likes to remind me, I once ate a meal of *rognons à la moutarde*, kidneys in mustard sauce, spent all night on the bathroom floor, shivering, sweating, and expelling, and then woke up proclaiming the dish "excellent" and wanting more. I do not forget to eat.

Now, though, my stomach was wound so tight that there seemed to be no room for food. Whatever I put in my mouth felt like dry newspaper; I was unable to swallow.

Just by way of topping things off, I was broke. Which is why, though I felt incapable of forming a coherent thought, much less writing one, I accepted an assignment from a sympathetic friend at this magazine. It was a short sidebar, to be included in a package about home cooking: Ask Jacques Pépin, one of the world's first celebrity chefs, for his tips on designing a home kitchen. 400 words. Even in my profoundly stunted state, it was the kind of thing I couldn't screw up too completely.

I'm embarrassed now to admit that I was only dimly aware then of who Pépin was. I knew he belonged to the pioneering generation of food personalities that predated the current celebrity-chef revolution. I associated his name with Julia Child's. (Their TV show *Julia & Jacques Cooking at Home* was, in fact, one of the great culinary vaudeville acts of all time.) I suppose that the editorial statute of limitations has expired and I can admit: I did not overly prepare for this interview.

However I did manage to set an alarm for that hot, late spring morning, shower, and haul myself out of the basement. My friend's four-year-old son, Caleb, was on the couch, eating cereal, one hand working the spoon while the other was tangled in his thatch of sandy hair.

"Do you want to play?" he asked.

"Sorry. I have to go to work," I told him.

"Why?"

"Because that's what grown-ups do sometimes."

He looked at me. "You're not a *grown-up*," he said, attempting to work it out. "I mean, you're not a *kid* . . . " He trailed off. I understood completely.

An hour later, I emerged from the subway and stood blinking in the hot sun at Grand Street and Broadway. Across the street, on the corner, sat the International Culinary Center. Pépin had been a dean at the school since 1988, when it was still called the French Culinary Institute. I hadn't eaten, and I felt shaky and weak. With ten minutes to kill, I went looking for something to stabilize my stomach. At a bodega, I scanned the refrigerator case for anything I could choke down. Blindly, I settled on some kind of protein drink. Undoubtedly, there are worse bottoms to hit, but this, in retrospect, was mine—what I can only hope will remain the worst meal of my life. White, chalky, it was like swallowing wallpaper paste. I gagged as much down as I could before throwing the rest away. Then, I crossed the street and went upstairs.

I knew enough about Pépin's stature to feel sheepish about taking up his time for such a small story. I expected to spend a quick twenty minutes, ask my questions and get out of there. An assistant led me to the cluttered office where Pépin waited. He was wearing chef's whites, having just given a demo to students in one of the downstairs kitchens, and his gray but thick hair was swept dashingly upward from his forehead. He extended a hand to shake, one of the most extraordinary hands I'd ever seen: angular and bony, with an exceptionally long middle finger, thick pads at the tip of each digit, and a thumb that protruded at an odd angle upwards. It seemed at once wrecked by years of kitchen work and oddly delicate; the hand of a workman and an artist. Later, I would come to know the kind of elemental alchemy Pépin's hands were capable of: transforming a liquid mass of eggs into an omelet with a few sharp pulls of a fork, trussing a roast with lightning-fast knots as elaborate and tight as a sailor's, deftly dismantling a whole chicken with whatever implement happens to be at hand—a knife, a spoon, for all I know the daily newspaper. For now, I shook hastily and muttered an apology for taking up his time.

"No, no. Don't be ridiculous," he said. His accent was almost comically French, despite nearly five decades in the United States.

So I settled in, between the filing cabinets and teetering stacks of paper, and we talked about the finer points of kitchen design: how he, at his Madison, Connecticut, home, had a wall made of reclaimed barnwood on which most of the pots, pans, and other implements he used hung within easy reach. How one should, of course, have a gas stove but opt for the consistency of an electric oven, preferably placed high on the wall, to avoid excessive bending. How, contrariwise, a side-by-side fridge and freezer is a waste of space and the freezer as bottom drawer is preferable. How most gadgets are useless and fail the Closet Test—i.e., that anything you stick in one will never be used. How there should be good light, good music, and a good view, if possible, and a place for your guests to perch to drink wine and watch you work.

These were all simple, concrete, tactile tips based on a fundamental view of eating as a central part of life and the effort of cooking as an integral part of the pleasure itself. What I noticed most, though, was how completely Pépin was granting me his attention, how present and engaged he was, despite the banality of my questions. It was a simple thing, but weirdly magical, allowing the rest of the world to fade away as we chatted. Twenty minutes passed quickly, then forty, then an hour. I was aware that my shoulders were starting to relax.

It was now approaching noon and finally I got up to leave. "Would you like something to eat?" Pépin's assistant asked. I assumed this was just a courtesy and prepared to beg off. I couldn't imagine sitting downstairs, in the student-manned restaurant L'Ecole, by myself, trying vainly to eat.

"Will you join me?" I asked Pépin, sending the courtesy back.

He looked at me as though I might have hearing problems.

"Of course," he said. "It's lunchtime!"

We took the long way downstairs, so that Pépin could walk me through ICC's facilities. Every time we entered a kitchen classroom, the young men and women in their starchy whites and toques would stiffen over their cutting boards and mixers, stealing glances at Pépin. He did his best to put them at ease, laying a hand on a shoulder and offering bits of advice. "Yes, chef," they murmured. In the stairwell, a breathless young man stopped us to gush about an egg demo Pépin had led the day before, in particular a technique in which the chef deep-fried an egg by cracking it into hot oil and gently herding it into shape with a pair of spoons. "I'll never be able to do that, Chef" the student said. "You will," Pépin told him. "You will."

At L'Ecole, we were ushered to a seat and given menus. Pépin ordered: a list of newish items on the menu that he wanted to check up on, and a bottle of Sancerre. Conversation came easily. We talked about his arrival in New York, in 1959, a time when it was possible to land in town and, within weeks, know everybody who mattered in the food world. Pépin had done just that, quickly meeting such legendary figures as James Beard; Pierre Franey, chef at Le Pavillon; *New York Times* restaurant critic Craig Claiborne; and, of course, Julia Child, whose *Mastering the Art of French Cooking* was still a pile of type-written pages.

The food came and I took a few tentative sips of consommé. "What do you think?" Pépin asked. This was not a test, but genuine curiosity. I said it was good but could use some salt. He reached over and took a spoonful. "I think you are right," he said.

I was pleased, but I had not told the whole truth. Yes, from a technical standpoint, I thought the soup needed more salt. But I also thought it was the most delicious thing I had ever eaten. I was aware, as more food arrived, that I had started breathing for what seemed like the first time in weeks. And I was *ravenous*. I grabbed hunks of bread and slathered them with paté, wolfed down delicate, pink lamb chops, gnawing the bones. If Pépin noticed, he didn't say. We reached over to each others' plates to take tastes, ordered another bottle. Alain Sailhac, the longtime chef at Le Cirque and another dean at the school, with his silver hair and bushy eyebrows, passed through the dining room and sat for a glass. He and Pépin swapped stories of coming up in France's old *brigade* system: the yelling, the smack of a pan hurled across the room, the chore of pressing ingredients through a massive sieve in the back of the Plaza Athénée in the days before food processors. Pépin showed the bulbous tips of his fingers, still inured to heat after a summer spent in Aix-les-Bains as the *grillardin* for a chef who prohibited the use of utensils to flip his steaks, chickens and chops.

I sat in a state of wonder. At a time when I had forgotten the possibility of pleasure, Pépin had effortlessly, instinctively brought me back to life. Without knowing it, he had extended a hand to a drowning man. For dessert we had crème brûlée and an apple tart, coffee, and one more glass of wine. And then I was shaking that hand again, the other clasped warmly atop mine. And then I was out on the street, dazed and floating.

That night, my newly ex-girlfriend was out of town, so I was able to go back to my house. I bought a six-pack of Tecate in cans, a half-pound of *prosciutto di parma*, sliced thin, and a loaf of bread. I sat in my backyard, in the dark, drinking the beer, listening to a Mets game on the radio and breathing the warm, humid air. I had swum back to myself.

Things continued to happen. I made it through that summer, slowly rejoining life. I had another relationship, a better one, though it also ended. Not as badly, but badly enough. I did well professionally; I wrote a couple of books. Just after New Year's, 2011, I got on a train and moved to New Orleans where, eventually, I bought a house with the woman I intend to spend the rest of my life with. We built a big, open kitchen that is the center of the house, with space for stools at the counter, a thick, green stand of birds of paradise outside the French doors, and a freezer stacked underneath the fridge. Last August, I became a father.

Along the way, I've cooked an awful lot from Pépin's cookbooks: squab with lettuce, roast leg of lamb, leafy salads with mustardy vinaigrette and boiled potatoes, *poulet à l'estragon*—chicken simmered in white wine and tarragon, served beneath a velvet blanket of cream and egg yolk sauce. (This was the first dish Pépin had ever been allowed to prepare alone at the stove—for late night arrivals at Le Grand Hôtel de l'Europe in Lyon—and some version of it appears throughout his cookbooks since.)

I've roasted dozens of chickens according to his method, which, among an infinite number of competing philosophies, I believe to be the only truly foolproof one. (Cast iron pan; 425 degrees; 20 minutes laid on one side, leg down; 20 minutes on the other; breast up for 20 minutes, or until the juices run clear.) I've turned countless times to one or another iteration of *La Technique*, Pépin's revolutionary series of illustrated cooking lessons, to learn what to do with, say, a bundle of leeks, a membranous pile of sweetbreads, a few pounds of frogs legs dropped off by a New Orleans neighbor. (Shaken in a paper bag with flour and black pepper—I add cayenne in a nod to Louisiana—then flash-sautéed in frothing butter.) I am hardly alone in my dependence on these books; Tom Colicchio taught himself to cook by reading *La Technique*.

I learned quite a bit more about Pépin the man, too, starting with his lovely 2003 memoir, *The Apprentice: My Life in the Kitchen*. His has been a life too varied and rich to be quickly summarized: from apprenticeships in the provinces, to the kitchens of Paris, to the palace itself, where he served three prime ministers, including Charles de Gaulle. He made the fateful passage to New York, where he landed in the kitchen of the legendary Le Pavillon restaurant. He met Craig and Jim and Julia. And he fell in love with America. There was plenty to dislike about how we ate in those days of canned vegetables and condensed soups, but Pépin fell for Oreos and Jell-O, for Maine lobster, fried chicken, sweet summer corn, and Reuben sandwiches—for the country's democratic, openhearted approach to food. His accent may be Pepé Le Pew's but his heart is pure Capra.

He turned down a chance to be John F. Kennedy's White House chef, in favor of going to work for Howard Johnson, the man and the restaurant chain. Cooking for presidents and visiting dignitaries was something he had done before. Serving good food—with real milk, real seafood, real vegetables—to ordinary Americans? That turned him on. He wrote a Master's thesis, at Columbia, on Voltaire. He endured a devastating car accident in the Catskills, after which he was not expected to walk again, much less cook. He became a teacher, giving two and three classes per day across the country, and then conquered television. He settled finally in Connecticut where, in my favorite of his cookbooks, *Chez Jacques: Traditions and Rituals of a Cook*, he can be seen living what can only be described as the good life: gathering mushrooms in the spring and fall, catching fish and frogs in his pond, painting watercolors when the spirit takes hold, standing at the kitchen counter eating roast chicken with knife and fingers.

I can think of no better summary than an interview conducted by the photographer Melanie Dunea for her book *My Last Supper: 50 Great*

Chefs and Their Final Meals. His answer to the question of what his final meal would be begins:

The menu for my last meal would be eclectic, relaxed, informal, and would go on for a very, very long time—years! . . . I cannot conceive of anything better than the greatest baguette, deep golden, nutty, and crunchy, with a block of the sublime butter of Brittany and Bélon oysters. I would consume tons of the best beluga caviar with my wife, dispose of the best boiled ham and the most excellent Ibérico ham, and would eat eggs cooked in butter, scrambled, mollet-style or sunny-side up, with the ham.

And the list continues: fingerling potatoes cooked in goose fat, pâté of pheasant with black truffles, a lobster roll, a hot dog, apricots, cherries, white and wine peaches. "I would pile homemade apricot jam onto thin, buttery crêpes, hot from the pan and accompany them with a Bollinger Brut 1996 champagne."

Who would be your dining companions? Dunea asks.

My family, a few close friends, and my dog, Paco, would stay until the end, while many other good friends would come by and have a few drinks, eat, and leave

Who would prepare the meal?

We would cook, drink, and eat together until the end—weeks or months later—when I would die from the *péché de gourmandise* (sin of gluttony)!

The Last Supper he was describing, in other words, had begun years ago. It had in fact been the entirety of his life.

Meanwhile, through the years, I told the story of my own meal with Jacques. Often. It's a good story—heavy but not too heavy, semi-confessional, a dash of celebrity, a happy ending. One evening, occasioned by a shared plate of prosciutto at The Tasting Kitchen, a restaurant in Venice Beach, I told it to an especially sharp friend. When I was done, he looked at me for a long time. You should write about that, he told me. Sure, I plan to, I said.

Then he said, "Don't make it an obituary."

Another steamy day. Back on the corner of Grand and Broadway. I was about to go inside and take up more of Jacques Pépin's time. Another year or so had gone by since that Venice Beach meal, but I had thought often about what my friend had said: "Don't make it an obituary." It had made me instantly ashamed. In the back of my head, I knew, I had always thought of it as just that: a story to tell in tribute someday, when it would be a feather in my cap—if an earnest, heartfelt one—but of little use to Jacques Pépin.

It amazed me, the more I thought about it, that it had never occurred to me to simply reach out and say thank you. Why? Well, a lot of time had passed. Pépin is famous and, like many people, I harbor the irrational superstition that part of becoming famous is a kind of cognitive retardation that prevents one from remembering anybody who is not also famous.

And there was no easy definition for what Pépin had become for me. He was not my father, certainly, nor a friend, nor even a mentor. "Role models" were for college essays, not grown men. Any of those relationships would have been recognizable, with its own protocol for behavior and for expressing gratitude. But Pépin and I had met only glancingly, at a moment that had obviously meant vastly more to me than it had to him, itself something hard to admit. I *had* learned, over time, that I was not alone. Many other men had had similar experiences—even equally surreal ones. Not enough of them had ever said thanks.

So I called Pépin's office and asked to meet. I was invited to watch him give a demo at the ICC and then have dinner. As it happened, it was the same egg demo that the student had gushed about in the stairwell six years earlier—the equivalent of a free-throw clinic taught by Michael Jordan. About twenty students were gathered in the small auditorium when Pépin entered, looking more or less the same as I remembered.

The demo began. "I am Jacques Pépin, I am one of the deans here," said Pépin. "If you ever see me when I am around and want to talk about food, please do."

As he talked, one hand idly scraped at a block of yellow butter on the counter in front of him, pulling up long, flat strips. A twist, a flourish with the fingers, and he had transformed them into a rose, which he dropped into cold water. He wore the barest smile of a master magician.

Indeed, the show had just begun: For the next 45 minutes, Pépin spun gold out of the base elements of yolk and albumen. He created perfect poached eggs, summoned two omelets—one the traditional fluffy French kind, the other the hard, American diner version; there was a time and place for each, he said. He made a mayonnaise, intentionally broke the emulsion and then brought it, Lazarus-like, back to life. The money shot, true to the admiring student's promise, came when he cracked an egg into hot oil, using a pair of spoons to shepherd the spreading white until it was a perfect fried orb. This was an almost primitive magic, a mastery of the physical world—though rooted in a plain-spoken stream of scientific fact.

When it was over, Pépin patiently answered questions at the front of the room. He signed books. Slowly the room emptied until it was just Pépin, me, and a few assistants cleaning up. He took me by the arm: "Let's have dinner."

To answer my first question: I did look familiar, though he couldn't remember exactly why we had met. "It was silly," I said. "A waste of your time."

"We had lunch didn't we?" he said. "So I was not suffering."

We sat at a table at L'Ecole, a few feet from where our first meal together had been. A woman approached the table, one of a stream throughout the evening, to say hello and thanks for a cooking lesson she had attended years before. Pépin ordered some wine and bread—requesting the hard heel of the loaf—the *croûton*—which, to his chagrin, he had noticed being thrown out the day before.

"This is my favorite part," he said, cradling a handful of crumbs in his hand and shaking them ruminatively, like dice, before funneling them into his mouth.

We ordered charcuterie and homemade cavatelli with rock shrimp and two whole Fourchu lobsters—a special variety found only in the cold waters around an island in Nova Scotia. The ICC was housing a pondful of them somewhere in Bushwick.

We talked about the state of modern chefdom. He was clear-eyed but uncranky. The undercooking of everything, especially vegetables, drove him crazy. So did excessive culinary piety: "I've been in restaurants where they bring over a carrot and say 'This carrot was born the ninth of September. His name is Jean-Marie ...' Just give me the goddamned carrot!'"

Young chefs, he said, had become overly concerned with self-expression. *Nouvelle cuisine* had been about many things: fresher ingredients, new techniques, a sensitivity to place and season, healthier preparations, creativity, innovation. Out of all those mandates, chefs sometimes seemed to have only heard the final two. "That's how you wind up with a slice of rock salt in a bowl of raspberry ice cream," he said.

He sighed. "But we tend to do that. This is America. We go totally from one end of the spectrum to the other end." In the end, the job was still and would always be the same. "We are the mashed potato makers," he said. "We are here to please people."

I was stalling. Twice I opened my mouth to tell my story and twice I was surprised to find my heart beating wildly. The lobsters came and Pépin used two hands to pry open the shell with a resounding crack. He pressed the leggy bottom of the body to his mouth and inhaled a blast of brine. I took a deep breath.

"So, the reason I came here today," I began, "I wanted to tell you a story about the last time we met and . . . for reasons . . . there's no reason you should have known this, but it was a difficult time in my life, I was at a real low point. I was in a terrible state of anxiety and unhappiness and . . . I had stopped eating. And, well, it was just such a lovely day that it really turned me around." This was inadequate in the extreme, but apparently my tremble did a better job of conveying the depth of my feeling.

Pépin put down his lobster. He dipped his napkin in his water glass and used it to wash his fingers.

"Well, thank you very much," he said, finally. "But I just happened to be there. I was . . . what is it, from Aristotle? I was just the *medium*."

"I never said thank you," I said.

"But it was not me, it was you," he said. "*You* did it."

At that moment, another woman came over to shake Pépin's hand, giving me a chance to collect myself. As simple and obvious as Pépin's assessment seemed, it confused me. I felt both giddy and queasy.

When the woman left, Pépin sat back and took a thoughtful sip of wine.

"I think I know what you are talking about," he said. "After my years in Paris in the 1950s, reading Camus and Sartre, I am a bit of an existentialist at heart." (He had, in fact, served Sartre at La Rotonde, the Paris brasserie.) "I think that the point is that you do things in life where you are moving . . . often without realizing it."

He knew what it was like to meet somebody who changed your life. For him, it had been Claiborne, the first food critic at the *Times*—the inventor, really, of modern restaurant criticism—and a guru of the nascent food scene of the 1960s. Weekends at Claiborne's house in the Hamptons were long parties filled with food and drink, in which guests came and went and ate and cooked. To a buttoned-down Frenchman, it was a revelation.

"In France you would invite someone for the weekend or for dinner, it was an ordeal, as much for them as for you. You would organize what you were going to do and what you were going to eat, for breakfast, lunch, dinner," he said chopping at the air like a military bandleader. "I came to Craig and we went to the market. He poached eggs and kept them in a bowl of ice water; you woke up and had one, whenever you wanted. Fine. At lunch, there's some ham, you stuff a sandwich. And then in the afternoon we started cooking, maybe have a cocktail, maybe finish up at one or two in the morning, halfway drunk. But it was such a free, casual way, an open way of seeing people, of receiving people, which for me had always been very structured. It changed my life. It made me stay in America. I . . . " He searched for the words. "I came out of my carapace."

He had told Claiborne thank you, but under unhappy circumstances. The critic's last days were marked by dementia and alcoholism; their last dinner had been at Le Cirque with Ed Giobbi, the artist, gourmand and reputed inventor of pasta primavera. Claiborne, wheelchair bound, had been cranky and displeased.

"Craig was great," Pépin said, tenderly. "But he could be a bitch."

Claiborne's sense of generosity and conviviality, Pépin believed, had come from his upbringing in Mississippi—another argument for the notion that Southerners have always made the best New Yorkers. It occurred to me that whatever strain of his philosophy had been passed along to me through Pépin had circuitously sent me to live in the South myself, where I had come out of *my* carapace. For the first time, I felt my experience might be a link in a chain.

We turned to our lobsters and ate, silent for a few minutes, except for the cracking of shells and sucking of flesh.

I realized that, rudely, I hadn't asked what the past six years had been like for him. Not much, he said: A couple of shoulder and hip surgeries, another cookbook. A grandchild. His mother, close to 100, was still alive in Lyon. His poodle, Paco, loved him ever more each day. He and his wife Gloria had now been married for nearly 50 years. "When you get older you hope that things slow down a bit but continue the same," he said. "If things continue the same, it is a great miracle." (This March, he survived and recovered from a minor stroke.)

Pépin folded the corner of his napkin contemplatively. "I go back to Lyon. Or, I look at my daughter. I see paintings that I did in 1962 . . . Sometimes, I look and I say, *It's not me,*" he said. "I would love to be able to taste the food I did forty years ago. It would be quite fascinating. The painting is still on the wall. I can see it. But the beauty of food in many ways is that it's so evanescent. It comes and it disappears. And all you have is your memory."

Suddenly I was seized with the urge to spill more: "I've tried, Jacques," I wanted to say. "Honestly I've tried. To live with an open heart. To give more than take. To work joyfully. To be awake to the world always. To live up to our lunch. But, it's hard. And I fail all the time."

What I said instead, was, "I've tried. Over and over. But . . . I just can't debone a chicken."

"Ah, well," he patted my arm. "That's probably okay too."

And now our time was up. Pépin would go upstairs and change into street clothes. He would spend the night at the Yale Club, as he did when he found himself in Manhattan late. In the morning, he would get on the train, back to the house in Madison. And I would go my way, too.

"Perhaps we'll catch up in another six years?" I said, as we shook hands again.

"Sooner, I hope," he said, ushering me toward the door. He pressed two packages, wrapped in brown paper, into my hands. I did not fully register what they were until I was alone, on the street, and Jacques Pépin had disappeared: two warm, long loaves of bread, for the walk ahead.

Life, on a Plate

Sonoko Dreams of Soba

By Francis Lam

From *Saveur*

⚴

Francis Lam is a star on many platforms—a book editor at
Clarkson Potter, a columnist at the *New York Times Magazine*,
a judge on *Top Chef Masters*. Busy as he must be, he never
neglects to pay honest attention to the soul of a food experience.
Which includes letting a Japanese noodle master press the reset
button....

I had the first line of this story written before I even got out of the car.
"Dogs smell your fear," it said at the top of my notebook. "But soba
smells your anxiety."

I'd been snarled in L.A. traffic, late on my way to meet Sonoko Sakai,
the woman waiting to show me the way of soba, but there was one
thing I already knew about the meditative culture of Japanese noodle
making: Stressed out and road-ragey is not the way of soba. If ramen
is the pork-fat shock-and-awe of the noodle world, soba is what phi-
losophers slurp—a simple buckwheat noodle, a cuisine of purity and
contemplation. A soba restaurant's menu may include a tray of noodles
served with tempura, or maybe a tangle bathed in a lean, coffee-dark
duck broth, as austere as duck gets. But always, there will be an offering
of plain soba, just-cooked, chilled cold, served with only a small cup of
seasoned stock for dipping. It's completely fireworks-free, but in simple
things lie complex pleasures, if you choose to discover them, which is
why you often find this most naked of dishes offered as a course on
its own in refined *kaiseki* tasting menus. Slip a few strands between

your chopsticks and dip them—ideally no more than a third of their length, to really taste the noodle. Slurp them up, feeling the way they glide toward you; the Japanese have a word for what you're looking for—*nodogoshi*, which means "good throat-feel." Chew, and think about their texture—how firm, or yielding, or firm-but-yielding. Take in their flavor—do they taste nutty and earthy or round and mild, like buckwheat or wheat? Do this over and over, learning to notice the unnoticed: how evenly the master cut each strand; how much sauce clings to them; how the noodles change from day to day, season to season, as the flour ages and new crops replace old.

Buckwheat is second only to rice as the traditional grain of the Japanese diet; the word soba means both "buckwheat" and "noodle," so it is the foundational pasta of Japanese cuisine. It is a craft perfected through meditative union between dough and maker, and an art when there is an eater to receive and make sense of it.

So I knew how my time with Sakai was supposed to go: I'd get a crash course in soba making and maybe find it surprisingly easy, at least until I got a little better and realized how little I actually knew. I'd understand that the masters adjust their dough according to the humidity in the air, according to the variety of buckwheat, according to the grind of the flour, probably according to the song of the birds in the wisteria above. I'd fall into a trance while rolling out the sheets, while cutting the noodles. I'd learn to make better soba, and making better soba would make me a better person: more present, more grounded. This was going to be a story of losing myself in the particulars, of mindfulness and detail and learning to see how big the world is by learning to see its smallest alchemies. I've seen *Jiro Dreams of Sushi*. That's how Japanese food is supposed to work.

I finally arrived at Sakai's sunbaked olive house, and she greeted me with her wide, smiling face, a scarf tied around her head, prepared for work. "My house is a little buckwheat monastery," she said as she led me through its airy rooms: blond woods and cool, angular surfaces displaying little more than a book here, a book there, some pieces of art by her husband, Katsuhisa. I went to wash my hands in the bathroom and struggled to find the mirror.

"Soba saved me," she said. A movie buyer and producer raised in New York, Mexico, and Japan, Sakai lived a big life in the presence of stars. But seven years ago, she finished producing a difficult film, one that burned her out, and she took more and more satisfaction in learning about noodles on her business trips to Japan. The day Sakai thought it would be a good idea to leave her clothes behind and fill her luggage with buckwheat flour was the day she knew her life had changed. "I stripped everything out of my life that I didn't need." Now she teaches the meditation of noodle making. "I like the scale of making food," she said, and so she committed herself to the intimacy, the humanness, the smallness of a simple craft that you make, serve, and watch disappear over and over again.

Talking with her, you're immediately impressed with how centered, how balanced, she seems. In her studio, a plain room with a work table and two windows letting in lemonade light, she showed me some of her flours: this one American, by Anson Mills, with rustic shards of husk; this one Canadian; this one Japanese, milled at an impossibly slow pace of two kilos an hour to make a flour so fine, so heavy, it feels like cream when you put your hands in it. That Japanese flour, she said, makes supremely supple and refined noodles, but America actually grows far more buckwheat than Japan. Farmers here usually plant it as a cover crop, essentially a by-product, harvested and stored carelessly since there is little domestic market for it.

She stirred some flours in a massive lacquered bowl, its black expanse as wide as her arms could stretch around. Mostly she makes soba in the *ni-hachi* style, which usually means that it's roughly 20 percent wheat and 80 percent buckwheat. For soba lovers, the higher the buckwheat percentage, the truer the flavor, but since buckwheat is gluten-free, most noodle makers will add some wheat to help give the dough strength and elasticity. She added water carefully, then repeatedly jabbed her fingers into the bowl in sharp motions, making spätzle-like strands as the flour began to come together. Then, with force in her forearms, she pressed into the bowl with broad swipes, rolling the strands into pebbles, rolling the pebbles into a dough. Through this, I noted how the ivory buckwheat turned a gravelly gray when it took in water and how it gave off, I swear, the scent of black sesame. "That's good," Sakai said. "You have to talk to your dough. If you're treating it right, it has a real glow."

Sakai worked in elegant, nearly ritualistic movements. With one hand, she rotated the dough, using the other to gently pull in its corners, forming a disk with inward pleats; it looked a bit like a millstone to me, but she referred to it as "the chrysanthemum." She rolled this on its side, the pleats stretching to meet one another at the point of a cone, which she then gently pressed into a near-perfect circle. Then came a series of passes with a rolling pin, a way of curling the dough around the pin like a scroll and stretching it to make squared edges, and finally folding and cutting. By the end, as she grasped her soba in little ponytails, patted them to puff away the dusting of starch she used to keep them separated, her noodles were not only beautiful and precise, they looked cared for. There was no waste, no scraggly edges, no subtly wavy noodles where the rolling pin landed a little heavy. They were not perfect, not quite, but I could see how close Sakai was to getting them there.

"Sometimes, my students ask, 'Can I roll these through a pasta machine?'" she said to me. "And I say yes, of course, but that's not the point. The practice, connecting with your hands, is the point." Some forms of perfection you chase because they are objectively perfect, as far as you can tell, with your palate and your training and your nerve endings, which feel the resistance between your teeth and fire off the precise information to your brain to make you use the words "chewy" or "al dente" or "silky." And some you chase not just because you want their deliciousness, but because there is joy in losing yourself to them.

I scaled out some flour and made a few batches of my own soba with Sakai's gentle words of guidance: "The chrysanthemum should look like a flower. Yours looks a little like a face. That's been punched." And so I worked on the pleating, again. Worked on the rolling, again. Worked on the folding and worked on the cutting, until she said, "Hey, your noodles look really nice!" Only I didn't dust them with enough starch, and they glued themselves together. Start over. Again. But with each batch, knowing Sakai was watching me, I could focus on feeling the stretch of the dough, feeling every movement, feeling the pauses when I lost my rhythm. In that sense it was like yoga, a practice based in the sensation of being a physical being. Only there was lunch to eat at the end of it.

I came home from my lessons eager to start my own little soba life. I acquired. I scoured shops; bought flours, dashi, and dip ingredients, a sweet extra-long rolling pin, a beautiful knife, a traditional cedar cutting guide; and eyed one of those lacquer mixing bowls that would make a mortgage payment blush. I invited a friend over.

The humidity was like a living creature that night, and I couldn't tell whether that meant I should reduce the water in the dough, or whether the fact that I was literally sweating into it was going to overhydrate it. But the water hit the flour, I could smell that sesame scent again, and I pushed on. I kneaded and rolled, but after half a dozen tries, my chrysanthemum looked again less like a flower and more like a face, maybe a pug's face. I looked at it, looked at the clock, looked at my hungry friend, and skipped the part where I roll the chrysanthemum into a cone altogether. I rolled out the noodle sheets like an errant pie dough, tearing it in places where I rolled over my own fingers. Who rolls over their own fingers with a rolling pin? I folded the dough up and cut through it not with the even, rhythmic strokes that Sakai says should sound like a horse's trot, but with a halting, awkward series of *ca-chunks*, worrying that each cut would be too wide or too thin. I was a mess by the end, cursing my oafish hands, ridiculing myself for not being able to remember how the twist of the wrist should feel when handling the dough. "What kind of hack cook are you?" I sneered at myself.

My friend loved the noodles, chewy and nutty alongside some tempura mushrooms. A great cook and eater, he even asked me to teach him how to make them, so he could make them for his wife. Still, with each batch, better or worse than that night, I found myself furious at too-wonky edges, too-clumsy cuts. My soba life was lame, and I put my tools away in the cupboard.

Weeks later, I was talking with another friend. She'd lost the company she ran a few years ago in one brutal, bewildering morning. She wrote a book about it, about re-finding her life by retreating to the kitchen. In it, there's a passage where, to get herself out of a funk, she spends the day making an exquisite kind of Chinese dumpling. They sounded impossible: The wrappers are actually tiny, crepe-thin omelets, wrapped delicately around the filling so that they don't tear. "You made those to calm yourself down?" I asked her. "Because I would be ripping them, driving myself crazy, throwing things across the room."

"Well," she said, "I feel like it's okay to make mistakes. I cook to learn. That's the pleasure, not to perform."

That word grabbed me: Performing and doing can be entirely different things. Performance is about projection, not acceptance, and even when I was all alone with my soba, I realized I was still performing the making of them—putting myself on stage, watching myself, criticizing every move. It wasn't just that I didn't have Sakai's guidance on the technique, it was that I didn't have her calm, her letting go. Meditation, it turns out, is not a spectator sport.

But then I got home and looked around. My wife and I were waiting for our baby to be born. I looked at a pile of toys, a wireless monitor, a trash can just for diapers. Speaking of diapers, which ones should we get? Because what I'm hearing is that getting your kids the wrong kind of diaper will mean they will grow up to hate you, or at the very least not get into college. Wait, sorry, there it is again. My anxiety. My fear that I'm always stressed about work, that I don't see my friends enough, that I have no idea how to be a father, that my world is actually getting smaller and smaller even as I write about how it's supposed to get bigger when you learn to see its little alchemies.

I suppose I shouldn't add the stress of cooking for perfection on top of that. Not for noodles, not for this story. Next time, when the water hits the buckwheat and I smell the scent of sesame again, it will just be dinner, and that will just have to be enough. That's a kind of meditation, isn't it?

How to Make Fresh Soba Noodles at Home

Step 1

In a large bowl, whisk 10 oz. light buckwheat flour (not whole-grain) and 2½ oz. all-purpose flour until evenly combined. Pour ¾ cup lukewarm water over the flour sand, using your fingers, toss and rub the flours with the water until crumbly, like muddy sand.

Step 2

Scrape the dough onto a work surface and press and knead until smooth, about 6 minutes. Press the dough into a disk, then rotate the disk clockwise as you pinch portions of the dough on top of the disk and fold them over in a counterclockwise motion to form pleats.

Step 3

Arrange the dough pleated-side-down and mold into a cone. Flatten the dough around its perimeter until it is ½-inch thick, keeping a slight bump in the center of the disk. Transfer the dough to a work surface dusted lightly with tapioca starch and lightly dust the dough with starch.

Step 4

Using a thin rolling pin or wooden dowel dusted with more starch, roll the dough using back-and-forth strokes, rotating it as needed. (You can also use a pasta machine for this task by cutting the disk into quarters and feeding each through the machine on its thinnest setting.)

Step 5

Once the dough is flattened to ⅛-inch thick (you can roll the dough around the rolling pin to check for even thickness), dust the flattened dough generously with starch and fold in half. Dust the sheet with more starch and fold it again in the same direction to make four layers.

Step 6

Using a sharp slicing knife, slice the dough into ⅙ -inch-thick noodles and toss in the starch to ensure they don't stick together. Use the cut soba noodles immediately or transfer to a parchment paper–lined sheet, cover with plastic wrap, and refrigerate for up to 3 days.

So Long, Menus; Hello, Pots and Pans

By Pete Wells

From the *New York Times*

New York Times restaurant critic Pete Wells has one of the
food world's most enviable—and most highly fraught—jobs.
In early 2016, his precise and unflinching demotion of NYC
gastronomic temple Per Se made headlines. After all the
firestorms, who wouldn't grant him a summer month off?

There are people who plan their vacations around restaurant reservations that have to be secured months in advance. I am not
one of them. When I need to get away from it all, competing for a
table is one of the main things I'm getting away from. That, and meals
longer than a filibuster, and hearing that "Chef" would like me to eat
this particular taste in one bite while rubbing my stomach and patting
my head.

You can put down your tiny violins; it doesn't take much to see that
the problems of an overfed restaurant critic don't amount to a hill of fava
beans in this crazy world. I have lucked into a job that's more interesting than I am, one that gives me a front-row seat to a runway parade of
generosity and egomania, innovations and knockoffs, money-minting
empires and tiny bootstrap operations that struggle to pay the rent.

Eating in a different restaurant almost every night, I am rarely bored.
But I do get a little misty-eyed for the civilian life I've left behind. I start
to miss those heartwarming scenes of domestic bliss around the family hearth: bleeding on the chopped onions, raising welts the size of
hamsters on my arms each time I get near an oven rack, and erupting

in language that my children would otherwise have to learn from Judd Apatow movies.

Summer vacation is my chance to bleed on the onions again. It's also my chance to forget about celtuce and sea buckthorn, to revert to stuff I've been eating all my life. We stay in a shack on the beach near the part of New England where I was raised.

All the markets have the ingredients I grew up with. When I need salt pork, oyster crackers, brown bread in a can and hot dog buns split along the top so the exposed white sides can be toasted on the grill (I can't tell you how crucial this is), they will be there. And I will find what I think of as the holy trinity of New England-Portuguese food products: linguiça, its spicier cousin chouriço and bolos levedos, sweet, flat muffins that are always a half-inch too wide to fit in the toaster.

When I manage to cook at home, it is usually a one-night stand. My vacation cooking is a longer commitment. Tonight's dinner may start with last night's leftovers, and the remnants of a cilantro bunch I chopped on Monday may come in handy on Thursday. With a whole week at hand, I find my kitchen rhythm again.

With the salt pork, along with dried beans and molasses, I am on my way to a pot of Boston baked beans, which I'll stash in a warm oven right after breakfast. They will be soft enough to eat in a couple of hours, or about the time it takes me to apply a primer coat of sunscreen, go for a fast swim, then put on a second coat.

I have been taking liberties with a recipe from the Boston chef Jasper White for years. I don't know any New York restaurants that specialize in Boston baked beans. They sound too Nathaniel Hawthorne, I guess, although I sometimes wonder why so many of my city's chefs try so hard to replicate beans from Texas or Mexico or Tuscany and so few bother to root around in old cookbooks from the Northeast.

If the beans don't turn into lunch, they'll cool their heels in the refrigerator until a night when my sun-baked brain can't think of anything more creative than Portuguese sausage on the grill (top-split buns optional, but recommended). I like baked beans with fish, too, although I'll concede that it may take a New Englander to appreciate seafood with molasses.

Experts in beach vacationing agree that one of the best practices in the field is to spend as little time as possible in the car. I make an exception for fried clams; everyone should make an exception for fried clams. I also allow myself a daily run to one of the local seafood markets, which swim circles around anything I've seen in New York.

They all sell quahogs. These are the size of a woman's purse and should not be eaten raw unless you are a sea gull. This makes them useless on the half-shell but perfect for the clam chowder I'll cook with potatoes, onions, a few more slabs of salt pork and enough cream to drown a kitten. Cream mixed with the cloudy, salty juices that spill from opened quahogs gives me more strength than any superfood I've ever heard of.

Fishermen back their pickups up to the doors of these markets to unload ice chests full of striped bass, fluke and bluefish. This summer, there aren't as many striped bass in the water, so I gave them a year off, with best wishes for a speedy recovery. Bluefish is never in short supply. I eat as much of it as I can stand, and I can stand a lot more than most people.

Because of its unpopularity and its uncanny talent for smelling like cat food after a night or two out of water, bluefish almost never turns up in restaurants. To me, a shiny raw bluefish fillet on ice is more exciting than foie gras. I will cook it skin-side down a few inches away from a small pile of charcoal with the lid on the grill.

Hot smoked like this, it can push back against the most overbearing sauce I can think of: lemon, Dijon mustard, maple syrup and horseradish; a salsa verde of tomatillos, jalapeños and onions, all softened on the grill; or, easiest of all, cherry tomatoes cut in half and left to relax for a few minutes with salt, chives, olive oil and sliced fresh chiles.

Before the end of the week I will buy a small fleet of lobsters. Eating whole lobsters in a restaurant is a Tom Sawyer deal; you do all the work, then you pay. It's a messy, chaotic demolition zone, with shell fragments zinging around like shrapnel and hot juice squirting in your eyes. It's a meal for the beach, for T-shirts and bathing suits that will be washed in the sink.

The best lobsters I ever made were boiled in salt water I carried up from the bay, but usually I just steam them. More important than technique is quantity: There must be too many lobsters, or else the next day there will be no cold lobster salad for lunch.

Because I have the time and because my two boys will hate me if I don't, I make dessert. My summer vacation desserts are not geometric or asymmetrical. If they contain crumbles or streusel, they will be baked on top, not scattered across the plate like a Martian soil sample. My shortcakes and cobblers are as attractive as a pile of wet beach towels. They are also gone before anyone notices.

Before anyone gave me an expense account to write about restaurants, I did almost all my eating at home. Cooking was a hobby that metastasized into a career. The people who advise you to find a job doing what you love never tell you that if you do that job long enough, you will rise up and out of the thing that you loved in the first place. These days, I need to take a vacation to get back to the thing that got me into this mess.

Then I come home. This year I returned with a chunk of the beach shack's back porch lodged deep inside my left foot, but I still had a bounce in my step that first night when I shampooed the sand out of my scalp, shaved off my vacation beard, remembered how shoelaces work and headed out to a restaurant.

Before vacation, restaurant kitchens sometimes strike me as hermetic environments. After, I remember that professional cooking builds on what we civilians do, adding a different set of pleasures. These may be pleasures of refinement and simplicity, or ones of elaboration and complexity. Either way, my time at the stove helps me to see just what's on the plate in front of me. Then at the end of the night, all those plates go away and somebody else washes them. Civilization!

Boston Baked Beans

Squat, glazed ceramic bean pots lurk in cabinets all over New England. They're traditional for Boston baked beans, but enameled cast iron is faster. Beans in cast iron can be brought to a boil over a burner before the dish goes into the oven; this saves about an hour.

1 pound dried navy or Great Northern beans
½ pound salt pork or bacon, rind removed, cut into ¼-inch dice
1 onion, chopped
4 garlic cloves, peeled
½ cup dark molasses or maple syrup, preferably Grade B
¼ cup ketchup

3 tablespoons mustard powder
1 tablespoon Worcestershire sauce
1 teaspoon pepper, plus more to taste
1 thyme branch (optional)
1 bay leaf (optional)
1 teaspoon salt, plus more to taste
1 tablespoon cider vinegar, plus more to taste

Pick through the beans for stones, rinse them thoroughly and soak in water overnight. (Leave soaking until ready to cook; you'll need the water.)

Heat oven to 300 degrees. Place a Dutch oven, 5-quart size or larger, over low heat. Add the salt pork or bacon and fry until crisp, 12 to 15 minutes. Raise heat to medium and stir in the onion. Cook until onion is translucent, stirring occasionally, 5 to 8 minutes.

Add the beans to the pan along with enough of the soaking liquid to cover them by ½ inch, adding fresh water if needed. Add the garlic cloves, molasses or maple syrup, ketchup, mustard powder, Worcestershire sauce, 1 teaspoon pepper and the thyme branch and bay leaf, if using. Stir well and bring to a boil. Cover the pot and put in oven.

Check the liquid level in the pot every hour or so, and add hot water as needed to barely cover the beans. Cook until beans are very soft but not falling apart, 2 to 3 hours. Remove from oven. Stir in 1 teaspoon salt and 1 tablespoon vinegar; let sit at room temperature for 30 minutes, then taste a bean and some liquid, adding more salt, pepper or vinegar, if you like. Serve, or cool completely and reheat.

Dinner Party Diaries

By Andrew Sean Greer

From *Saveur*

Novelist Andrew Sean Greer (*The Confessions of Max Tivoli, The Impossible Lives of Greta Wells*) has lived all over the United States, from New York City to Missoula, Montana, Seattle, Washington, and San Francisco, California. In this essay, a simple notebook triggers memories of his Washington DC childhood.

This January, my mother turned 70, and, in a mood of giddy nostalgia, she brought out an old college-ruled notebook: one of the journals in which she's kept a record of all the dinner parties she's hosted since 1976. Ever my mother's son, I have a similar journal. But I am a writer and she is a chemist. Mine features stories and narratives and feelings about the dinners I've hosted, whereas hers reads like laboratory notes—just the meal plan and who was invited. No digressions, no extraneous comments.

"Salmon mousse," she announced, reading the first entry. "My God, I must have made that a hundred times. For the Kaufmans and Hurleys, do you remember them?" I did not; I was five and could barely tell apart the scientists she entertained in those years. But I did remember that salmon mousse. Pink, jiggling, molded in the curved shape of a fish.

"How do you plan a meal?" I asked my mother. She considered this, sipping her red wine. "You start with something you want to make, and you round it out with old favorites. Like salmon mousse," she told me. "Same as a lab experiment: only one variable at a time."

How fascinating to go over the decades with her, there on the couch with the wine. First, the adventurous period of youth: making *pirozhki* by hand in 1977; serving quiche Lorraine and a roast leg of lamb while raising twin boys, running a laboratory, and teaching; attempting Peking duck because she saw it on Joyce Chen's PBS show. Then the middle-aged period, where ham was the "old favorite," complemented by variables of crab in phyllo and Jockey Club salad; a time of simplicity, less showing off. And the recent era of rediscovered adventure: Thai food and mango salad, taken from one of her 200 cookbooks.

And yet, despite the wide variety of her cooking, she was right: There were dishes that repeated throughout the years, and they were rarely the most extravagant ones: honey chicken, a recipe from her best friend in college; broccoli bread, from another friend's mother in South Carolina; crab cakes. Despite all the foods collected from other regions and sources, what the journals showed most of all were my mother's Southern roots. She would never think of herself as a Southern cook; her own mother refused to teach her, and mine refused to make the fried chicken and macaroni salad of her childhood. Yet there it was, on almost every page: ham, biscuits, spoon bread, pecan pie. How do you plan a menu? You start with what intrigues you, yes. Something new. But you fill in with old favorites.

"Thoughts for a crowd," my mother read aloud as we passed into the entries from the '90s. A list of possible meals for large groups: boiled shrimp, jambalaya, hot dogs, and hamburgers. She laughed: "I had to write down *hot dogs*?"

Old friends came and went in her journal. Childhood pals, visiting our Maryland home from the South for a reunion. Her graduate-school friends (one of whom gave us the pound cake recipe that is still a favorite). My mother remarked how many of her old dinner guests were now dead. New friends arrived; new favorites joined the rotation. My husband's name first shows up at Christmas in 1997, along with a Christmas Eve meals of just hors d'oeuvres that, because he loved it, we have kept as a tradition ever since. My sister-in-law's name arrived in 2006, and with it, all shellfish vanished from family menus (she is allergic). Her influence is also clear in a dish of peach, ricotta, and lemon that showed up with frequency after that. There is my mother's partner,

Ruth, who appeared in 1991, heralding almost five years of vegetarian dishes before she succumbed to my mother's ham. And there is my father, who, despite being her ex-husband, appeared every year or so after their divorce, including on the most recent page: a family lunch of *salade niçoise*.

I've kept my journal since 1996, but I have never shown it to my mother; I think it would strain her heart. In it, there is no menu planning. Often I get the date wrong, sometimes the *year*. That is because, while my mother has always written in her journal before a dinner party, I write in mine *afterward*. Or during. "MEAL OF DISASTER," reads one entry, with a drawing of flames. There are almost no repetitions, no old favorites, no salmon mousse of my own. It is *all* variables. My life has reached the point where dinner parties occur spontaneously, and I run to the grocery store to get something bubbling by the time eight, ten, or more people arrive. There is no plan, only the tipsy record of what happened. I think these kinds of dinner parties visit my mother in anxiety dreams.

It is too bad that there are large gaps and strange indecipherable entries in my journal, whereas in my mother's books everything is clear. Hers pass from early motherhood through divorce and the deaths of friends without a break. I, on the other hand, have three entire years unaccounted for. Was I too content to put anything down? Too distracted? My journal chronicles the meals of a moody, passionate person; hers are efficient and calm. I see her row of journals and I am envious: this is what being an adult looks like. By 44, I should not be winging it at dinner. I should not be spilling wine over the pages. I should learn to plan a menu. I should practice with old favorites. I should have a salmon mousse.

And so, I am putting this resolution into practice at a dinner party this week for writer friends. The menu is already written in my book—chicken with sunchokes and spinach salad. To start, a favorite of mine already curing in the fridge: salmon gravlax. And for this I must apologize to my mother: It is as close as I can get. I love you, I do. But I have always hated that salmon mousse.

Orange-Marinated Gravlax

Serves 6 as a starter

Active: 25 min.; Total: 1 hr. plus 1 day.

1 whole salmon fillet, skin on (1 to 1¼ pounds)
2 tablespoons kosher salt
1 tablespoon sugar
1 teaspoon freshly ground black pepper
1 teaspon sweet paprika
1 teaspoon sumac (amazon.com)
1 orange
2 tablespoons olive oil
1½ teaspoons honey
Rye or pumpernickel toast, for serving

On a work surface, dry the salmon thoroughly with paper towels and then remove any small bones still in the flesh. Transfer the salmon to a 9-by-13-inch baking dish. In a small bowl, stir the salt with the sugar, pepper, paprika, and sumac. Rub the spice mix all over the flesh and then wrap the whole dish in plastic wrap. Refrigerate the salmon for at least 24 hours, or up to 48 hours, to cure.

Meanwhile, for the marinade, use a Microplane grater to finely grate half the orange's zest into a small bowl. Using a vegetable peeler, peel the zest from the other orange half and slice it lengthwise into very thin strips. Juice the orange and measure out 6 tablespoons; reserve remaining juice for another use. Stir the orange juice into the grated zest along with the olive oil and honey until the honey dissolves.

Unwrap the salmon and transfer to a cutting board. Gently pat dry the flesh of the salmon and then cut across the grain into ¼-inch-thin slices. Arrange the slices to overlap on a large serving platter, and then spoon the marinade over the slices. Sprinkle with the orange zest strips and let stand for 30 minutes in a cool place to meld flavors before serving with toast.

Churnin'

BY CAROL PENN-ROMINE

From HungryPassport.com

Seattle-based food writer, editor, and culinary tour guide
Carol Penn-Romine has evolved in so many ways from her rural
Tennessee upbringing. (Not many farm girls have a Le Cordon
Bleu degree!). Still, there are moments when her connection to
those Southern foodways trump everything else.

In my credulous preschool days the Beatles just wanted to hold my
hand. That was about as racy as the radio ever got then. But before
the Top 40 concept reached the hinterlands of rural, churchgoing Tennessee, you never could tell what sort of risqué business might ooze
into your world on the airwaves. While it was nothing on a par with
today's no-holds-barred lyrics that could make a porn star blush, it was
enough to stoke the imagination of a child brimming with more questions than the adults were willing to answer.

Once when I was about five, my momma and I were shopping in the
general store just down the road from our farm when a chipper voice on
its tinny speaker instructed:

"Keep on churnin' till the butter come . . .

Keep on pumpin' make the butter flow.

Wipe off the paddle and churn some more."

I asked her about it because I couldn't understand why anyone
would sing about making what we smeared onto our toast for breakfast.

She grew ashen, pointed across the store and blurted, "Look! There's
a kitten!"

I raced over and began scouring the dry goods section but didn't see it anywhere. By the time I returned to her side the song was over, and my questions shifted from the significance of those dairy-centric lyrics to the whereabouts of the mysteriously vanished kitten that I failed to find playing amongst the bib overalls and nubby work gloves.

Her diversionary tactics worked for a little while. Then I heard "I Like Bread and Butter" and decided it was my new favorite song after the luster had faded from the not-quite-so-snappy "Jesus Loves Me." I'd prance around the house singing the sad story of the fellow whose girl feeds him bread and butter, and everything is hunky dory until he comes home early one day and finds her eating chicken and dumplings with another guy.

"Does this mean you can eat chicken and dumplings with your honey but not with anybody else?" I asked as she stirred a generous dollop of bacon drippings into the iron skillet filled with blackening green beans. "Or that it's okay to eat bread and butter but it's not okay to eat chicken and dumplings?" She told me I asked too many questions and that I'd understand when I was older. When those responses didn't satisfy and I pressed the issue, she explained that children who were too inquisitive were in danger of going straight to H-E-double-L.

This made me wonder if there was some moral objection to dumplings that was simply too wicked to discuss. Our family didn't eat them, and honestly, I wasn't sure exactly what a dumpling was. There was no one I could turn to for clarification of these finer points of culinary propriety. My momma clearly wasn't up to the task, and I figured if she couldn't explain them to me, no one else could either. While my daddy was a farmer, and I'd witnessed plenty of hanky panky going on amongst the hogs and cattle, we never discussed the similarities between what the livestock was doing and what humans might get up to. Were any of those extra parts I saw while they were carrying on "dumplings?"

As concerned as my momma seemed to be about me skipping down the murky path to Aitcheedubulel, wherever that was, I decided this question should remain unasked. Singing about food was inexcusably naughty. Period. But the issue lingered in my mind, and I began looking everywhere, musing over song lyrics and searching for clues to this conundrum. At church I browsed through the hymnal during sermons and was surprised to find that even the hymns we sang at Thanksgiving, the season for conveniently overlooking the sin of gluttony, made only scant and unhelpful mention of food. The holiday table at church groaned from the weight of turkey, dressing, brown-and-serve rolls, countless congealed salads and plenteous desserts. There, as everywhere else, we talked about food, obsessed over it and packed it away in huge quantities.

We just didn't sing about it.

Then one day a woman's smoky voice spilled out of our lunchbox-sized, leather-bound transistor radio. "I need a little sugar in my bowl," she sighed. "I need a little hot dog between my rolls." I held my tongue until the singer of "All That Meat and No Potatoes" bemoaned that he was "waitin', palpitatin'." Picking judiciously through the food references, I focused on the non-food word.

"Momma, what's 'palpitatin'?"

"It's a ten-dollar word for goin' to the devil," she snapped, her face crimsoning to the shade of our rooster's crown, and switched off the radio with such vehemence I thought the knob would break off in her hand.

So proximity alone was enough to get a word barred from discussion. This was a difficult time for a child enamored of words and already stoking her vocabulary for life as a writer.

Finally I started school, with each day beginning and ending on the bus, surrounded by kids of all ages and backgrounds. The worldly high school men sat on the back three rows and snickered about things like "makin' bacon." Their obsession with food puzzled me, until finally I began putting the clues together, noting that somehow it involved s-e-x and that this stuff was supposed to be fun. But they clammed up every time they saw me glancing back their way, so I got only, um, snatches of the mystery.

By second grade I decided the playground was the only sensible place to learn what "doing it" was all about, when my worldly, town-dwelling friend Patty promised to explain it to me during recess one day. I counted the miserably slow minutes until we hit the playground.

We hung upside down on the monkey bars in silence for what seemed like forever, when suddenly she heaved herself over, grabbed my shoulders, pressed her lips against my ear and whispered: "A boy pulls down his pants, and a girl pulls down her panties, and he sticks his you-know-what into her you-know-what." Then she let go of my shoulders, and I swung back into my solitary upside down space, more knowledgeable but feeling cheated.

That was it? I had to hang by my knees until I was lightheaded just to hear that? I had a brother and a raft of boy cousins, so it wasn't like I'd never caught a glimpse of their equipment when someone had left the bathroom door open. But her account sounded too matter-of-fact, basic "insert Tab A into Slot A" business, and not like the kind of knowledge that needed to be so carefully guarded. And not like any fun at all, certainly not like something you'd want to sing about.

Before I could react the bell rang. We unhooked our knees, turned the requisite flip and dropped to the dusty ground.

"But what about butter?" I called after her as she raced ahead of me to the schoolhouse door. "And potatoes . . . and dumplings?" She stopped in her tracks and looked back at me in bewilderment, her authority dissolving. She was just as baffled as I was.

Further complicating matters were whispered suggestions that sex and babies were somehow connected. One day as I set the table for dinner, a boy called in to "Swap Shop" on the radio and offered to trade his rock-n-roll records for a baby bed. Momma let out a hoot but then sucked it back in, as quick as the cord retreated back into our fancy new Electrolux vacuum cleaner.

So there was a clue. I knew women carried their babies around under their baggy dresses until they got tired of that. Then they pulled the babies out from under their dresses, wrapped them in blankets and carried them around in their arms. But how did they get there in the first place? Did singing about food cause them to get the babies? How was that possible?

Deepening the mystery was the introduction of Better Than Sex Cake. Every upstanding churchwoman and neighbor lady had a recipe for it, but they always whispered its name with a blush and a titter. Being a kid, I had nothing to compare it to. Even my stately grandmother began bringing this cake to church potlucks, and she whispered and tittered with all the rest. I had no appreciation for it simply because it wasn't chocolate. I'd look at her cake, pale yellow and loaded with crushed pineapple and instant vanilla pudding and topped with canned whipped cream and flaked coconut, and I'd shudder. It was the sum and substance of everything I despised in a dessert, because there were flavor issues. And texture issues. It was supposed to be better than sex, so I held out scant hope that sex would be worth the bother.

No evidence remains to confirm my doubts because at some point these recipes vanished from the collections of both grandmothers. I think all venerable Southern women make a pact so that whenever one of them dies, the others will sneak into her kitchen, ninja style, spirit away her Better Than Sex Cake recipe and destroy it.

What did I learn about sex from all this vagueness, from the tittering and whispering about cake and the pretend kitten spotting? And from all that cryptic music in which the mysteries of food loomed so large?

Not much, but by the time I was in junior high and the boys were embarrassing the girls with their most obnoxious renditions of Robert Plant singing, "Squeeze my lemon 'til the juice runs down my leg," I realized Led Zeppelin's take on that old Howlin' Wolf tune wasn't about fruit at all. What adults couldn't accomplish with averted eyes and evasive responses, teenaged boys reeking of Hai Karate and cigarettes could, and I began to appreciate that it's through music and food that sex finds some of its most imaginative and playful expression. At least it gave us a way to speculate in public about things we otherwise didn't dare discuss in polite society—and eventually develop our own savory vocabulary as we engaged in the fevered backseat exploration of lemons, potatoes, dumplings and all.

It turned out that churnin' had nothing to do with dairy products and farm chores. It had everything to do with frosting the cake.

Better Than Sex Cake

The list of recipes for Better Than Sex Cake is endless, and like other sensual activities, completely open to interpretation. Essentially the idea is to load one cake with as much decadence as it can bear, and then add some more. While I believe no cake baked from pre-made, packaged ingredients is going to be better than sex, every recipe I've ever seen for it contained nothing homemade. So in the spirit of my Better Than Sex Cake–baking forebears, mine is also a combination of store-bought ingredients.

1 box of Betty Crocker Devil's Food Cake mix, plus the ingredients
   listed on the box: 1¼ cups of water, ½ cup of vegetable oil and
   3 eggs
½ of a 14-oz. can of sweetened condensed milk
1 small jar of caramel sauce
1 8-oz. container of Cool Whip
chocolate chips, as needed
peanut butter chips, as needed
Butterfinger candy bars, as needed

Bake the cake according to the directions on the box.

Leave it in the pan, and let it cool partially on a wire rack, about 10 minutes.

While it is still warm, poke holes in the cake about an inch apart with the handle of a wooden spoon, and drop a few chocolate and peanut butter chips into each hole.

When the cake has finished cooling, pour the sweetened, condensed milk into the holes. Next pour the caramel topping over the cake and spread to cover. Then top the cake with the whipped topping (use it all!). Sprinkle with enough crushed Butterfingers to completely cover the whipped topping.

If any cake survives the initial assault, cover it tightly with plastic wrap and keep it in the refrigerator.

The Breakfast Club

By Rachel Levin

From *Lucky Peach*

It's food writer Rachel Levin's job to chronicle the
San Francisco food scene, for such publications as
San Francisco magazine, *Pacific Standard, Food & Wine,*
The New Yorker, and *Sunset.* But amidst the hipster buzz at
one hot spot, something different caught her attention—
those two old guys at the back table....

Scrawled across the chest of every server at Sweet Maple is a tribute
to its signature item. "I ♥ Millionaire's Bacon," the T-shirts tout.
Indeed, the sales tactic works—as plates of the thick, brown sugar-
tinged slabs adorn pretty much every one of the twenty-five tables in
the place. But not Billy's and Bob's.

"*Pork?*" scoffs Billy Cohen, when I ask if it's the bacon that brings
him and his friend Bob Bransten here every Saturday morning. Definitely not, they say.

At eighty years old, they don't touch the stuff. Oh, sure, maybe
thirty years ago—when they were college buddies who became Pacific
Heights neighbors and began what's become a weekly breakfast tradition. Sweet Maple wasn't always their spot. Neither can recall the name
of the first San Francisco diner they went to together, just that they've
outlived it. "Remember that other place on Fulton, where we could
never find parking?" probes Bob, like one half of a long-married couple.
"What was it called?"

Another of their spots was Eats, a classic on Clement Street. "But frankly, by the time we got there, it was already packed with families," says Billy. "I don't do lines anymore. I gave up that up in the army."

The Internet is filled with raves about Sweet Maple ("OMG, the millionaire bacon. Let's talk about that first!" Yelps Karen S. of Sacramento. "As I took the first bite, my eyes rolled back like I was having an orgasm."), but for Billy and Bob, the food here is just "fine." Ultimately, they chose it as their go-to place simply because of its size. It's one of the largest breakfast spots in the city. Plus, they quickly figured out that if they showed up by eight a.m., they'd "beat the mobs." After four years, the staff knows their names, their window table, and their order. "Granola and fruit, no yogurt, low-fat milk for Billy; one egg white scrambled with tomatoes and mushrooms, no toast, no potatoes, and a glass of orange juice [with a straw] for Bob," says the smiley server as she presents their plates and refills their coffee mugs. Billy pours in three packets of Splenda and passes Bob the ketchup, which he squeezes beside his egg white. For Billy and Bob, it's not about the cuisine, but the company.

Bob came from a big West Coast coffee family—*MJB* it was called; founded in 1881, it rivaled Folgers and Hills Bros. back in the day. He worked in mass-produced coffee for decades, but admits he likes Blue Bottle now. Still, he doesn't seem to mind the generic Italian roast at Sweet Maple; he accepts a third, then a fourth, then a fifth topper.

Back in New York, Billy took his Harvard MBA to Broadway, where he was a producer. He still is, in that semi-retired, successful way. He co-produced the current hit *Beautiful*, about Carole King. "I've spent my life theoretically working in a creative industry," says Billy, "but none of it has rolled off on me as far as my culinary habits."

Bob agrees. "Let me suggest that Billy also likes to go to the same place *at night*," he teases. That place is Izzy's Steak & Chop House, a Marina mainstay since 1987. They go about once a month, with their wives, which means they sometimes end up eating breakfast and dinner together in the same day. "He likes the potatoes and the creamed spinach there," explains Bob.

After thirty years sitting across from each other, there's still plenty to talk about: They gossip about their kids (Billy's son, who's thirty-two, "is about to cohabit with a young woman," beams Billy); rib each other about their prestigious business schools ("You know what they call Harvard," says Bob. "Preparation H."); and roar with laughter about their lucky, lackluster military experience. "My friend here, was a member of the distinguished 353rd and Leaflet Battalion!" Billy guffaws over his granola. Apparently, Bob's role was to drop leaflets for civilians when the occasion called, but turns out his battalion never even had to do that. "They called us 'Legs,'" says Bob, "A deprecatory term that means guys who walked as opposed to guys who jump out of airplanes." "You know, on Veterans Day, when you're at the 49ers game and they ask those who served to stand, I'm always a little hesitant," says Bob. "I don't think we're really the ones they mean to honor."

The real draw of Sweet Maple every Saturday, say Billy and Bob, is the desire to get out of the house, to talk, and to try to make sense of the sort of life-stuff that happens. "Let me be clear, Billy is my psychiatrist," says Bob, only half-joking. "My wife, forget it. He's heard all of my trials and tribulations. It's painful, but it's cheaper than therapy."

Billy puts the point of their weekly breakfast date a little more bluntly: "It keeps us alive," he says.

With collared button-downs beneath their wool sweaters, gray hairs on their balding heads, and cute comments about grandkids (Bob has six; Billy's "still waiting"), this two-top sticks out at Sweet Maple. In fact, they stick out in San Francisco, where signs of life over sixty are becoming more and more rare. But sit and talk with these guys for an hour on a Saturday morning, and their wrinkles and their years seem to fade away. Suddenly, it's easy to see Billy and Bob as they still see themselves.

"Sure, we have more physical concerns now," says Billy. "But we also wake up every morning and know it's a hell of a lot better than the alternative." He peers around the restaurant, at the fitted plaid shirts, the soft hands sparkling with newly donned engagement rings, the new fathers cutting their toddler's pancakes, and the hung-over crews devouring deep-fried French toast and sucking down Sweet Maple's bottomless soju Bloody Marys. "We think, *Gee, that guy over there certainly looks old*, when he's probably ten years younger!" (Or fifty years younger.)

Oh, kids today. They text and bail and reschedule and hover for hours, holding out for the perfect poached eggs at the most popular spot—but Billy and Bob know better. They know what matters isn't so much where you go—bacon be damned—but that you show up. "We just call each other and say, 'Eight a.m.' and hang up," says Billy. "Ninety-five percent of Saturdays, you'll see us here."

The bill arrives, which they split, and scramble together a 20-plus percent tip. "I don't like owing this guy anything," teases Bob. It's getting close to ten a.m. A few more swigs of coffee and the old friends shuffle out. In their loafers and pressed-yet-sagging khakis, they cut through the throngs waiting for a table, San Francisco's hipster youth parting like the Red Sea. "What's going on the rest of the day?" asks Bob. Not much, replies Billy. "I think I'll go home and take a nap."

Filter Fish

By Oliver Sacks

From *The New Yorker*

In books such as *Awakenings*, *The Man Who Mistook His Wife for a Hat*, and *The Mind's Eye*, the great neurologist and writer Oliver Sacks proved himself equal parts clinician and poet. Shortly before his death in August 2015, he wrote this elegiac essay, choosing one beloved food as a prism to review his life.

Gefilte fish is not an everyday dish; it is to be eaten mainly on the Jewish Sabbath in Orthodox households, when cooking is not allowed. When I was growing up, my mother would take off from her surgical duties early on Friday afternoon and devote her time, before the coming of Shabbat, to preparing gefilte fish and other Sabbath dishes.

Our gefilte fish was basically carp, to which pike, whitefish, and sometimes perch or mullet would be added. (The fishmonger delivered the fish alive, swimming in a pail of water.) The fish had to be skinned, boned, and fed into a grinder—we had a massive metal grinder attached to the kitchen table, and my mother would sometimes let me turn the handle. She would then mix the ground fish with raw eggs, matzo meal, and pepper and sugar. (Litvak gefilte fish, I was told, used more pepper, which is how she made it—my father was a Litvak, born in Lithuania.)

My mother would fashion the mixture into balls about two inches in diameter—two to three pounds of fish would allow a dozen or more substantial fish balls—and then poach these gently with a few slices of carrot. As the gefilte fish cooled, a jelly of an extraordinarily delicate sort coalesced, and, as a child, I had a passion for the fish balls and their rich jelly, along with the obligatory *khreyn* (Yiddish for horseradish).

I thought I would never taste anything like my mother's gefilte fish again, but in my forties I found a housekeeper, Helen Jones, with a veritable genius for cooking. Helen improvised everything, nothing was by the book, and, learning my tastes, she decided to try her hand at gefilte fish.

When she arrived each Thursday morning, we would set out for the Bronx to do some shopping together, our first stop being a fish shop on Lydig Avenue run by two Sicilian brothers who were as alike as twins. The fishmongers were happy to give us carp, whitefish, and pike, but I had no idea how Helen, African-American, a good, churchgoing Christian, would manage with making such a Jewish delicacy. But her powers of improvisation were formidable, and she made magnificent gefilte fish (she called it "filter fish"), which, I had to acknowledge, was as good as my mother's. Helen refined her filter fish each time she made it, and my friends and neighbors got a taste for it, too. So did Helen's church friends; I loved to think of her fellow-Baptists gorging on gefilte fish at their church socials.

For my fiftieth birthday, in 1983, she made a gigantic bowl of it—enough for the fifty birthday guests. Among them was Bob Silvers, the editor of *The New York Review of Books*, who was so enamored of Helen's gefilte fish that he wondered if she could make it for his entire staff.

When Helen died, after seventeen years of working for me, I mourned her deeply—and I lost my taste for gefilte fish. Commercially made, bottled gefilte fish, sold in supermarkets, I found detestable compared to Helen's ambrosia.

But now, in what are (barring a miracle) my last weeks of life—so queasy that I am averse to almost every food, with difficulty swallowing anything except liquids or jellylike solids—I have rediscovered the joys of gefilte fish. I cannot eat more than two or three ounces at a time, but an aliquot of gefilte fish every waking hour nourishes me with much needed protein. (Gefilte-fish jelly, like calf's-foot jelly, was always valued as an invalid's food.)

Deliveries now arrive daily from one shop or another: Murray's on Broadway, Russ & Daughters, Sable's, Zabar's, Barney Greengrass, the 2nd Ave Deli—they all make their own gefilte fish, and I like it all (though none compares to my mother's or Helen's).

While I have conscious memories of gefilte fish from about the age of four, I suspect that I acquired my taste for it even earlier, for, with its abundant, nutritious jelly, it was often given to infants in Orthodox households as they moved from baby foods to solid food. Gefilte fish will usher me out of this life, as it ushered me into it, eighty-two years ago.

Recipe Index

Permissions Acknowledgments

About the Editor

HOLLY HUGHES is a writer, the former executive editor of Fodor's Travel Publications, and author of *Frommer's 500 Places for Food and Wine Lovers*.

Submissions for Best Food Writing 2017

Submissions and nominations for *Best Food Writing 2017* should be forwarded no later than May 1, 2017, to Holly Hughes at *Best Food Writing 2017*, c/o Da Capo Press, 44 Farnsworth Street, Boston MA 02210, or emailed to best.food@perseusbooks.com. We regret that, due to volume, we cannot acknowledge receipt of all submissions.